Golden Retrievers For Dummies®

Cheat Sheet

Emergency Symptoms and Medica...

- Know the symptoms of a true emergency and when you...
- Recognize signs of serious illness that require veterinar...
- Post this list where it will remind you to take emergency ... of the symptoms in the following sections.

Emergency!

- Diarrhea for more than 24 hours
- Bloody diarrhea, diarrhea with vomiting, fever, or other symptoms
- Vomiting for more than 24 hours (save the vomitus)
- Excessive panting, drooling, rapid pulse, dark red gums, frantic glazed expression (heatstroke)
- Abdominal swelling, discomfort with labored breathing, restlessness, roaching the back, drooling, gag vomiting (bloat)
- Very pale gums, shivering, lowered body temperature (under 100 degrees) (hypothermia)
- Depression, shivering, weak pulse, listlessness, lowered body temperature (shock from loss of blood or injury)
- Sudden swelling around the head or other body part

Signs of serious health problems:

- Poor appetite
- Prolonged or pronounced limping
- Shortness of breath
- Extreme lethargy or sleeping habits
- Frequent urination
- Sudden weight loss
- Excessive water intake
- Straining to move the bowels
- Lumps or black mole-like growths on any body part
- Unexplained change in attitude: fearful, shy, or aggressive

Common medication dosages for common ailments (no Tylenol or Ibuprofen for dogs!):

- Buffered aspirin or Ascriptin: Five mg per pound every 12 hours (65 pounds = one 325 mg tablet) for pain relief
- Hydrogen peroxide: One to 3 teaspoons every 10 minutes to induce vomiting
- Kaopectate: One ml per pound every 3 hours (65 pounds = 3 to 4 tablespoons) for diarrhea
- Imodium: One mg per 15 pounds, 1 to 2 times daily (1 cap per 25 pounds) for diarrhea
- Benadryl: One to 2 mg per pound every 8 hours (65 pounds = 2 to 4 25 mg tablets) for allergic reaction

For Dummies™: Bestselling Book Series for Beginners

Golden Retrievers For Dummies®

Dog-Proofing Your Premises

Dog-proof your home to keep it safe for your puppy and your adult Golden. Keep these reminders handy in case you forget and leave the trash uncovered or toilet lid open.

- ✔ Keep medication bottles and cleaning supplies out of reach.
- ✔ Don't toss dental floss where your puppy can get into it.
- ✔ Unplug electrical cords.
- ✔ Beware of coins, socks, needles, and tinsel.
- ✔ Watch out for stringy stuff like yarn and sewing gear.
- ✔ Do not use roach or rodent poison or other pesticide in areas accessible to your puppy.
- ✔ Keep the toilet lid down and never use toilet bowl cleaners.
- ✔ Keep the diaper pail lid shut tight.
- ✔ Hide all trash.
- ✔ Hide your underwear.
- ✔ Beware of certain chemicals, such as treated lumber products and flea control products.
- ✔ Watch out for windows.
- ✔ Hide the antifreeze.
- ✔ Store weed killers, pesticides, and herbicides out of reach.
- ✔ Ban cigarettes or at least keep those ashtrays clean.
- ✔ Watch out for poisonous plants, such as Lily of the Valley, Oleander, Rhododendron, Japanese Yews, and Poinsettia.
- ✔ Beware of herbicide hazards.

For Dummies™: Bestselling Book Series for Beginners

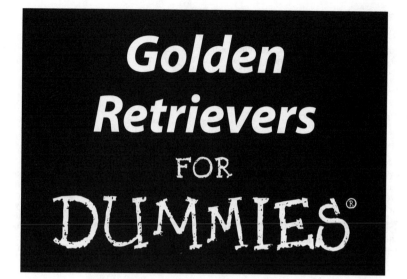

Golden Retrievers FOR DUMMIES®

by Nona Kilgore Bauer

IDG Books Worldwide, Inc.
An International Data Group Company

Foster City, CA ◆ Chicago, IL ◆ Indianapolis, IN ◆ New York, NY

Golden Retrievers For Dummies®

Published by
IDG Books Worldwide, Inc.
An International Data Group Company
919 E. Hillsdale Blvd.
Suite 400
Foster City, CA 94404
www.idgbooks.com (IDG Books Worldwide Web Site)
www.dummies.com (Dummies Press Web Site)

Library of Congress Control Number: 00-104222

ISBN: 0-7645-5267-8

Printed in the United States of America

10 9 8 7 6 5 4 3 2 1

1B/RR/QZ/QQ/IN

Distributed in the United States by IDG Books Worldwide, Inc.

Distributed by CDG Books Canada Inc. for Canada; by Transworld Publishers Limited in the United Kingdom; by IDG Norge Books for Norway; by IDG Sweden Books for Sweden; by IDG Books Australia Publishing Corporation Pty. Ltd. for Australia and New Zealand; by TransQuest Publishers Pte Ltd. for Singapore, Malaysia, Thailand, Indonesia, and Hong Kong; by Gotop Information Inc. for Taiwan; by ICG Muse, Inc. for Japan; by Intersoft for South Africa; by Eyrolles for France; by International Thomson Publishing for Germany, Austria and Switzerland; by Distribuidora Cuspide for Argentina; by LR International for Brazil; by Galileo Libros for Chile; by Ediciones ZETA S.C.R. Ltda. for Peru; by WS Computer Publishing Corporation, Inc., for the Philippines; by Contemporanea de Ediciones for Venezuela; by Express Computer Distributors for the Caribbean and West Indies; by Micronesia Media Distributor, Inc. for Micronesia; by Chips Computadoras S.A. de C.V. for Mexico; by Editorial Norma de Panama S.A. for Panama; by American Bookshops for Finland.

For general information on IDG Books Worldwide's books in the U.S., please call our Consumer Customer Service department at 800-762-2974. For reseller information, including discounts and premium sales, please call our Reseller Customer Service department at 800-434-3422.

For information on where to purchase IDG Books Worldwide's books outside the U.S., please contact our International Sales department at 317-572-3993 or fax 317-572-4002.

For consumer information on foreign language translations, please contact our Customer Service department at 800-434-3422, fax 317-572-4002, or e-mail rights@idgbooks.com.

For information on licensing foreign or domestic rights, please phone +1-650-653-7098.

For sales inquiries and special prices for bulk quantities, please contact our Order Services department at 800-434-4322 or write to the address above.

For information on using IDG Books Worldwide's books in the classroom or for ordering examination copies, please contact our Educational Sales department at 800-434-2086 or fax 317-572-4005.

For press review copies, author interviews, or other publicity information, please contact our Public Relations department at 650-653-7000 or fax 650-653-7500.

For authorization to photocopy items for corporate, personal, or educational use, please contact Copyright Clearance Center, 222 Rosewood Drive, Danvers, MA 01923, or fax 978-750-4470.

About the Author

If there is one thing that defines Nona's life, it's this: She could not live without her Goldens. For the past 30 years, they have been her best friends and the inspiration for her books. They have also blessed her with friends from all corners of the dog world: breeders, veterinarians, dog writers, professional trainers, great training partners, and so many good dog friends who adore all furry creatures great and small.

Nona's special love is working with her Goldens in the field, and she trains them for field trials and hunt tests as well as for obedience competition. She has trained several of her dogs to the Master Hunter level and Qualified All-Age status in the field, and many others to obedience and other working titles. Nona also judges field events and enjoys nothing more than watching a stylish retriever doing what he loves best.

Several of her Goldens also work as furry therapists at local nursing homes. Each monthly visit proves that friendly paws and wagging tails are the world's best tonic for the sick and lonely.

Nona studied journalism at Truman State University and began writing to help make the dog community a better place to live. She has written over a dozen dog books, and this is her fifth book about her beloved Golden Retrievers. Her very first Golden book captured the coveted Dog Writer's Association of America Best Breed Book of the Year award in 1993.

Her passion for her dogs colors everything she does, especially her books and writing projects.

If she can teach, motivate, or inspire her readers to do it right or better, the world will be a happier, safer place for dogs. And that will make her dog life even more golden than it already is.

ABOUT IDG BOOKS WORLDWIDE

Welcome to the world of IDG Books Worldwide.

IDG Books Worldwide, Inc., is a subsidiary of International Data Group, the world's largest publisher of computer-related information and the leading global provider of information services on information technology. IDG was founded more than 30 years ago by Patrick J. McGovern and now employs more than 9,000 people worldwide. IDG publishes more than 290 computer publications in over 75 countries. More than 90 million people read one or more IDG publications each month.

Launched in 1990, IDG Books Worldwide is today the #1 publisher of best-selling computer books in the United States. We are proud to have received eight awards from the Computer Press Association in recognition of editorial excellence and three from Computer Currents' First Annual Readers' Choice Awards. Our best-selling *...For Dummies®* series has more than 50 million copies in print with translations in 31 languages. IDG Books Worldwide, through a joint venture with IDG's Hi-Tech Beijing, became the first U.S. publisher to publish a computer book in the People's Republic of China. In record time, IDG Books Worldwide has become the first choice for millions of readers around the world who want to learn how to better manage their businesses.

Our mission is simple: Every one of our books is designed to bring extra value and skill-building instructions to the reader. Our books are written by experts who understand and care about our readers. The knowledge base of our editorial staff comes from years of experience in publishing, education, and journalism — experience we use to produce books to carry us into the new millennium. In short, we care about books, so we attract the best people. We devote special attention to details such as audience, interior design, use of icons, and illustrations. And because we use an efficient process of authoring, editing, and desktop publishing our books electronically, we can spend more time ensuring superior content and less time on the technicalities of making books.

You can count on our commitment to deliver high-quality books at competitive prices on topics you want to read about. At IDG Books Worldwide, we continue in the IDG tradition of delivering quality for more than 30 years. You'll find no better book on a subject than one from IDG Books Worldwide.

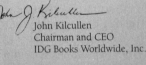

John Kilcullen
Chairman and CEO
IDG Books Worldwide, Inc.

**Eighth Annual
Computer Press
Awards ⪴1992**

**Ninth Annual
Computer Press
Awards ⪴1993**

**1995 COMPUTER CURRENTS
READERS' CHOICE**

**Tenth Annual
Computer Press
Awards ⪴1994**

**Eleventh Annual
Computer Press
Awards ⪴1995**

IDG is the world's leading IT media, research and exposition company. Founded in 1964, IDG had 1997 revenues of $2.05 billion and has more than 9,000 employees worldwide. IDG offers the widest range of media options that reach IT buyers in 75 countries representing 95% of worldwide IT spending. IDG's diverse product and services portfolio spans six key areas including print publishing, online publishing, expositions and conferences, market research, education and training, and global marketing services. More than 90 million people read one or more of IDG's 290 magazines and newspapers, including IDG's leading global brands — Computerworld, PC World, Network World, Macworld and the Channel World family of publications. IDG Books Worldwide is one of the fastest-growing computer book publishers in the world, with more than 700 titles in 36 languages. The "...For Dummies®" series alone has more than 50 million copies in print. IDG offers online users the largest network of technology-specific Web sites around the world through IDG.net (http://www.idg.net), which comprises more than 225 targeted Web sites in 55 countries worldwide. International Data Corporation (IDC) is the world's largest provider of information technology data, analysis and consulting, with research centers in over 41 countries and more than 400 research analysts worldwide. IDG World Expo is a leading producer of more than 168 globally branded conferences and expositions in 35 countries including E3 (Electronic Entertainment Expo), Macworld Expo, ComNet, Windows World Expo, ICE (Internet Commerce Expo), Agenda, DEMO, and Spotlight. IDG's training subsidiary, ExecuTrain, is the world's largest computer training company, with more than 230 locations worldwide and 785 training courses. IDG Marketing Services helps industry-leading IT companies build international brand recognition by developing global integrated marketing programs via IDG's print, online and exposition products worldwide. Further information about the company can be found at www.idg.com.

1/26/00

About Howell Book House
Committed to the Human/Companion Animal Bond

Thank you for choosing a book brought to you by the pet experts at Howell Book House, a division of IDG Books Worldwide. And welcome to the family of pet owners who've put their trust in Howell books for nearly 40 years!

Pet ownership is about relationships — the bonds people form with their dogs, cats, horses, birds, fish, small mammals, reptiles, and other animals. Howell Book House/IDGB understands that these are some of the most important relationships in life, and that it's vital to nurture them through enjoyment and education. The happiest pet owners are those who know they're taking the best care of their pets — and with Howell books, owners have this satisfaction. They're happy, educated owners, and as a result, they have happy pets, and that enriches the bond they share.

Howell Book House was established in 1961 by Mr. Elsworth S. Howell, an active and proactive dog fancier who showed English Setters and judged at the prestigious Westminster Kennel Club show in New York. Mr. Howell based his publishing program on strength of content, and his passion for books written by experienced and knowledgeable owners defined Howell Book House and has remained true over the years. Howell's reputation as the premier pet book publisher is supported by the distinction of having won more awards from the Dog Writers Association of America than any other publisher. Howell Book House/IDGB has over 400 titles in publication, including such classics as The American Kennel Club's *Complete Dog Book*, the *Dog Owner's Home Veterinary Handbook*, *Blessed Are the Brood Mares*, and *Mother Knows Best: The Natural Way to Train Your Dog*.

When you need answers to questions you have about any aspect of raising or training your companion animals, trust that Howell Book House/IDGB has the answers. We welcome your comments and suggestions, and we look forward to helping you maximize your relationships with your pets throughout the years.

Dominique C. De Vito

Publisher

Howell Book House/IDG Books Worldwide

Dedication

For China, Arrow, Apache, Ginnie, and Ms. Schatzie, and all my Goldens at the Rainbow Bridge.

Author's Acknowledgments

I have never written a dog book on my own. So many people (including the four-footed variety) make each venture possible. Thank you to my publisher, Dominique De Vito, for your faith, support, and understanding about my personal dog voice — I cannot thank you enough! And Kelly, you were a peach to put up with my OCD (Obsessive Compulsive Disorder!) about this project, and Scott for hanging in there with us all. Mickey, you were a huge help with your keen eye and "golden" tips and pointers that will help our readers stay on track. Thanks loads to all of you! And a final hurrah to Chris Gonnerman, my computer repair genius who saved my computer and this book!

A very special thanks to my human family, who always grant me extra space when I am obsessing over another dog book project.

And, of course, I can't forget my Golden family — past and present training partners, hiking pals, and couch cushion buds, who have blessed my life for the past 30 years. You are the inspiration behind every single word.

Publisher's Acknowledgments

We're proud of this book; please register your comments through our IDG Books Worldwide Online Registration Form located at http://my2cents.dummies.com.

Some of the people who helped bring this book to market include the following:

Acquisitions, Editorial, and Media Development

Project Editor: Kelly Ewing

Senior Editor: Scott Prentzas

General Reviewer: Mickey Strandberg, Mioak's Retrievers

Illustrator: Barbara Frake

Editorial Manager: Pamela Mourouzis

Editorial Administrator: Michelle Hacker

Production

Project Coordinator: Regina Snyder

Layout and Graphics: Heather Pope, Brent Savage, Jacque Schneider, Brian Torwelle

Proofreaders: Corey Bowen, Susan Moritz, Christy Pingleton, Toni Settle, Sossity Smith

Indexer: Sherry Massey

General and Administrative

IDG Books Worldwide, Inc.: John Kilcullen, CEO; Bill Barry, President and COO

IDG Books Consumer Reference Group

  Business: Kathleen A. Welton, Vice President and Publisher; Kevin Thornton, Acquisitions Manager

  Cooking/Gardening: Jennifer Feldman, Associate Vice President and Publisher

  Education/Reference: Diane Graves Steele, Vice President and Publisher; Greg Tubach, Publishing Director

  Lifestyles: Kathleen Nebenhaus, Vice President and Publisher; Tracy Boggier, Managing Editor

  Pets: Dominique De Vito, Associate Vice President and Publisher; Tracy Boggier, Managing Editor

  Travel: Michael Spring, Vice President and Publisher; Suzanne Jannetta, Editorial Director; Brice Gosnell, Managing Editor

IDG Books Consumer Editorial Services: Kathleen Nebenhaus, Vice President and Publisher; Kristin A. Cocks, Editorial Director; Cindy Kitchel, Editorial Director

IDG Books Consumer Production: Debbie Stailey, Production Director

IDG Books Packaging: Marc J. Mikulich, Vice President, Brand Strategy and Research

◆

The publisher would like to give special thanks to Patrick J. McGovern, without whom this book would not have been possible.

◆

Contents at a Glance

Cartoons at a Glance

By Rich Tennant

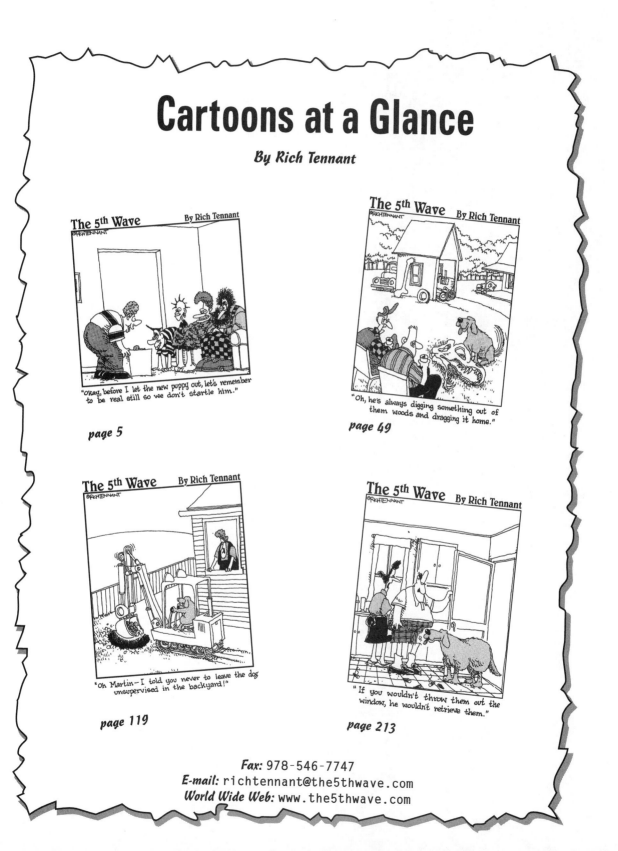

The 5th Wave — By Rich Tennant

"Okay, before I let the new puppy out, let's remember to be real still so we don't startle him."

page 5

The 5th Wave — By Rich Tennant

"Oh, he's always digging something out of them woods and dragging it home."

page 49

The 5th Wave — By Rich Tennant

"Oh Martin — I told you never to leave the dog unsupervised in the backyard!"

page 119

The 5th Wave — By Rich Tennant

"If you wouldn't throw them out the window, he wouldn't retrieve them."

page 213

Fax: 978-546-7747
E-mail: richtennant@the5thwave.com
World Wide Web: www.the5thwave.com

Table of Contents

Introduction

● ●

*W*hether you're thinking about making a run for the gold or already own one or a dozen Golden Retrievers, you've come to the right book stop. Through these pages, I explore all the elements of your Golden Retriever's life (present and future company included), from the joyous days of puppyhood to the sweet serenity of the senior years.

Before you turn to the next page, I must warn you in advance. I will occasionally nag a bit. That's because certain dog facts and rules are important enough to bear extra emphasis, and I will lose sleep if you don't understand them. If you notice it, I'm proud of you because it means that you remember what I said.

About This Book

This book is actually intended for busy 21st century dog owners who don't have time to sit down and read through 300 pages at a crack. This is a reference you can jump in and out of as dog questions rear their furry heads. Just flip to the index to find the pertinent pages on that topic.

That's not to say you shouldn't read this entire book! Every chapter offers golden nuggets of information that I believe every Golden owner needs to know. But you don't need the details on senior dog food when your Golden's just a pup, so that's the real beauty of the *For Dummies* formula. You can go directly to the information you need at the time.

What You're Not to Read

In case you're wondering about those little gray boxes you see throughout the book, these sidebars contain bonus information — kind of like puppy treats. These goodies are not essential to the overall content of each chapter, so don't feel guilty if you skip past one or two!

Foolish Assumptions

I made a few assumptions when I wrote this book:

- ✔ You are hooked on Golden Retrievers and either own one or you're thinking about taking the plunge.
- ✔ You want to find out the best way to raise and train your Golden, as a loving family dog and well-behaved golden citizen.
- ✔ Lastly, I assumed that you want your Golden to not just survive, but thrive, and you bought this book to help you make that happen.

How This Book Is Organized

This book is divided into four parts, each one made up of chapters.

Part I: Finding Your Soul Mate

If you're thinking golden thoughts and haven't taken that big step, you'll need this part to discover more about the breed, whether it's the right fit for your family, and how to find that special breeder. You can also find important tips on puppy selection to be sure that your puppy will match your goals and lifestyle.

Part II: Welcome Home!

Your puppy's homecoming should be a safe and happy time — safe for you as well as for the pup! This part shows you how to puppy-proof your house and introduces your puppy to his crate. There's a lot to learn in puppy's first weeks home, but hang in there; this part helps you get through this time unscathed.

Part III: Keeping Your Pal Healthy and Happy

Your Golden needs a well-rounded health care plan, one that includes proper diet, exercise, and veterinary care. This section covers all of that and also covers those emergency situations where your dog's life may be at risk. It also covers the gamut of canine-world activities that are tailored to your Golden's many talents and abilities.

Part IV: The Part of Tens

For the Part of Tens, I've chosen fun stuff like great puppy games to play, sensible ways to help your Golden live healthier and longer, and Web sites you can explore to discover all sorts of neat doggy stuff. Happy surfing!

Icons Used in This Book

Throughout this book, various icons appear in the margin to highlight different types of information.

See this icon, and you'll discover ways to make your life easier.

The Warning icon means just that!

Remember icons are memory boosters so that you won't forget important doggy details.

This icon marks pure canine pleasantries that dog folks like to know.

Where to Go from Here

Where you start in this book depends on what you want at any particular moment. If your Golden just dug into the trash for the umpteenth time and you're counting to ten, then check out Part II. Other needs and questions will point you to other sections of the book. It's all just the flip of a page away! So go ahead, indulge yourself!

My goal in writing this book was to make you the smartest Golden owner in your neighborhood, heck, even the entire town! If I succeed, everyone will be richer for it — you, your Golden, and, of course, I'll sleep a whole lot better, too!

Part I
Finding Your Soul Mate

The 5th Wave   By Rich Tennant

"Okay, before I let the new puppy out, let's remember
to be real still so we don't startle him."

In this part . . .

Golden Retrievers are great dogs. But just because you see one in every neighborhood doesn't mean that the breed is right for everyone. And before you rush out and find one, you need to make sure that the two of you are a good match. You also need to know where to look for your puppy and then how to go about choosing the one that's meant for you.

Chapter 1

Are You Meant for Each Other?

*I*f you live in a typical neighborhood, then you're probably neighbors with at least one Golden Retriever. Goldens seem to be everywhere — down the block, on television, and in every magazine. These big blonde beauties are the most popular advertising gimmick of the '90s. Not only are they huggable, they're trainable as well. What other dog can leap so high or smile so wide into that camera lens? As one of AKC's five most popular dog breeds, Goldens are no doubt the most photographed subject in the media. Of course, Golden fanatics don't see anything strange about this and love every doggy moment. Heck, even abnormal nondog people will admit (under their breath) those Golden Retrievers are kinda cute.

More proof of the Golden's popularity — for the past decade the Golden Retriever has ranked among the five most popular breeds registered with AKC with over 65,000 Goldens registered every year.

This chapter gives you the inside scoop on this special breed. If you haven't fallen in love with your neighbor's dog already, you will by the time you're done browsing this book.

But — and this is a big *but*. Although Golden Retrievers are great dogs, here's a wake-up call: They're not for everyone. This chapter also tells you how to determine whether you're one of those lucky persons who is perfect for the breed.

The Name Game

The Golden Retriever is aptly named — especially the golden part. What began as a description of his yellow coat more appropriately describes his sunny disposition and his 14-karat value to his owner and society. Goldens are great

Are all Golden Retrievers golden?

The color of that lush Golden Retriever coat dates back to the breed's four original yellow ancestors crossed with a few selected hunting breeds sprinkled here and there during the late 19th century. Today, the breed color can range from very pale blond to reddish gold to deep Irish Setter red.

Keep in mind that the color of the Golden's coat has nothing to do with his intelligence or equally golden temperament. Color matters occasionally in the conformation ring. Show judges of the '90s seem to prefer blondes, which only means they probably spent too much time watching reruns of old Marilyn Monroe movies.

family dogs and all-around good sports who think they were created purely to please their person. This happy, funny, friendly fetcher of anything not nailed down has captured a permanent corner of the 1990s American heart, home, and marketplace (see Figure 1-1). Give them a couch cushion with a human on it, a puddle to play in, and a stick or tennis ball to fetch and carry (maybe not in that order), and you've made their day. As a bonus, throw in an occasional duck or pheasant — after all, retriever is 50 percent of this dog's name!

Figure 1-1: Golden Retrievers are friendly, fun, and as American as apple pie.

Nance Photography/AKC Stock Images.

Forgive and forget

Goldens have the dog world's most forgiving disposition and will blithely dismiss all those dumb mistakes you're bound to make. Whether you come home two hours late, forget his dinner bowl, or accidentally step on his tail, he'll forget it ever happened once you smile at him. (A hefty scratch behind his ears, and he's your slave forever.) That does not imply that you have his permission to do stupid things. It just means he understands you're only human.

Likewise, you should follow his good example and forgive your dog his trespasses. In dog terms, they're not mistakes because he's just a dog and is the product of his instincts and your training, good or bad.

More than Beauty

The Golden Retriever's personality is as golden as his outer coat. The Golden was bred to please, and please he does. He started out as a hunting partner who delivered birds to hand and has evolved into modern times delivering whatever suits his owner's fancy. He's always happy to oblige.

Because Golden Retrievers were originally bred to work in tandem with humans, they are also highly trainable and eager to please. These creatures are a breath of fresh air in an era of too many wild and crazy dogs who drive their owners nuts.

 Trainable doesn't mean that Golden Retrievers are born already trained. It just means they're very willing fellows who like to work as a team, and if you're the captain of the team, your Golden will be delighted to do your bidding. Remember the part about the captain; it's important! (See Chapter 7 for more on training.)

Beauty, Brains, Personality — and the Sporting Life

If the Golden Retriever were a human, you'd be envious. Not only are Goldens beautiful, intelligent, and friendly, they're also natural athletes who have dipped their paws into every canine sporting discipline. These dogs are joyful companions who are willing to try anything as long as they can enjoy it with someone fun to be with.

The do-it-all Golden Retriever

Beyond sportsmanship, that famous Golden nose has nudged its way into almost every other facet of the human-animal connection. Today, Golden Retrievers serve as assistance dogs for the physically disabled, guide dogs for the blind, and hearing dogs for the deaf. And those Golden noses keep on sniffing, working for law enforcement as drug and arson detectives, and as search and rescue dogs who find victims buried under snow and earthquake rubble. Beyond that, they also excel as therapy dogs in hospitals and nursing homes where, unlike the average hourly employee, they love their jobs. (Just watch our Golden Retriever, Apache, race for the front door of the nursing home.) And they work for free, unless you count dog biscuits as a paycheck.

Why Not a Golden Retriever?

Of course you want a Golden Retriever. What person in his right mind wouldn't? And you firmly believe you and the dog would be a golden combination.

Well, maybe. Despite their high-profile status in the media, Goldens aren't for everyone. This is a sporting breed, folks. These high-energy dogs require training. On the other hand, Goldens are easily trained and love to learn, so training could and should be a fun but very busy experience.

With no offense intended to my favorite breed, the following sections outline some reasons that you may want to think twice about life with a Golden Retriever.

Hair, hair, everywhere

The Golden Retriever has what's called a *double coat,* which means that he has a soft downy undercoat to insulate him from the cold and heat and a longer outer coat of guard hairs. These hairy critters shed their downy undercoat in huge quantities every spring and drip a little dog hair all over the house all year long. The resulting clouds of dog down all over the house can make you tear out your hair as well.

Brushing will help keep that nuisance dog hair to a minimum (see Figure 1-2). Daily brushing is best — twice weekly is a must. If you use a professional groomer, expect to pay $15 to $25 per grooming session. Pretty is seldom cheap. (For more on grooming, see Chapter 13.)

Do you really want a puppy?

Golden Retriever puppy fever isn't a dog disease; it's a people condition that most often occurs in spring when humans become infected with an uncontrollable urge to add a puppy to the family. It can lead to dog heaven or, heaven forbid, a nervous breakdown if the affected person thinks all Goldens are like the ones they see on television. The cure — getting that cute puppy immediately — can be worse than the disease.

If you're serious about this golden business and not just caving in to the kids or some other wild and crazy impulse, follow the advice of responsible dog owners and breeders. Look deep into your dog-loving soul and check out the big picture. Love alone is not enough.

Move over!

If you want to live with a Golden Retriever, make sure that you have room for one. These big sprawling fellows easily occupy at least one couch cushion or easy chair. Everything's big, including their muddy paw prints on your kitchen floor and their nose prints on the window. That happy Golden tail can easily clear your coffee table. (Sorry, move your Waterford.)

Figure 1-2:
Daily brushing keeps nuisance dog hair to a minimum.

Close Encounters of the Furry Kind.

Born to retrieve

The Golden Retriever is a Scotsman, a hunting dog bred and born in Scotland over 100 years ago. To the Golden's credit, he has surpassed Scottish tweeds and kilts in popularity and today performs well beyond the duck blind he was born for. Overdosed with talent and versatility, the 20th century Golden consistently outperforms other breeds in every discipline in dog sports, including more mundane activities like sock and shoe theft. (Just ask my personal Golden Retriever crew about that!)

In short, Goldens need space, and lots of it, both in-house and out. A yard is a must, and good fencing is preferred.

Daily dose of exercise

A normal Golden usually creates a little happy chaos, which is part of its irresistible appeal. These spirited dogs have a great sense of humor and love to retrieve, play, chase, and chew (see Figure 1-3). They need exercise to expend all that sporting energy, or they will entertain themselves in typical canine fashion. (Think destruction!)

The typical Golden Retriever household usually has few ragged chew marks on the chair legs, dog toys strewn about the living room, piles of shredded sticks in the backyard, and one or two large sticks at the front or back door, the ones he delivered to you as his special prize.

Your Golden will not exercise without you. You are his incentive to romp and play. Daily walks and jogs, Frisbee games, and bumper chasing (those large, hot-dog shaped canvas or plastic retrieving objects sold in pet stores for retrieve-a-holic dogs) can help keep your Golden tired and content. For more on exercising with your dog, see Chapters 10 and 17.

Lively or laid back?

Just like people, you can't stereotype Goldens. If you're discouraged about all this talk about active, high-energy Golden Retrievers, don't worry. You can still find a quiet(er) Golden companion who won't disrupt your household. Some lines (or families) of show-type Goldens produce a more laid-back animal who doesn't act like Robo Cop. See Chapters 3 and 4 for more details.

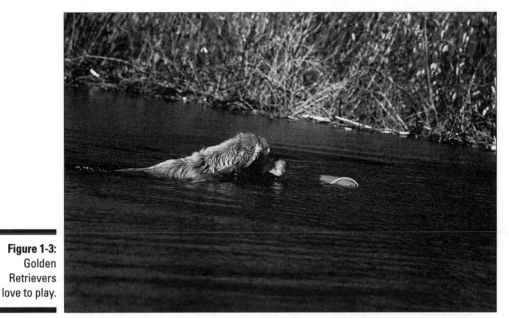

Figure 1-3:
Golden
Retrievers
love to play.

Kent and Donna Dannen/AKC Stock Images.

Get up and go!

If you're on the go and never home and he's alone most of the day, your Golden will be stressed and most unhappy. That's not fair to the dog and may be disastrous for you. Goldens need to be with people, and an isolated and lonely Golden can easily suffer from separation anxiety, which will lead to destructive behavior. It's a natural canine stress reliever.

If you're an active family who loves the outdoor life and plan to take your Golden to soccer practice and baseball games, then the two of you are probably a good match

Train, train, train

Smart as he is, a Golden Retriever will not train himself. Good manners are not included in his pedigree. It's up to you, the team captain, to teach your dog acceptable behavior — what he may and may not do at home and in the neighborhood. Obedience training is the only way to accomplish that. Few pet owners have the know-how, expertise, or motivation to do it solo, so training classes must be part of your golden agenda. That also means practicing every day, or your once-a-week classes will be wasted.

Don't be misled by the over-used 10-minutes-a-day obedience slogan. That rule may apply to the Sit or Stay command, but training is an ongoing process whenever you're with your dog and he's awake. If you can't or won't commit to raising your Golden as you would an infant or toddler, don't blame your Golden if he's wild or disobedient.

Love-'em-all

If you're looking for a guard dog, get rid of this book and investigate another breed. Most Goldens are complete love sponges who would happily lick the boots of an intruder. You can encourage them to bark at people who approach your house, but you can't — and shouldn't — teach them to intimidate or bite. Their very size may deter a home invader, but anyone familiar with a Golden's love-'em-all attitude knows that a scratch behind Golden ears means instant friendship.

On the other hand, I firmly believe that my Golden family would sense any danger to me personally and would defend me to the death. Stories abound about Golden Retriever heroes who have protected children and adults who were in danger or threatened by some adversary.

Kids or dogs?

If you have kids under age 3 or 4 and you get a puppy, you will now have the equivalent of two or three kids under 3! Double your pleasure, and, you got it, twice the work. And a major communication problem.

Because neither pup nor child have learned the house rules yet, almost everything they hear will be a no-no, which creates a negative learning environment for both kid and dog. Puppies nip and chew, and kids pull tails and sit on furry bodies. Both require 24-hour attention. And face it, when you have to prioritize, the puppy naturally loses. That's not fair for the dog. Some breeders may recommend that you wait until your child is older before they let you have one of their prize packages. My personal age limit is 4 years old.

A Golden Price Tag

Dogs are not a bargain if you think long term. Even if you find a pup for free, you still need to pay for food, veterinary care, training, equipment, and possibly doggie day care. And there are no laters or maybes. A sick dog, like a sick child, needs attention now, not when you have the money. In both the short term and the long haul, dogs, especially large ones, add up to mega bucks. So before you fall in love with some blond cutie, consider these figures provided by the American Kennel Club.

- ✔ **Veterinary expenses:** Initial veterinary care, (shots, worming, and other healthy stuff) runs about $150 to $200, with lifetime vet care totaling more than $1,000. That's without the cost of spay/neuter surgery ($75 to $200) and the possibility of other surgery due to accident or illness. Factor in preventive medications for typical canine illnesses, and the total medical care can run over $2,000 during the lifetime of your dog. For more on preventive care, see Chapter 11.

- ✔ **Obedience classes:** Training fees for puppy classes and early obedience instruction start at $50 to $100, the same for the additional classes you'll need to make your dog bomb-proof, and will run well into the hundreds if you continue formal training. For more on training, see Chapter 7.

- ✔ **Food:** Good quality dog food for an average-size Golden can cost up to $500 a year. That's $5,500 over an 11-year period. Imagine feeding a Great Dane!

- ✔ **Wardrobe costs:** Dog supplies, grooming equipment, leashes, collars, and toys carry an initial cost of $250, with a lifetime estimate of $2,500 if you take good care of your dog. (And, of course, you would!) Registration fees vary by state and county, and there's usually flea and pest control, which every Golden owner faces more than once. Hands-on flea treatment and yard care are estimated at $900 lifetime cost.

The grand total comes in at $10,000 to $15,000, the approximate 10- to 13-year lifetime cost for the privilege and pleasure of living with a Golden Retriever. And don't forget the initial purchase of the dog, which can range from a $100 donation to an animal shelter or up to $1,000 for a decent to competition-quality Golden with health guarantees.

If your Golden damages or destroys your possessions (bet on it!) or a neighbor's (probably), you can add hundreds more to annual living expenses.

The Midas puppy

Some breeders who raise competition Goldens may have "pet quality" pups from certain litters. Pet-quality pups are ones that don't make the cut for competition in the field or show ring but still possess all the other important "golden" qualities and thus may be less expensive. But that $200 Golden pup is not a bargain and may end up costing a fortune in medical bills, not to mention heartbreak.

Chapter 2

Knowing What to Look for in the Breed

All breeds must have a standard. After all, that's what makes a breed a breed. Without a standard, you could breed a dog with big black or white spots to another spotted dog, and a few generations down the road you'd have a leopard-spotted Golden. That's what genetics are all about.

It's the job and purpose of every breed's parent club to decide how to preserve the purity of its chosen breed. Goldens were originally hunting dogs, and the standard says so. The standard also dictates other characteristics of the Golden, like its color, coat type, size, and temperament.

In this chapter, I explain the intricacies of the Golden Retriever standard as approved by AKC. Ignore the funny wording — just like the U.S. Constitution or other complex legal document, it has its share of funny terms and language.

Officially Golden

The American Kennel Club first recognized the Golden Retriever in 1925. By 1938, the breed had gained enough popularity that Golden fanciers formed a national breed club. Thus was born the Golden Retriever Club of America to help direct the future of the breed in the United States. By the late 1990s, the GRCA had about 50 member clubs across the country.

Those local Golden Retriever clubs are a major resource for Golden Retriever owners. You don't have to be a canine expert or good at anything doggie to join a dog club. Just loving your dog like crazy is reason enough. You can get lots of good dog advice and information from more experienced club members, and it's a great place to share the dog tales and brags that your other friends are sick of hearing.

AKC Standards

The AKC has certain standards when it comes to each breed. The following sections, along with Figure 2-1, tell you what to look for when you're shopping for a Golden Retriever. Please keep in mind that the language is like a canine legal document and difficult for the lay person to understand.

While a breed standard is necessary to define the ideal Golden Retriever, dogs who are poor specimens still make wonderful pets, but they should not be bred.

Throughout the following sections, I include parentheses that interpret terms in my words.

Figure 2-1:
The profile
of a Golden
Retriever.

Beauty, brains, and bird dogs

Always great showmen and competitors, Goldens trip the light fantastic in the conformation ring, beguiling the judges and the spectators with their beauty and performance (see figure). Goldens consistently outshine all other breeds in the obedience ring, winning trials and wowing the audience with their high-stepping strut. And a lucky minority still pursue their birthright in the field, in hunting tests, field trials, and doing the real thing with their hunter-owners. Beyond even that, Goldens also steal the show at agility events and flyball competition. With all those fun activities, no wonder these Golden dogs are always smiling!

It was inevitable that a dog this versatile and talented would be embraced by sporting specialists and bred for specific qualities for various canine competitions. Today, the conformation crowd breeds Goldens for their grand good looks. The obedience enthusiasts prefer high-stepping Goldens who love teamwork, and the bird dog division looks for Goldens who still love birds and water.

As a result, there are often a huge difference in how each type of Golden looks and acts. They're all Golden Retrievers, but be careful which you choose. While each type should have a heart of gold, remember there are gold-plated and several varieties of solid gold.

Mary Bloom/AKC Stock Images.

General appearance

A symmetrical, powerful, active dog, sound and well put together, not clumsy nor long in leg, displaying a kindly expression and possessing a personality that is eager, alert, and self-confident. Primarily a hunting dog, he should be shown in hard-working condition. Overall appearance, balance, gait, and purpose to be given more emphasis than any of his component parts.

Faults: Any departure from the described ideal shall be considered faulty to the degree to which it interferes with the breed's purpose or is contrary to breed character.

The Faults definition is intended primarily to guide those who judge the dogs in the conformation ring.

Size, proportion, substance

Males 23–24 inches in height at withers; females 21½–22½ inches. Dogs up to 1 inch above or below standard size should be proportionately penalized. Deviation in height of more than 1 inch from standard shall disqualify.

Length from breastbone to point of buttocks slightly greater than height at *withers* (top of shoulder) in ratio of 12:11. Weight for dogs 65–75 pounds; bitches 55–65 pounds.

Head

Broad in skull, slightly arched laterally and longitudinally without prominence of *frontal bones* (forehead) or *occipital bones* (top back point of the skull). *Stop* (between the eyes, where the top of the nose and forehead meet) well defined but not abrupt. *Foreface* (front of face) deep and wide; nearly as long as skull. Muzzle straight in profile, blending smoothly and strongly into skull; when viewed in profile or from above, slightly deeper and wider at stop than at tip. No heaviness in *flews* (the skin that hangs from the dog's muzzle or his lip). Removal of whiskers is permitted but not preferred.

Eyes friendly and intelligent in expression, medium large with dark, close fitting rims, set well apart and reasonably deep in sockets. Color preferably dark brown; medium brown acceptable. Slant eyes and narrow, triangular eyes detract from correct expression and are to be faulted. No white or *haw* (lining inside the lower eye lid) visible when looking straight ahead. Dogs showing evidence of functional abnormality of eyelids or eyelashes (such as, but not limited to, trichiasis, entropion, ectropion, or distichiasis) are to be excused from the ring.

Snow nose

Don't worry if your Golden's nose turns a little pink in winter. It's called a *snow nose* and will turn black or brownish-black again in spring. Some dogs get it, and some don't. Others get it later in life, and some never do.

Ears rather short with front edge attached well behind and just above the eye and falling close to cheek. When pulled forward, tip of ear should just cover the eye. Low, hound-like ear set to be faulted.

Nose black or brownish black, though fading to a lighter shade in cold weather not serious. Pink nose or one seriously lacking in pigmentation to be faulted.

Teeth scissors bite, in which the outer side of the lower incisors touches the inner side of the upper incisors. *Undershot* (the lower front teeth protrude beyond the front upper teeth in bite or closed position) or *overshot* (just the opposite; the lower jaw is shorter, so the upper front teeth bite down over the lower teeth) is a disqualification. *Misalignment of teeth* (irregular placement of incisors) or a level *bite* (incisors meet each other edge to edge) is undesirable, but not to be confused with undershot or overshot. Full dentition. Obvious gaps are serious faults.

Neck, topline, body

Neck medium long, merging gradually into well-laid back shoulders, giving sturdy, muscular appearance. No throatiness.

Back line strong and level from *withers* (top of the shoulders, just behind the neck) to slightly sloping *croup* (the lower back, from the front of the pelvis to the base of the tail), whether standing or moving. Sloping back line, *roach* (humped up) or sway back, flat or steep croup to be faulted.

Body well balanced, short coupled (not an excessively long body), deep through the chest. Chest between forelegs at least as wide as a man's closed hand including thumb, with well developed *forechest* (top of the chest). *Brisket* (lower chest under the breast bone extending to between the front legs) extends to elbow. Ribs long and well sprung but not barrel shaped, extending well toward hindquarters. *Loin* (from the rib cage to the pelvis) short, muscular, wide and deep, with very little tuck-up. *Slabsidedness* (a flat or caved-in chest), narrow chest, lack of depth in brisket, excessive *tuck-up* (underneath the rear part of the body) to be faulted.

Tail well set on, thick and muscular at the base, following the natural line of the croup. Tail bones extend to, but not below, the point of *hock* (the joint between the lower thigh and rear *pastern* (sort of the rear elbow). Carried with merry action, level or with some moderate upward curve; never curled over back nor between the legs.

Forequarters

Muscular, well coordinated with hindquarters and capable of free movement. Shoulder blades long and well laid back with upper tips fairly close together at withers. Upper arms appear about the same length as the blades, setting the elbows back beneath the upper tip of the blades, close to the ribs without looseness. Legs, viewed from the front, straight with good bone, but not to the point of coarseness. *Pasterns* (on the leg, just above the foot, where the foot, or wrist/carpus bends into the leg; metacarpus in front, metatarsus in rear) short and strong, sloping slightly with no suggestion of weakness. *Dewclaws* (a nail on the small fifth toe on the inside of the front leg above the rest of the toes) on forelegs may be removed, but are normally left on.

Feet medium size, round, compact, and well knuckled, with thick pads. Excess hair may be trimmed to show natural size and contour. *Splayed* (the toes or digits are split apart or separated) or *hare feet* (center toes are more than a hair longer than the outer toes) to be faulted.

Hindquarters

Broad and strongly muscled. Profile of croup slopes slightly; the pelvic bone slopes at a slightly greater angle (approximately 30 degrees from horizontal). In a natural stance, the femur (thigh bone, rear leg) joins the pelvis at approximately a 90-degree angle; *stifles* (a joint in the thigh, sometimes called the knee) well bent; *hocks* (tarsus — the joint between the lower thigh and rear pastern) well let down with short, strong rear pasterns. Feet as in front. Legs straight when viewed from rear. *Cow hocks* (hind legs that bend in), *spread hocks* (just the opposite), and *sickle hocks* (hocks with angulation in sickle shape) to be faulted.

Coat

Dense and water repellent with good undercoat. Outer coat firm and water resilient, neither coarse nor silky, lying close to the body; may be straight or wavy. Untrimmed natural ruff; moderate feathering on back of forelegs and on underbody; heavier feathering on front of neck, back of thighs, and underside of tail. Coat on head, paws and front of legs is short and even. Excessive length, open coats, and limp, soft coats are very undesirable. Feet may be trimmed and stray hairs neatened, but the natural appearance of coat or outline should not be altered by cutting or clipping.

Golden myths and history

A charming tale existed years ago about a group of Russian circus dogs who evolved into the very talented Golden Retriever.

Okay, so maybe not. The truth is you can thank a Scotsman for your lovely breed. Sir Dudley Marjoriebanks — later elevated to Lord Tweedmouth and so named because his estate rested on the Tweed River in the hills of Inverness, Scotland — was an avid sportsman with a special passion for waterfowling. Apparently collecting the ducks he shot over those rough coastal waters wasn't easy, because he longed for a canine hunting companion who would not only swim out to retrieve his birds, but also deliver them to hand. And he had a yen for a yellow dog to do the job. Sounds like a good idea to me, too.

So in 1868, Tweedmouth launched his first experimental yellow breeding, mating a liver-colored Tweed Water Spaniel (the name begs no explanation) named Belle to a yellow Wavy-Coated Retriever named Nous, which in Greek means wisdom. See anything prophetic in that name? Nous was the only yellow pup, in those days called a "sport," out of a litter of all blacks, which was the standard color for the Wavy-Coat.

Surprise! Nous and Belle produced four yellow furries, which Tweedmouth promptly named Cowslip, Ada, Crocus, and Primrose. He kept Cowslip for himself and gave the other pups to good friends who shared his passion for breeding a yellow sporting dog.

Tweedmoth's kennel records show a detailed history of Color-Me-Yellow canine marriages dating back to Cowslip and his littermates. Linebreeding of this nature was pretty radical in those days, so Tweedmouth was a true vanguard of his time.

So where did red-gold and rust-colored Goldens come from? Okay, carry that a little further. Who were the parents that produced so many other shades of gold? Surely not just the yellow dogs that Tweedmouth was so avidly promoting.

Enter the Irish Setter (sorry, Scotland), the Bloodhound, and the yellow Labrador. Breeding reliable retrieving dogs also meant improving and preserving essential sporting qualities like scenting ability and other important hunting talents. So along the way these retriever pioneers occasionally outcrossed their yellow dogs to other popular hunting breeds. It's often said the Golden nose is one of its most famous parts, and you can thank the Bloodhound cross for that.

The Golden's destiny eventually took them across the Atlantic into the United States and Canada. In the early 1900s, British military officers and other professionals often traveled with their hunting dogs so that they could do a little shooting on their business trips. (Sort of like today's political junkets.) Eventually, the dogs merged into the U.S. population, growing especially popular in the bird-rich areas of the northern states and coastal areas. The breed is still abundant in those states where pheasant stock is plentiful and that Golden nose can track them down.

Tweedmouth really did his homework. His yellow retrievers had such sweet and winning personalities they just naturally wiggled their way into the house after a hard day of hunting. Always smiling, great with kids, and eager to please, the Golden was as good in the house as he was afield. By 1950, the breed was becoming well known as a dual purpose dog.

Color

Rich, lustrous golden of various shades. Feathering may be lighter than rest of coat. With the exception of graying or whitening on face or body due to age, any white marking, other than a few white hairs on the chest, should be penalized according to its extent. Allowable light shadings are not to be confused with white markings. Predominant body color that is extremely pale or extremely dark is undesirable. Some latitude should be given to the light puppy whose coloring shows promising of deepening with maturity. Any noticeable area of black or other off-color hair is a serious fault.

Gait

When trotting, gait is free, smooth, powerful, and well coordinated, showing good reach. Viewed from any position, legs turn neither in nor out, nor do feet cross or interfere with each other. As speed increases, feet tend to converge toward center line of balance. It is recommended that dogs be shown on a loose lead to reflect true gait.

Temperament

Friendly, reliable, and trustworthy. Quarrelsomeness or hostility toward other dogs or people in normal situations, or an unwarranted show of timidity or nervousness, is not in keeping with Golden Retriever characteristics. Such actions should be penalized according to their significance.

(For more information on a Golden Retriever's temperament, see Chapter 1.)

Disqualifications

Deviation in height of more than 1 inch from standard either way. Undershot or overshot bite.

Chapter 3

Finding a Golden Breeder

· ·

In This Chapter

▶ Quizzing your prospective breeders

▶ Evaluating your puppy alternatives — older puppies and adult Goldens

▶ Understanding pedigrees

▶ Analyzing health clearances

· ·

*E*ver take a look at your family tree? Just like humans have family trees, dogs have pedigrees. And just as your ancestry can reflect bank robbers or other unsavory people, so, too, can a dog's pedigree contain some very common, even crummy, parents, grandparents, aunts, or uncles. And their genetic influence will determine what kind of dog your Golden will grow up to be. So when you're looking for a Golden, pedigree is the first order of the day.

And because good breeders build good pedigrees, finding a good breeder is actually the most important ingredient in your puppy search. In this chapter, I outline a breeder search plan.

Finding a Breeder Who Is Golden

References are a good start to finding a reputable breeder. If enough people say positive things about a breeder, you're probably moving in the right direction. But if you don't know someone who knows a breeder, don't despair. There are other ways to get referrals:

✔ **Ask your veterinarian.** If you don't have a veterinarian, ask a friend's vet.

✔ **Ask other Golden owners.** Talk to people who own Goldens you admire and ask them where they got their dogs. But be careful — you still want to evaluate the source, even if another Golden owner recommends it, especially if his breeder is questionable and he just got lucky with his dog.

✔ **Go to dog events.** Spend the day at a dog show, an obedience show, or field event. You'll see a wide variety of Goldens and can get up close and personal with the ones you like. Most dog owners who show their dogs in the various dog activities enjoy nothing better than talking about their special Goldens and where they got them.

✔ **Check with a local kennel or dog training club.** You can also call, write, or e-mail the AKC, 51 Madison Ave., New York, NY 10010, for contacts in the Golden Retriever Club of America. You can also visit the GRCA Web site on the Internet (see Chapter 18). These sources can refer you to a Golden breeder in your area.

For openers, do not check newspaper ads to find a puppy. Good breeders seldom advertise. They usually have reservations in advance and depend on referrals from other dog friends or previous puppy clients. They also don't want to sort through all the riffraff to find proper homes for their puppies and will keep puppies past the normal 7- to 8-week placement age until the right person comes along.

If you don't already have a breeder reference from someone you know and trust, you may want to ask the breeder you're visiting about previous litters and where you can meet other dogs she's bred and the people who own them. A reputable breeder should be more than willing to offer references.

In addition, a reputable breeder:

✔ **Understands the genetics behind the mating of a particular sire (father) and dam (mother).** A reputable breeder also has reasonable expectations for what the breeding will produce and plans a litter for specific reasons. She never does it just because her Golden is sweet or beautiful and her neighbor's Golden is a handsome guy and they'd have such pretty babies, and so on. That's the stuff unhealthy and unsound dogs are made of.

✔ **Has a puppy contract that specifies health guarantees.** Usually, she agrees to take the puppy back, replace the puppy with one of equal value, or refund your purchase price if the pup fails to meet the health guarantees in the contract. The contract should include a spay/neuter clause and indicate whether the pup is being sold on a limited registration. See the section "The Paper Trail — Pedigree and AKC Registration Papers" for details on limited registrations.

✔ **Breeds no more than one or two litters a year (see Figure 3-1).** The reputable breeder does not keep several different breeds of dogs on premises who spend their entire lives in pens, cages, or kennels, popping out puppies every year. Golden breeders are devoted to their breed. Their dogs are members of the family and usually live in the house (at least most of the time) and enjoy the same privileges as the kids. (Okay, maybe they don't all sleep on the bed like mine do.) Make sure that any breeder you consider fits that description.

Your breeder should be involved

Expect a breeder who specializes in show, field, or obedience Goldens to be involved in activities related to those disciplines. If she isn't, ask whether she can refer you to someone who is. It's not likely you'll find the perfect litter on your first try.

Figure 3-1:
One to two litters a year is typical for most reputable breeders.

Close Encounters of the Furry Kind.

 You may have to travel to find a good quality litter. If the breeder is too far away to visit, ask her to send a video of the puppies and her other dogs. Today, even Golden Retrievers are high-tech!

Visiting a Breeder

The puppy environment is one important indicator of the breeder's level of care and expertise. You'll want to check out not only where but how the puppies are raised. The puppies should be in the house or an adjoining room, not isolated down in a basement, or kennel or kennel building, or a dark corner of the garage. (The key word here is isolated.) They need to be near family areas where they can be raised and socialized with people every day, or they'll be fearful and intimidated by humans. The greater their exposure to household sights and sounds between 3 and 7 weeks of age, the easier the transition from canine family to human.

In addition, the puppy area should be reasonably clean, but don't forget to consider the nonstop food chain in a litter of healthy pups. What goes in keeps coming out all day long, so scrupulously clean is pretty tough, but your overall impression of "clean" is a good clue.

The puppies themselves should have clean thick coats and feel solid and muscular. You don't want to see crusted or runny discharge from their eyes, ears, or nose or watery or bloody stools. Their dewclaws should have been removed soon after birth, and they should have had one or two wormings and a parvo-distemper shot before 7 weeks and before they leave their litter.

If your breeder passes the preceding initial tests, it's quiz show time. Start with the following questions:

How long have you been breeding Golden Retrievers?

Experienced breeders are more knowledgeable than a novice who is breeding for the first or second time. If it's a first-timer, she should have an experienced mentor she can refer you to.

Do you belong to a breed or kennel club?

Breeders who are truly involved in their breed usually belong to one or more dog clubs.

Do you screen your breeding dogs for genetic defects?

Both sire and dam of every litter should have OFA, CERF, and cardiology clearances.

Are you involved in any dog activities or events with your Goldens?

Most reputable breeders of quality Goldens show or train their dogs for some type of performance event or dog-related activity.

Have your Goldens earned any titles?

Breeders who earn titles in various canine competitions prove their experience and commitment to the breed.

When do you allow your puppies to go home?

A breeder who releases puppies under 7 weeks of age may not have the best interest of the puppy in mind.

What do you require or demand of prospective puppy buyers?

Good breeders have certain requirements about *who* will raise their puppy, *how,* and *where.* They may even act like a Watergate prosecutor.

Breeder interrogation

As you visit breeders, you'll discover that the good ones not only give you scads of information about the breed in general and, more specifically, their puppies, but they quiz you as well! That's great, because it means she knows her dog facts and wants to make you dog-smart, too, especially if you're going to raise one of her puppies. Good breeders care not just about their pups, but also about the families who will purchase them. Expect the breeder to ask you questions about your dog history, such as whether you ever owned a dog, what kind it was, and what became of it.

She'll also want to know about your family, the ages of your kids, and who will be home to raise the puppy. Some insist on meeting all family members before sending puppy home. (I do.) Don't be offended; she's not being nosy. It's just your typical job interview. How else can she determine whether or not you qualify as a good puppy parent? Her questions indicate she cares. If she doesn't ask questions, find another breeder. A good breeder is very protective of the puppies she brings into the world.

Do you give any guarantees with your pups, and are those guarantees in a contract?

Reputable breeders offer health guarantees and reasonable return policies in a written contract and explain the specifics of each guarentee.

Do you require that your puppies be spayed or neutered?

Reputable breeders frequently sell their pet quality puppies on spay/neuter agreements or on a limited registration basis.

Also realize that a reputable breeder should tell you what it's like to live with a Golden Retriever — the good and the bad. No breed of dog is perfect, and she should volunteer the disadvantages of Golden ownership along with all the happy news. (See Chapter 2 for more on the cons of Golden ownership.)

The puppies can't go home until they're 7 to 10 weeks old, depending on the breeder's policy. Most breeder's release their puppies at about 7 weeks of age, a few even keep their puppies longer. (If the breeder lets them go at 5 or 6 weeks, say good-bye and leave.) Breeders usually allow visitors after the pups are 3 or 4 weeks old, but you can't tell much about individual personality until they're at least 5 weeks of age. You can, however, get to know the breeder and the Momma Golden in the meantime and decide whether you want to join her Golden family.

Adopting an Older Golden

If the thought of struggling through housetraining and canine puberty appalls you, consider the joys of adopting an older Golden Retriever (see Figure 3-2). When you adopt a dog who has grown through the cute bouncy puppy stage, what you see is what you get.

With an adult dog, you don't have to guess about the coat type or adult size or the personality in a dog who has outgrown puppyhood. An older or more mature Golden may even be housebroken and have some degree of basic house manners or training. Of course, puppies are great fun, but they're also work, and you can spare yourself that struggle if you bypass adolescence and go directly to adulthood.

If you worry that an older Golden will not bond or relate to you because you didn't nurture him from infancy, forget it. An almost unfortunate fact about this breed is that they will love just about anyone who loves them back. As much as I hate to think about it, I know that my beloved Goldens would be just as happy with someone else who loved and cared for them the way I do. That's just the nature of this sweet beast.

Figure 3-2:
If you don't think you'd enjoy the puppy stage, consider adopting an older Golden.

Close Encounters of the Furry Kind.

You can sometimes find adult Goldens and older Golden puppies through a breeder, Golden Retriever rescue services, or animal shelters.

Breeders

Occasionally a breeder will keep more than one puppy from a litter to evaluate its potential as a future show dog or field prospect. If and when the pup doesn't fulfill her expectations, she places it in a pet home. These dogs are usually excellent companions, sometimes even fine competitors for a novice Golden owner. If they have been well socialized and cared for, they will bond easily to a loving human being.

Once in a while, a breeder also gets a puppy or older Golden back from a previous litter for some unfortunate reason. (Some reasons are legitimate, like divorce or allergies, while some are inexcusable, such as he barked too much, jumped on the kids, got hair in the pool, don't have time, and so on.) The breeder will evaluate the dog before placing him in another home to prevent another life change for the dog. If you work with a breeder, make your preferences known so that she can arrange a perfect match.

Rescue groups

Golden Retriever rescue services work with animal shelters, animal control agencies, and dog owners to assist in relocating and rehabilitating abandoned, abused, and confiscated (from puppy mills and brokers) Goldens into healthy, loving homes. At least 35 rescue services are affiliated with Golden Retriever clubs across the country that rescue and rehome thousands of Goldens every year.

The rescue process can range from very simple to extremely complicated, depending on the geographical area and the number of people and dogs involved in each rescue operation. Rescue volunteers provide health care and foster care and do personality and temperament evaluations before each placement. They want permanent loving homes for these golden victims, so they look for lifetime commitments from adoptive families.

If you work with Golden Rescue to find an older puppy or adult (puppies come along infrequently), you can usually rely on their evaluation of the dog, their choice for you, and their help in his adjustment to his new environment. The last thing they want is for this dog to be uprooted once again. Expect them to be firm and possibly intimidating to make sure that you're the right person for this dog. They already know the dog. They *don't* know you!

Animal shelters

Many animal shelters work with area breed rescue groups when a purebred dog arrives. If no Golden Retriever organization or dedicated volunteer is available to assist with the adoption, the dog goes into the general shelter population. Shelters in smaller communities of under 100,000 often work with a few reliable individuals who raise certain breeds and are willing to assist or act as an adoption agent on their own. The vast majority of shelters have the dog's best interests at heart and do their best to screen and evaluate their animals to determine whether they are adoptable and to assure a good match with the adoptive person.

For years I worked independently with local agencies and area veterinarians as a Golden Retriever Rescue committee of one. Now I act as an interim liaison between those sources and my Golden club's official Golden Rescue group, which is 200 miles away. I average two or three Golden strays a year from this rural community, and I am absolutely thrilled to tell you that over the past ten years, every single Golden who came into my home from who-knows-where was an absolute peach that I would have kept in a heartbeat if I wasn't already over-dogged. Each one went on to a good home with a family who swears this is the best dog they ever saw. I rest my case!

When you visit a shelter, bring a prepared checklist, just as if you were adopting a puppy. Don't be shy. Ask lots of questions and spend time alone with the dog before you agree to take him home. Your best choice is that middle-of-the-road guy we always talk about. Not too timid or too pushy, and never aggressive in any way. Don't cave in or feel sorry for a dog who isn't right for you or who could present more problems than you're prepared to handle. The awful truth is that you and I can't save them all.

There will be paperwork with each adoption agency, whether shelter or rescue organization, which is for the dog's protection as well as yours. They will charge an adoption fee, which may include certain health services for the dog. Almost all require that every adopted Golden must be spayed or neutered.

If you adopt or purchase an adult Golden or older puppy, bring him home during a vacation period or at least over a weekend when you can spend two or three days helping him adjust to his new home (see Chapter 5). All dogs, regardless of age, need reassurance and attention to make them feel safe and comfortable in a new environment.

After a reasonable adjustment period, take your new Golden to obedience school. Like all Goldens, he'll love doing something with his person, he'll enjoy learning new things, and he'll especially like knowing you're in charge, which is the main benefit of the obedience experience.

The Paper Trail — Pedigree and AKC Registration Papers

You've all heard those famous dog words, "Of course, he's a good dog; he's AKC." Or "He's a good dog, he has all his papers," or "He's purebred, his parents were AKC."

Don't buy into that. "Papers" and AKC-registered have absolutely nothing to do with a dog's quality or worth. They mean one thing only — that the dog's parents were recognized by AKC as being of the same breed. What it does not prove or guarantee is that those parents, or their offspring, were healthy, sound, stable, or even decent animals.

However, the AKC does its best to screen out dishonest and disreputable dog breeders. Every month the AKC Board of Directors fines and suspends dozens of individuals across the country for falsifying paperwork and keeping improper records (about who sired who and so on) in their dog-breeding business and affairs. What better reason to use caution when you look for Golden puppies?

Registering your dog

If you want the official paperwork from the American Kennel Club, you must first complete the registration form received from the breeder. You simply fill in the dog's name (25 letters or less), write in your name as the new owner, and sign and send to the AKC at 260 Madison Ave., New York, NY 10016 with the stipulated registration fee. Your confirmation usually arrives in four to six weeks.

AKC also offers an Indefinite Listing Privilege (ILP) for dogs who are purebred but have no proof of parentage. You can show ILP registered dogs in AKC licensed performance events, but they're not eligible to be shown in conformation. To obtain an ILP number, send good quality photographs of the dog, including frontal view and both sides, along with a spay-neuter certificate from a veterinarian. Contact the AKC for more details on how to present the necessary information.

Analyzing a Pedigree

An AKC registration form and a pedigree are two different documents. The *registration* is simply AKC's confirmation of a puppy's sire and dam and certifies you as the owner of that pup. It is *not* the dog's *pedigree*, which is a three- to five-generation list of all its ancestors.

The *sire* and *dam* are your dog's father and mother. In the next generation, you have two *granddams* and two *grandsires* and so on up the pedigree ladder. Your pedigree should list any titles and may list certain health clearances as well. (See the following sections.)

Steer clear of the breeder who tells you her dog doesn't need a hip clearance because he or she can jump a 6-foot fence in one great leap. Or one who tells you the pups are from "championship lines" when in fact you see only one solitary Ch. title (see Table 3-1) three generations back.

Look for titles

Titles may appear before and/or after certain dogs' names, indicating some great or small accomplishment in a particular area of the dog world.

Titles in a pedigree prove that a dog is as smart, beautiful or handsome, and talented as a breeder claims. Table 3-1 gives you a list of some common titles and what they mean.

If a pedigree lacks titles, it doesn't mean that the puppies have no potential as competitors or pets. But unless the breeder is very experienced and knows what she's doing, a nondescript pedigree offers little assurance that the pups are top-quality Goldens.

Note: In Table 3-1, the hunt test dog is judged against a standard of performance and is not eliminated because another dog had better work. Hunt test titles appear after the dog's name.

Cancer concerns

Cancer in Golden Retrievers has increased by leaps and bounds during the past ten years. Why? No one knows as yet, but it's being researched by the experts. Goldens today are dying at 2, 3, and 4 years of age from several common forms of cancer. Breeders and buyers now look for longevity and cancerfree ancestors in their pedigrees. Be sure to ask whether any dogs in the first three generations died of cancer and at what age.

Table 3-1	**AKC Pedigree Titles**
Title	*Meaning*
Ch.	Bench (show) champion. This title appears in front of the dog's name The dog has been declared a quality and breedable specimen of the breed by judges who are licensed to evaluate that breed. Dogs earn points toward their championship in accordance with the number of dogs defeated in the show ring. They must earn a total of 15 points, including two "major" wins of three or more points, with a maximum of five points awarded at any one single show.
Obedience titles	
OTCh.	Another prefix title, the Obedience Trial Champion is the ultimate title in competitive obedience. To become an OTCh. a dog must earn a total of 100 points, including one first place in the both Open B and Utility classes, another first place in either class, with three first places under three different judges.
CD	Companion Dog, an obedience title that appears after a dog's name. To earn a CD, the dog must qualify in the Novice class three times under three different judges, performing exercises such as heeling on and off leash, stand for a brief hands-on exam by the judge, come into front and heel position when called (recall), and sit and lie down in place during a group exercise with other dogs.
CDX	Companion Dog Excellent. The CDX dog competes in the Open class and must qualify three times under three different judges. He must heel off leash (heel free), retrieve a dumbbell thrown across the ring (retrieve on flat) as well as over a high jump, drop into a down position on command during the recall, jump over a broad jump on command, and sit and lie down in place during a group exercise with the owner/handler out of sight.
UD	Utility Dog. In the Utility exercises (three qualifying scores, three different judges), the dog must respond to hand signals, do scent discrimination, a directed retrieve, directed jump, and a group examination.
UDX	Utility Dog Excellent. Awarded to the UD dog who obtains qualifying scores (a minimum of 170 points out of a perfect score of 200) in both Open and Utility classes at the same trial, at ten different trails.
Tracking titles	
TD	Tracking Dog. All tracking titles appear after a dog's name. To earn the TD, a dog must follow a 440- to 500-yard track, which includes at least two right angle turns on a track that is 30 minutes to two hours old, and retrieve the glove or wallet dropped at the track's end.

(continued)

Table 3-1 *(continued)*

Title	Meaning
Field titles	
FC	Field Champion, a prefix title that is earned in all-breed (meaning all retriever breeds) field trial "Open" competition, a stake that is open to professional handlers as well as amateur handlers. Untitled dogs also compete against dogs who have already earned their championship, making the field extremely hard to beat. The dogs are tested in four series on both land and in the water under a wide variety of difficult conditions. Points are awarded for first through fourth place, with 10 points required for the title.
AFC	Amateur Field Champion. In the Amateur stake, only amateur handlers are allowed to compete. As in the Open stake, dogs compete against both titled and untitled dogs, making the competition equally tough. The dogs are tested on land and in water under similar arduous conditions. An AFC must earn a total of 15 points to title.
Hunt test titles	
JH	Junior Hunter. A suffix title. A JH requires four qualifying scores or "legs." Dogs must complete two single retrieves on land and two in water at a maximum of 100 yards.
SH	Senior Hunter, a title requiring five legs, four if the dog already has a JH. Senior dogs complete more difficult double retrieves on land and in water, do single land a water blinds (birds the dog had not seen shot) and honor another working dog (remain steady while the other dog retrieves).
MH	Master Hunter, the highest hunt test title offered. The MH dog needs six legs, five if he has an SH. He must complete multiple land, water, and combined land-water retrieves, do multiple blinds on land and in water, and work under more difficult and complex conditions.

Healthy parents, healthy pups

The sire and dam of any Golden litter you consider should carry the standard health clearances for hips, eyes, heart, and, if at all possible, elbows. All these dog parts can be defective. If either parent has *hip dysplasia* (poor development of the hip joint), cataracts, heart disease, or shoulder or elbow disorders, it's a good bet they could pass that condition along to their kids. (See Chapter 15 for more on hereditary concerns.)

Here are some specific areas to keep a watchful eye on:

- ✔ **Hips:** An updated or current AKC registration will show an *OFA rating* after a dog's name, indicating it has been declared free of hip dysplasia by the Orthopedic Foundation for Animals (OFA), which is the official hip clearing house for dogs. Example: Dam: Chances R Gingersnap, SF123456 (AKC registration number) (8-98) (date of evaluation) OFA24E (OFA rating).

  In the OFA number OFA24E, the *24* indicates the dog's age in months, and the letter *E* following that number indicates a rating of Excellent. *G* means Good, and *F* is Fair. Dysplastic ratings of Mild, Moderate, and Severe indicate the degree of hip dysplasia and will not appear on the registration.

  OFA ratings were not recorded with AKC prior to the 1990s, so the breeder will have to produce OFA certificates if the dog's AKC registration certificate lacks an OFA clearance. OFA also certifies elbows, and because elbow disease has become so common (see Chapter 15), many breeders include elbow clearances on their breeding stock.

- ✔ **Eyes:** Eye clearances are registered with the Canine Eye Registry Foundation, which provides its own numbered certificate of clearance. However, some dogs with eye clearances may not registered with CERF. In those cases, the breeder should be able to produce Board-certified ophthalmologist certificates stating that both parent's eyes have been examined and found to be free of hereditary cataracts.

- ✔ **Heart:** Even the dog's heart needs another letter of approval. This time, the letter should be from a Board-certified cardiologist stating that both parents' hearts were tested and found to be free of a heart disease called *Subvalvular Aortic Stenosis* (SAS). This horrible disease involves a stricture in the left ventricle of the heart, which restricts the blood flow out of the heart, leading to sudden and unexpected death after normal activity or exercise. (For more on SAS, see Chapter 15.)

- ✔ **Allergies and thyroid problems:** Avoid pups from parents who have chronic allergies or are on thyroid medication.

It's great if you can find health clearances on a puppy's grandparents and other ancestors. The stronger the gene pool, the healthier the offspring.

Gold Links — Mom and Dad

Always make sure that you meet your potential dog's parents. Good temperament also is inherited. (Okay, face it. Just about everything is inherited.) If the sire or dam or other close relative is aggressive with other dogs or even people, it's a good bet that some of the puppies will reflect those qualities. When you visit a litter of pups, interact with one or both parents if you can. Quite frequently the sire lives elsewhere, but the dam is usually present.

If the breeder won't let you meet the Mom or either Mom or Dad is surly, growly, overly shy, or slinky, look elsewhere for a pup. Good litters are worth waiting for.

Chapter 4

Selecting Your Special Puppy

* *

In This Chapter

▶ Deciding what kind of Golden fits your lifestyle

▶ Testing and selecting your puppy

▶ Choosing between two pups

* *

*T*here's more to finding the right puppy than just finding a good breeder (see Chapter 3). Golden Retrievers can have as many different personalities and talents as they do coat colors. This chapter explores the different types of Goldens and helps you decide which one is the perfect match for you. That way, you won't just fall in love with the first pretty face you see!

A Golden Partnership

When you think about life with a Golden Retriever, what vision comes to mind? Is your red-gold athlete flushing dove or pheasant from the field? Are you and your Golden chasing tennis balls and Frisbees on the beach (see Figure 4-1)? Or are the two of you nestled in front of the fireplace, snoozing the weekend away?

Before you begin your golden search, you should have some idea of your future life together.

Consider the following questions:

▶ **Do you hunt, or would you like to?** If so, you'll need to research field and hunting lines to find a Golden who can share your duck blind and shag those pheasants from the fields and hedgerows (see Figure 4-2).

▶ **Are you a sports nut, a camping enthusiast, or a dedicated jogger?** If so, you'll probably want a typical spirited Golden who would fit well into your outdoor activities.

Close Encounters of the Furry Kind.

Figure 4-1:
Will you and
your Golden
spend fun
days at the
beach?

✔ **Are you a sedentary person who spends most of your leisure time curled up with a good book, or a senior citizen who wants a Golden mostly for its huggability?** You don't need a high-powered Golden who craves action and would be bouncing off the walls from boredom. Better to look for a laid-back animal, possibly from show lines, where the breeder's priorities lean more toward looks than to athletics.

Be specific when looking for your ideal Golden. If the breeder raises field-type Goldens and you want a career in conformation, look elsewhere for your pup. The reverse is also true. Don't purchase a show dog if you want to hunt, run field trials, or excel in the obedience competition. Pretty dog, yes. Hunting partner, nope.

Be realistic

No matter what you decide you want in a pet, your golden goals should be realistic. What can you reasonably do compared to what you'd like to do? Dogs aren't superhuman, so you need to make sure that the real world doesn't get in the way of what you want and what you can actually accomplish.

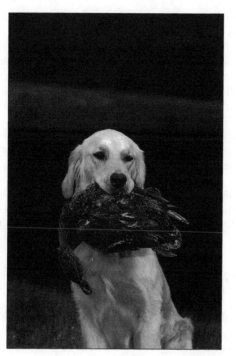

Figure 4-2:
Some dogs enjoy hunting and retrieving more than others.

Close Encounters of the Furry Kind.

Forewarned is forearmed! Those little yellow fuzzballs will steal your heart with one sweet puppy kiss, and suddenly you own one. Unless you are absolutely positive this is *the* litter, don't fall in love with the first pup who licks your cheek (yeah, right!) and try to visit more than one litter. That's the only way to find out the differences in Golden personalities and how each breeder raises them. Remember, all Goldens are not created equal.

Male or Female?

Males and females both make excellent pets, and any differences depend more on individual personality than on gender. Males, of course, are about 10 to 15 pounds bigger, and therefore stronger, and may display more male dominance unless they're neutered at an early age. And they do lift their leg when urinating, putting your prize shrubs and flower beds at risk. Some males also take a little longer to mature, stretching their teenage rowdiness into their second year.

Females, on the other hand, mature more quickly and tend to become lady-like before they're 2. (They squat to urinate, which saves your bushes but kills your grass.) They are usually about 10 pounds smaller and thus may be a bit easier to handle. While some females may be to be more sensitive and easier to discipline, others tend to pout or sulk when disciplined. Personally, I've raised plenty of both — wild and wooly females, and soft, tender males — and it all depends on personality.

No matter what the sex of your dog, you need to make sure that you spay or neuter it as soon as your veterinarian recommends it. (See Chapter 11 for more details on spay/neuter.)

If you already have an adult dog of any breed, you should get the opposite sex from your present dog. Males tend to get into dominance wars at certain life stages, and dogs of opposite sexes usually cohabit better.

Eenie, Meenie, Miney . . . YOU!

Who's the fairest of them all? How do you know which one is the one, the pup who will fit into your family scheme of things just like a glove? Listen to your breeder. Her observations are often a good criteria in evaluating puppies. After all, she has spent the last seven weeks living 24 hours a day with her furry charges and can point out the alpha pup, the middle of the road guys, and a shy, quiet wallflower if there is one. She can help you match a puppy to your goals and lifestyle. (If you don't have a breeder, you should check out Chapter 3.)

If you want a particular coat color, blond or gold or dark red golden, look at the puppy's ear. A Golden puppy's ears are often slightly to moderately darker than the rest of his coat. The ear color is the best indicator of the color of his future adult coat. Some coats will take a year or longer to reach their permanent adult Golden hue.

A rose by any other name . . .

Breeders often use some form of identification when each pup is born: colored rickrack, elastic pot holder rings, a touch of nail polish on a toe. Newborn pups resemble a pile of skinny wriggling rodents, and the breeder needs some way to tell at a glance which pup always finds the best end of Mom's dinner table, and which one does something first or last. I prefer colored ribbons, and when I have a litter, my usual puppy conversation is always about what Pink or Blue or Orange did today.

Many people still rely on puppy tests. Puppy testing is certainly not a science and is a questionable art at best. Test results are influenced by who performs the test, where the test occurs, the time of day, and whether the pups are hungry, tired, or reacting to immunizations. And puppies mature at different rates, with one pup precocious at 5 or 6 weeks, while a littermate may not blossom until several days later. Many experts discount test results and point out that some of the great dogs of this time have been leftover pups the breeder either gave away or kept because no one wanted them.

Still, some testing can't hurt and often just confirms what a dedicated breeder already knows about her pups. Most breeders and trainers have their favorite testing methods, using similar tests labeled with their own different or exotic names.

Ideally, testing should be performed when the pup is close to 7 weeks old, by an experienced Golden Retriever owner or breeder who has some knowledge of canine behavior and testing procedure and who has had little or no exposure to the litter. Testing should also be conducted in an area that is unfamiliar to the pups.

You and the tester should record a detailed description of each pup's reactions (tail up, body crouched down, and so on) as well as apply a numerical grade. These notes will help you remember why you gave a particular score, and is especially helpful when testing a large litter. It's easy to forget how puppy No. 2 reacted an hour earlier. Be familiar with the stated reactions before you begin to score the pups.

Remember that a testing process offers no guarantees. It's just one more way of trying to beat the odds.

1-2-3 testing

These first series of tests are a composite of tests developed by well-known canine behaviorists and are the most widely used among hobby breeders. Here's how they work:

- **Attraction:** The breeder takes the puppy to a quiet testing area and sets it down about 10 feet from the tester. The tester squats down and claps her hands while bending toward the pup, saying nothing. Observe how the puppy comes and score according to the chart below.

- **Handling:** The tester strokes the puppy from head to tail for about 30 seconds. Again, record the pup's response and assign a score.

- **Holding or cradling test:** The tester picks up the pup and cradles it upside down with all four legs skyward, in her arms for about 20 to 30 seconds and scores accordingly.

✔ **Following:** The tester releases the puppy, stands up, and then walks away without a word. If the pup follows, the tester chats with him to see whether he will come along. If he doesn't follow at all, keep walking for a few more feet to see whether he'll finally come along. Allow about one minute for this test and score accordingly.

Table 4-1 explains how to score each reaction.

Table 4-1	Puppy Test scores	
Category	*Reaction*	*Score*
Attraction	Comes at once, bites or nips at your hands or feet	1
	Comes quickly, licks but does not nip or bite	2
	Comes slowly but without hesitation or shyness	3
	Comes reluctantly or not at all, sits, and observes instead	4
	Does not come, turns, and goes the other way	5
Handling	Nips, growls, becomes agitated or excited	1
	Jumps up happily, paws up, no nipping or biting	2
	Wiggles around, licks at your hand	3
	Rolls over on his back	4
	Slinks away or walks away	5
Holding/Cradling	Struggles fiercely, nips, bites, or growls	1
	Struggles, then settles down or wiggles happily	2
	Settles down first, then wiggles or struggles	3
	Does not resist or struggle at all	4
	Wiggles a little the entire time	5
Following	Chases your feet, jumps on you or your feet, nips or bites	1
	Follows happily, stays with you	2

Category	Reaction	Score
	Follows willingly, but slowly	3
	Does not follow, sits and watches	4
	Does not follow, walks away	5

Scores of mostly 1s indicate an extremely dominant and aggressive pup with a strong and willful personality. He will require an experienced trainer who must be prepared for constant challenges to authority. This puppy will not be good with children and will need expert socialization by a very dominant owner. Not recommended for the average pet or companion home.

A puppy with mostly 2s is also a dominant pup who also will require a strong leader with experience and will need consistent training to become a reliable family companion.

Bless the puppy who scores mostly 3s! He is a middle-of-the-road guy, friendly and outgoing, who will respond well to people and children. He will need more praise for confidence.

A puppy who scores mostly 4s is quite submissive and will need a gentle hand to build long term confidence. He may not socialize too easily and is probably not a good choice for children.

If the puppy scores mostly 5s, he is terribly shy and would resist training. Pups with too many 5s are potential fear biters and seldom make good family dogs. They need to live with owners who understand their special needs and will work to build the puppy's confidence.

These numerical categories are merely guidelines. Most pups will end up with combinations scores. Dogs who score 2s and 3s or 3s and 4s also make good family dogs. And remember, tests do not always reflect many aspects of the puppy's character.

The competition pup tests

This next set of exercises happens to be one of my personal favorite and is often used by obedience competitors. They should also be conducted by a stranger.

> ✔ **Confidence and courage:** Set up a large nonskid-surface table in an quiet area or a room that is completely new and foreign to the pup. The tester should carry the pup and place him on the table without a spoken word. Gauge the pup's reaction according to Table 4-2.

Pups who score 1 or 2 are bold, courageous, and outgoing and will accept challenges and training with enthusiasm. These puppies are good choices for competition or a busy, active family.

Scorers of 3 or 4 are less confident puppies who would make good companions but will need more careful socializing and confidence building in their training. They will require a gentler, more patient hand in training.

Scores of 5 indicate puppies who are insecure and will require lots of extra TLC and training to become happy willing workers and family members. These puppies may not be good with young children.

✔ **Desire to retrieve:** This test is obviously more important to those who plan to hunt or field trial with their Golden. The tester takes the puppy to an unfamiliar area and sets him down without a word. Clear the area of all distractions, toys, paper, or anything that may attract his attention. The tester then teases the puppy with a dead pigeon or some highly visible retrieving object like a stuffed white sock. When the puppy is all excited, the tester tosses the sock (at the pup's eye level) about 6 to 8 feet in front of the puppy.

Grade the pup's reaction on a scale of 1 to 3 as described in Table 4-3. After the retrieve, the tester can call the puppy to return with the object, but the return does not affect the test results. Coming back is a response that is taught as the puppy matures, but the desire to retrieve is built into the pup genetically.

Table 4-2	Confidence and Courage Responses
Reaction	*Score*
Happy and fearless, tries to run around or jump off table	1
Tail high and wagging, investigates table, shows no fear	2
Tail wags slowly, curious but apprehensive, may crouch a bit, sniffs to investigate	3
Tail down or tucked under but wagging slightly, slinky, rather fearful, sniffs or investigates with much caution	4
Tail between hind legs, freezes, and won't move, does not sniff or investigate	5

Table 4-3	Retrieving Scores	
Reaction		*Score*
The puppy goes wild at the sight of the bird or sock bumper and strains madly to retrieve it when it's thrown		1
The puppy shows enthusiasm for the bird or sock and runs out happily to retrieve it		2
The puppy shows little interest in the retrieve object and merely wanders out to get it or fails to go at all		3

Puppies who score a 1 should make good hunters and good performers in field or obedience competition.

Puppies with scores of 2 should be adequate performers and with proper training and encouragement can reach competent levels of performance.

If you want a puppy that can do any type of hunting or retrieving activities other than a Frisbee game, do not consider a puppy who scores a 3. While some pups' hunting ability develops slowly with maturity, if you're hoping to enjoy hunt tests, hunting, or field trials, you need to narrow the field as early as possible. A promising puppy increases your odds of success in adventurous activities.

Realize that by the time you test puppy No. 9, the testing area has been compromised with lots of puppy scent, and the early pups tested may be more wide awake and energetic than the last. The test results should be only one part of your puppy selection process.

Your observations also factor into your choice of puppies. Watch them closely to see who's the boss pup, who seems precocious, who is the most inquisitive, and so on. If your breeder is involved in any type of performance competition, rely also on her evaluation of each pup.

If You Can't Decide . . .

If you can't decide between two equally adorable pups, don't even think about taking both. Puppies will always prefer the company of another pup to their human companion (see Figure 4-3). It's species selection, and your personal charisma is not involved. Furthermore, the more dominant puppy will assert himself over the submissive one and may even develop a bully personality. These patterns of behavior can magnify over time, and it will be harder to train either pup. Naturally, your puppy must learn how to behave around other dogs, but the two-puppy household is not the way to accomplish that. You're after that special human-canine bond.

If you still crave two Goldens, don't despair. Wait until your dog is 2 years old before getting a second pup. By then Golden No. 1 will be your soul mate. However, raising that second pup will present different challenges, because you'll have to separate him from your older Golden to prevent that canine selection instinct and maximize the human bond. In my own dog family, I keep a puppy with me almost exclusively until he's at least 6 months old.

Figure 4-3:
Pups instinctively prefer each other's company over a human's.

Close Encounters of the Furry Kind.

Part II
Welcome Home!

The 5th Wave   By Rich Tennant

"Oh, he's always digging something out of them woods and dragging it home."

In this part . . .

Adopting a puppy is a lot like having a baby. You can't just go to the breeder or hospital, come home, and let your puppy entertain herself. In this part, I clue you in on how to dog-proof your home, yard, and kids. I also give you the inside scoop on training — from the basics such as housetraining and feeding all the way to problem behaviors. (Hopefully, that last one is a chapter you'll never have to read.)

Chapter 5

Setting Out the Welcome Mat

In This Chapter

▶ Stocking up on puppy essentials

▶ Choosing healthy chews and toys

▶ Puppy-proofing your entire premises

Selecting your puppy is merely the first rung on your life-with-a-Golden ladder. Once you have your pup picked out, you may think you just plunk him in the car and head for home. Whoops, not yet! First you need to puppy-proof your entire premises from the ground up and give your kids a short course in canine safety. In this chapter, I delve into all the important (and fun!) things you need to know about laying the groundwork for your new family member.

Outfitting Your Puppy

Just like outfitting a newborn baby, your puppy will need his own layette of canine goodies — some necessary and others just plain fun. But hang on to your purse strings; shopping for puppies is a grand adventure and can easily spin out of control — and your budget. Make a list of essentials and the extra goodies so you know where to draw the line.

Puppy food

Lay in your own supply of a quality large-breed growth/puppy food (see Chapter 10). If the breeder has been feeding something different, take home a small bag of her food to mix with your new food so that your puppy can adjust gradually to the change in diet. Be sure to ask your breeder how much your puppy has been eating, although calculating that can be difficult when eight or nine puppies are sharing one large food pan. Start with a 20-pound bag. Does that sound like a lot? It won't last long!

Food and water bowls

Stainless steel food and water bowls are good choices for big guys like Goldens. They're indestructible and easy to sanitize. Buy the two-quart size right off and don't bother with tiny puppy pans; they outgrow them in a blink (see Figure 5-1).

If you crave those neat stoneware bowls, think about your back and how often you'll have to pick up those heavy dishes. Plastic bowls are too flimsy and do not sanitize as well.

Figure 5-1:
Don't forget food and water bowls.

Close Encounters of the Furry Kind.

Collars and ID tags

For immediate daily use, purchase a narrow adjustable nylon webbed collar with a plastic quick-release buckle. This collar will expand 2 to 3 inches in length as the puppy grows.

The 8- to 12-inch size will fit your little guy, but not for long. Your Golden puppy will grow faster than your crabgrass. You'll replace this collar at least twice during his first year.

If you prefer a leather collar, note that some leather dyes can stain the puppy's fur, especially if he plays in water (that includes big puddles!). It's a waste of money at this early age.

Protect your dog from fire

Stick Fire Alert stickers on all the entry doors to your home to alert emergency personnel that you have live animals in the house. You can find these stickers at most pet shops or make your own from 3 x 5-inch index cards. Make sure to include the number of animals and their names on the cards.

Never use a chain (or choke) collar on your puppy. Those collars are for older, bigger dogs, are intended for training purposes only and should never be worn beyond a training session. Tales abound about dogs who have been hanged or choked themselves to death when their chain collars tangled on furniture or a fence post. Your pup may graduate to a training collar at 4 or 5 months of age, depending on his size and temperament.

Always attach identification to your puppy's collar from day one. (Perish the thought, but what if he gets lost?) Never include his name (a thief could too easily call him) — just use your own name, address, and telephone number. After he is fully grown and is wearing a collar he won't outgrow, rivet a brass ID plate on the collar instead of the standard S-hook dangle tag. (Plates are available through pet supply catalogs.) Dangle tags get caught on carpeting and come off easily. The riveted plates are permanent and never snag.

On my own ID plates, I include my telephone number on the top name line and use the bottom fourth line for this message, "Dog needs medication." If the dog is stolen, the bad guys might think twice about the value of a dog who has some sickness or disease. If he's lost, that health "information" may motivate whoever finds the dog to return him promptly. It can't hurt, and it may even help.

Leashes

You probably always thought a leash was just a leash. Hey, dog life just isn't that simple! For training purposes and control, you'll need an entire wardrobe of "lines" with which to lead your dog:

- ✔ **A 4- to 6-foot nylon or lightweight leather leash:** You will use this shorter lead in the house, for tethering and teaching household manners.

- ✔ **A narrow 6-foot leather lead:** This is lightweight and easy to fold in your hand while walking. You'll need this size for obedience class in a few weeks. Get it before you bring your puppy home.

- ✔ **A 16- to 20-foot extendible (flexi) lead:** Flexi-leads are super for outdoor walks and on-leash playtime. I always have two — one for the house and one in the truck so that I don't inadvertently forget it!

✔ **A 20- to 30-foot long line plus a 50-foot long line:** You won't need this one for the first month or two, but once your Golden gains confidence in his new surroundings (it happens in a heartbeat!), you'll need a reliable method of controlling him away from you. The long line is a fabric leash available in pet stores or pet supply catalogs (as are most of the items in this chapter), or you can make your own as I do from a length of soft nylon or poly rope and a clip (for his collar), both available at the hardware or discount store. I frequently use both sizes (not at the same time, of course).

✔ **Collar tab:** You can make a collar tab or purchase one. This 6- to 10-inch length of leash or lightweight cord clips to your puppy's collar to wear around the house. He'll graduate into this short tab shortly after coming home. You may end up using the collar tab on your Golden throughout his first year.

In addition to the standard leash and collar, head gear worn with a leash can help control a puppy who adamantly resists a buckle collar when on leash. The Halti, the Come-Along, and the Gentle Leader-Promise Head Collar are different versions of the same type of head collar. Made from a webbed nylon material, the head gear goes over the bridge of the nose and the leash attaches to an O ring under the dog's chin.

A head halter is not a muzzle, although it resembles one. It offers more control than the slip or buckle collar. This device is used exclusively by many guide dog training schools. The head halter can transform an unruly pup into a gentleman and turn a war-of-wills-on-leash into a delightful stroll! (See Chapter 9 for more on obedience training.)

Bedding

You can go way overboard on bedding because bed choices are unlimited. Plush cushions, cedar pillows, and covered foam mattresses, all with patterns and colors galore to match your dog or match your color scheme. My preference always runs to ducks and geese. After all, my dogs are working retrievers, Golden variety!

Bed Note: A bed, plain or fancy, is not a canine necessity. Some pups will make confetti out of their designer beds. Test your pup first with an old blanket before you invest in expensive sleeping gear. Cutesy beds, if you so desire, can come later when your Golden has outgrown the chewing stage.

The scoop on rawhides

Rawhide chews are made from processed beefhide, so carnivorous dogs naturally love them.

Rawhides should be selected carefully. They are fine as long as your puppy or adult dog doesn't try to swallow it whole and choke on it. (It happened to one of my older Goldens. Ask your vet!) My dogs get them only under supervision. A newer type of molded rawhide is extra hard and safe and most dogs love it. The melting process in the new ones also sterilizes the material.

Other chew materials you may want to avoid include pressed rawhides, which are merely strips of rawhide material pressed together under pressure. These rawhides have been known to produce loose stools. Some meat-flavored rawhides also can stain your carpet. (I learned that one the hard way!) Pig's ears can cause upset stomachs, and cow hooves create a most unpleasant odor. We live in cattle country, and I still can't abide the smell of cow hooves in my house!

If you decide to give your Golden rawhides, buy only rawhide products made in the United States. In the U.S., rawhide is considered a food byproduct, and the processing is government controlled. That's not so in other countries where the chemical processing of rawhide materials is not regulated and the preservatives may contain formaldehyde, arsenic, and other toxic chemicals. My own dogs have become ill after munching on imported rawhides.

Toys and chewies

Golden Retriever puppies are really miniature chewing machines disguised as dogs. As a breed, Goldens tend to be very oral and possess a maniac desire to have something in their mouth. If they don't have toys to satisfy their chewing instincts, you know what will happen to your shoes and furniture. My own Goldens recommend these toys:

- ✔ **Nylabones and Gumabones:** These hard, bone-shaped chew toys are great chewcifiers, and they come in shapes and sizes to fit every age and breed. When the ends get spindly, just discard them.

- ✔ **Hard sterilized bones:** These bones are another retriever favorite. Like the Nylabone, these thick, hollow bones won't fragment or splinter. Because I live with five adult power-chewers, almost every room in my house is usually littered with these hard bones and Nylabones.

- ✔ **Woolly toys:** Puppies love 'em! Your pup will shake them and toss them around, and later snuggle up with them.

- ✔ **Braided rope:** Puppies love these rope toys, but they are for puppies only, not for people-tugging. Tug-of-war games (see Chapters 8 and 16) are definitely out of bounds.

Chew prevention

Get your chew deterrent before your puppy comes home and starts remodeling your furniture. You can spray woodwork and leashes with a product called Bitter Apple (or Bitter Grape). Test it before using it on fine wood furniture. Bitter Apple cream lasts longer, but is less convenient to use than the spray. Although Bitter Apple is really nasty tasting, a few puppies chew right over it. In those cases, you can try Tabasco sauce or hot pepper sauce (but not the kind that burns your tongue!).

You can also use a loud rattle to deter your little chewer. Fill an empty aluminum soda can with a dozen pennies and tape the opening shut. Use it only as directed later and only when your verbal or other methods fail. When you shake the can, the loud rattle will startle your puppy and make him stop what he's doing.

Rope toys have major shredding potential. If your pup or adult dog starts pulling them apart, or worse — ingests some of the threads — it can become a life-threatening surgical nightmare. Remove and discard chew ropes the minute they get stringy. If parts of it disappear and do not reappear in the dog's stool, suspect the worst and see your vet.

✔ **Empty gallon and half-gallon milk jugs:** These excellent puppy toys bounce around easily and make lots of noise. Puppies love to bat them about with their paws and will get crazy when they play with them. Replace as needed because they'll get chewed up in a hurry.

Be aware of the toys you shouldn't buy. Avoid cutesy toys with squeakers, tiny eyes, or fuzzy noses — your dog can chew them off and swallow them.

Of course, you're bound to go overboard with toys because they're all so doggone cute. Buy as many as your heart desires, but offer your puppy only two or three items at a time. Give him too many choices, and, just like a child, he'll get bored with all of them. Keep a couple of favorite chew toys in his crate and rotate a few others in his toy bucket. Incidentally, show him his toy container once or twice. That's one place he will not forget!

You also don't want to give your puppy any shoes or socks as toys. Do not *ever* toss your old or discarded tennis shoes or slippers into the toy bucket. This is so obvious I feel foolish even explaining it because I'm *sure* you know that puppies can't distinguish between old and new and will eventually chew up any and every shoe he finds. No socks either, even knotted ones. They shred, and if your pup swallows one, he can end up in surgery.

In addition, do not give your puppy squishy rubber toys. Although small pieces of shredded rubber toys can survive the digestive process, a whole rubber ducky would never make it through. If your pup's a bonafide chomping champ and one of his favorite toys disappears, suspect the worst and take him for a checkup.

Watch out for open windows

Dogs can and do jump out of open screened windows for reasons known only to the dog. Never leave a dog or puppy where he can climb up and push through an open window. Install safety grills on house windows or open them from the top. Open car windows are also dangerous.

Grooming tools

You don't need many grooming tools to start, but you should have a slicker brush to get your puppy used to the grooming process early on. A mild shampoo is also a good idea, just in case your puppy gets into something smelly, which is a favorite Golden trick. For more on grooming, see Chapter 13.

Great crates

A crate is your most important puppy purchase. Every puppy deserves his own private space, a place where he can escape from the hectic pace of human life. A crate is not a cage your puppy can't get out of. He thinks it's a place where humans can't get in, his very own safe house where he feels secure. Canines are natural den creatures, an instinct passed down from their wolf ancestors. Contrary to human perception, your puppy will not think he's looking at the world through a jail house window. In his dog's-eye view, it's a personal haven of security.

A pet crate is also good for child proofing; this is not a playhouse the kids can share with him. (At least for a while. After the kids and puppy are better acquainted, they may end up together in the crate — but only after he has fully adjusted to the kids and his new dwelling.)

Crates come in wire mesh or plastic, like the airline travel crate. Some wire crates conveniently fold up suitcase style to fit into the trunk of your car for traveling to grandma's house (or elsewhere).

My personal choice is the wire crate. I think my dogs feel less isolated and closer to their human family. Wire crates are also better ventilated, which is a bonus in warm weather. For privacy and nighty-night for puppies, I just drape a large towel or lightweight blanket over the top and sides. Make sure the covering is draped away from the sides to prevent the pup from snagging the fabric to chew or swallow (surgery!).

Purchase an adult-size crate; your puppy will soon grow into it. A 22-inch by 36-inch wire crate or a large size airline crate will be comfy for the average adult Golden. He only needs to lie down comfortably; he doesn't need a dance hall.

Children should never stick their hands into your dog's crate or poke any object at the pup. Whether he is sleeping or awake, children have to learn to respect their puppy's space and privacy.

Baby gates

Believe it or not, most puppy families can't survive without baby gates. Baby gates confine a puppy to his play room (usually the kitchen or utility room) and keep him out of rooms where he may get in trouble or make mischief.

Puppy-Proofing Your House and Yard

Before you bring your puppy home, you need to take a dog tour of your property. Your home, garage, and yard may be — and probably are — littered with hazards that can harm or endanger your new puppy. To change it into a pet-friendly domicile, check it out from your puppy's point of view. Complete an eye level inspection and then get down on your hands and knees and see what your puppy may find intriguing from his angle. Then hide it or get rid of it! If your neighbor shows up as you're crawling around on all fours, just ask him to join the fun.

To puppy-proof your house, just follow these tips:

- ✔ **Keep medication bottles and cleaning supplies locked up or out of reach.** The sound of pills rattling in a plastic bottle can intrigue a puppy who can easily chew the bottle open.

- ✔ **Don't toss dental floss where your puppy can get into it.** Dental floss will not digest and can become tangled in a pup's intestines. It's a surgical nightmare.

- ✔ **Unplug electrical cords.** You can also attach them inconspicuously to the wall or press them under baseboards. Puppies are especially attracted to loose cords. (I can't tell you how many computer or telephone cords I've replaced in my office because I trusted a rogue puppy as I worked right beside the pup!) Chewed cords are a common cause of household fires and electrical burns in canines. Think injuries and dollar signs.

  There is now an electrical extension cord on the market that automatically shuts off the power when chewed to prevent animal (and child) injuries. Cost: about $10 each.

- ✔ **Beware of coins, socks, needles, and tinsel.** Actually, beware of any miscellaneous objects small enough for a puppy to pick up and chew or swallow. Any veterinarian will gladly tell you horror stories about impossible trinkets they removed during surgery. (Dangerous, expensive, and unnecessary!) The common theme in these events is the owners never thought their puppy or dog would ingest such ridiculous objects.

- ✔ **Watch out for stringy stuff like yarn and sewing gear.** I know of one dog who died from swallowed twine that tangled in his intestines. If the worst happens and your Golden eats a no-no, immediately call your vet. (See Chapter 11 for more on first aid.)

- ✔ **Do not use roach or rodent poison or other pesticide in areas accessible to your puppy.** You can't be too careful. And remember, puppies wiggle into impossible-to-reach places.

- ✔ **Keep the toilet lid down and never use toilet bowl cleaners.** All puppies are born with toilet sonar and quickly discover the coldest water is in the toilet bowl. In my 30 years of 16 Golden companions, only one has never attempted to slurp from an open bathroom stool.

- ✔ **Keep the diaper pail lid shut tight.** Is there a baby in the house? There's not a dog afoot who doesn't love to ruminate in soiled diapers. It's not only disgusting, it's dangerous. Dogs have actually died from ingesting soiled diapers. They may vomit up part of the material, but the remaining toxins can send his body into a prolonged death spiral. Don't let diaper duty distract you from your dog's behavior.

- ✔ **Hide all trash.** Most Golden puppies are natural garbage explorers and will dig out chicken bones and other rotten stuff with serious potential for choking or tearing up your dog's intestines. My first Golden was a classic garbage dog who would empty our upright kitchen trash container every time we stayed out past the curfew she imposed on us. She would poke her head under the tilt-lid and make dozens of trips in order to carry every little-bitty piece out onto the family room couch.

- ✔ **Hide your underwear.** Puppies — and some adult dogs, too — love to chew up and swallow socks and other clothing items with your body scent that they find lying on the floor. Most puppies are underwear aficionados and will gobble up things like jockey shorts and pantyhose, especially unlaundered ones. If you value your Calvin Kleins, stash them in the hamper after wearing.

- ✔ **Watch cat litter boxes.** Pups love to snack on kitty droppings.

In addition to these safeguards, you should know about some uncommon chemicals that are also canine hazards. For example, the treated lumber used in decks and landscaping has been preserved with chemicals that are toxic and can be fatal for a dog who chews or eats the wood. Be careful, too, with flea control products on your carpet and on your dog. (See Chapter 12.)

Acorns are just for the squirrels

Certain varieties of acorns are so toxic to dogs that just one nut can cause death within a few hours. Outdoor birdbaths are also risky. (Come to think of it, who ever heard of an indoor birdbath?) The water contaminated from bird droppings can be dangerous to fatal.

Botanical dangers

Many years ago, I was surprised to learn how many plants could cause anything from diarrhea to death if my Goldens ate them. Yikes! I had to do some rapid replanting in my yard and garden. Lily of the Valley, Oleander, Rhododendron, Japanese Yews, and Poinsettia are just a few of more than 80 varieties of common house and yard plants that are toxic if ingested. Put house plants up high or move them where your puppy can't get into them. Always do a thorough greenery check inside and out before your pup comes home.

If the worst happens and your dog or puppy chomps on some forbidden plant or flower, call your veterinarian for instant help and then rush the animal to the clinic. If possible, take along a sample of the ingested plant or product. The bottom line here is never to underestimate your pet. (See Chapter 11) for more about poisoning, how to recognize the signs, and emergency action.)

Dispose of these dangers that may lurk in your garage:

- **Antifreeze:** Everyone knows (or should know!) the dangers of antifreeze. This bright green liquid has a sweet taste that attracts dogs and cats. Even a few drops can kill a large animal. Keep antifreeze containers tightly closed and out of reach and clean up spills immediately. Watch for leaks on your driveway or at the curb.

- **Weed killers, pesticides, and herbicides:** If you store these kinds of products in your garage, keep them well secured. Make sure that rodent traps or poisons are completely inaccessible. A curious puppy can be amazingly creative. He can dig into it-will-never-happen places and then chew apart and swallow last week's paint roller plus your turpentine brush.

- **Cigarettes:** Ingested cigarettes can lead to nicotine poisoning. Keep those ashtrays clean. Better yet, give up smoking. Second-hand smoke is bad for your dog's health.

- **Herbicide hazards:** A National Cancer Institute study found that dogs whose owners use the weed killer 2,4-D (dichlorophen-oxyacetic acid which kills broadleaf weeds like dandelions) on their lawns four times a year were twice as likely to develop canine lymphoma as dogs not exposed to that herbicide. Other studies showed that dogs exposed to 2,4-D-treated lawns had detectable amounts of the chemical in their urine, and that absorption of the herbicide through their skin occurred for several days after it has been used on your lawn. I hate to be a nag, but cancer is currently a huge threat to the Golden Retriever breed, so let your puppy play in the dandelions instead. He'll love it! If you absolutely must use 2,4-D, prohibit dog activity on treated areas for several days or until after the next cutting.

Chapter 6

Welcoming Your Puppy Home

- -

In This Chapter

▶ Introducing puppy to his new world

▶ Feeding your puppy

▶ Treating your puppy to pedicures and body rubs

▶ Socializing your puppy

▶ Creating golden bonds

- -

*T*he "how" of welcome home is as important as the "when." This is a tough time for your pup. Just think about it from your pup's perspective. He has no idea who you are or that you're going to love and care for him forever. He just knows he's leaving the only home he's ever known, not to mention saying good-bye to his mom and siblings. Don't let that wagging fuzzy tail deceive you. Beneath his furry chest, there beats an anxious heart that's wondering "Where's Mom?" In this chapter, you discover what you need to know to make his welcome home as calm as possible and also encourage all the good habits you want your adult Golden to have.

Bringing Your Puppy Home

To help your puppy with this major life change, arrange to pick him up over a long weekend or during your vacation so that you'll have several days to devote just to him. Arrive at the breeder's early in the day so that he will have more "awake" time to adjust to his new world. If possible, bring another person; one of you will have to drive, and the other can tend the puppy. If you do this solo, put a crate or carrier in your car. Driving and holding a puppy is a recipe for an accident!

Leave the kids at home (*if* you can swing it!). Their excitement and happy, squeaky voices will only add to the puppy's stress and make his departure still more difficult. If they do come along, make *sure* that they stay quiet and don't fondle or harass the puppy. (Oh yes, they will!)

The breeder should give you some type of puppy packet with your pup's AKC registration (which you both must sign), his pedigree, a health record of shots and wormings, and a list of instructions about food and general care.

You should also have your own list of prepared questions. In your excitement, you're bound to forget to ask a few important details. Ask about feeding and sleeping schedules and what kind of food he's been eating and how much.

Bring an empty gallon jug and fill it with water from the breeder. Mix that water gradually with yours at home. A change in water (well water to city water, and so on) can cause loose stools. Why take chances?

Bring along a couple of large towels. Toss one towel in with your puppy's littermates and let them drag it around to fully impregnate it with their special puppy scent. That towel will be your puppy's personal security blanket in his crate at home. Use the other towel to carry the puppy in your lap. A big towel will be snuggly, and you'll also have a safety net if puppy urinates or throws up during the ride. It may not happen, but you'll be sorry if you're not prepared. Chat calmly and softly to your puppy. A gentle voice will help to soothe his insecurity.

If you have to travel a long way, you'll need to make a puppy potty stop. That means you'll need his collar and leash or a long line to keep him safe and under control when he relieves himself. (See Chapter 5.)

Figure 6-1:
Let your puppy explore at his leisure.

Close Encounters of the Furry Kind.

Keeping His First Days Calm and Quiet

Even though your puppy was (should have been) socialized with humans at his breeder's, remember he's never been away from home. He will still be apprehensive in a new environment, and he'll need your full attention for reassurance. Keep the first day or two low-key and don't invite the neighbors over to see the new arrival. Ditto for your children's friends. Explain to the kids that your new puppy needs to feel comfortable and confident in his new surroundings before he meets too many people. Friends and other family members can visit in a day or two, after he feels at home.

This first day is *puppy* day! Let him sniff and investigate your yard and whatever rooms of the house you designate as his territory (see Figure 6-1). Show him his water bowl, crate, and toy box. Take it slow and let him set his own investigation pace. Make sure that the kids don't smother him to death. Too much hands-on attention can be stressful at this tenuous time. Calm, quiet, and relaxing — that's the cardinal rule for his first day at home.

Puppy-Proofing the Kids

Although most people lump kids and puppies into one big happy family (see Figure 6-2), they don't always co-exist peacefully. Child psychologists say that young children are not born with natural feelings of compassion or empathy toward animals, so they're often unintentionally cruel in their behavior with a pet. They don't mean to be unkind; they just don't know any better.

Consequently, it's your job to teach your children and their friends that your new Golden puppy is a living being who will love them and play with them if they treat him gently and with respect. Show the kids how to properly handle the puppy; don't let them drag him around by the tail or carry him by the neck or worse!

Teach your older children the correct way to hold the puppy. Show them how to grasp him under the chest and tummy so that he won't wiggle out of their arms. Toddlers and little ones should not be allowed to carry him under any circumstances. Rather, they should always sit on the floor when playing with the puppy. (With toddlers and youngsters, this play session will be brief and supervised.)

This is important! You should never leave any child and your puppy unsupervised together. If you do, you're begging for a problem. Puppy teeth are sharp, and even a playful puppy nip can easily break the skin, leaving the child or children frightened and resentful. The opposite is also true. Children can accidentally hurt the pup. They'll get along eventually, but you have to be the ringmaster for a while.

Figure 6-2:
Kids plus puppies don't always equal one big happy family.

In addition, the kids should not pester the puppy when he sleeps or eats. A puppy or adult dog who is eating may be possessive of his food and think that the child is going to take his food away.

Another important kid rule: Instruct your children not to wave their hands or holler when they approach the puppy. If they surprise the puppy from behind or wave and jiggle, they could scare him. He may also think that they're playing, and he'll jump on them and chase them, which is a normal response. This is also one of the toughest lessons to teach the children because silly antics are natural adolescent behavior.

Children should also never take a toy or bone from the puppy's mouth. It's your job, as the adult and puppy master, to teach the puppy to drop the object and give it willingly to you.

Dog-smart kids are less apt to become dog bite statistics, and as a bonus, they'll grow up to be best friends with your Golden.

Pulling Rank

If you have another dog or cat at home, you should know how your current pet responds to other dogs before you bring your puppy home. If he has had little or no social experience with other canines, you can (you should!) visit a local park or dog walk area to check out his response to other animals (see Figure 6-3). That way, you're not caught off guard if he's less than happy with his new playmate.

If you can, arrange to introduce your pup and older dog outdoors at a local park or on other neutral ground away from the home front where the older dog won't feel so territorial.

When you introduce your puppy to your adult dog, keep both dogs on leashes so that you can maintain control. It is most important that you also keep their leashes loose so that the two can sniff and feel comfortable with each other. In dog language, a tight leash may signal to the older dog that the puppy is a threat. Look for happy canine signs like play bows and tail wags and allow them to play together while they're still on leash. Your adult dog may growl and protest, even bare his teeth, if he feels it's necessary to pull rank, but for the most part, dogs work out their own pecking order.

If your two dogs don't reach an agreement you feel comfortable with or if you think your puppy's in harm's way, do not discipline your other dog. He's just being doggy. And playful puppies can be a real pain in the hindquarters for an older dog! Just keep them separated and continue this socialization process for the next couple of weeks. If your older guy continues to protest, consult your veterinarian or other behavior specialist.

Even if harmony reigns immediately, supervise their time together to prevent squabbles and make sure that some minor incident doesn't annoy your older dog. Dog fights often erupt for reasons known only to the dogs involved. Down the road, be prepared for changes in their relationship when your puppy approaches sexual maturity at 6 to 9 months of age.

Figure 6-3:
Your older dog has squatter's rights. Make sure that he's open to the idea of a new roommate — before your puppy comes home.

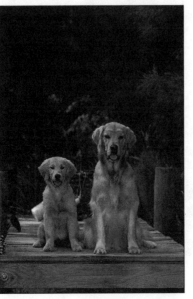

Close Encounters of the Furry Kind.

If your pet is a cat . . .

Cats are less problematic than dogs. They can escape to higher ground if things don't go their way. Some cats accept new puppies with aplomb, while others zip off to their favorite hiding place. Being independent creatures, cats usually work out cohabitation rules to suit themselves. Our own cat thinks he's a Golden because our 1-year-old (at the time) Golden adopted him and raised him as her own. He slept tucked in her tummy every night, and when she died 12 years later, he wandered through the house all night looking for her. Fortunately, one of our younger female Goldens took over, and now he sleeps curled up with her — in our bed, of course.

After the two are well acquainted, limit the amount of time the two dogs spend together. Puppies will quite naturally relate best to and bond with their own species (see Figure 6-4). You want your Golden to consider you his leader and become a people dog. I'm sure I have convinced my own Goldens they're just canine versions of my children! As a health precaution, understand that big-dog rough housing can injure a puppy's tender growing bones and joints, so it's best to keep wrestling and rowdy play to a minimum during those first six to eight months of rapid growth.

Figure 6-4: It's only natural for dogs to prefer each other's company.

Close Encounters of the Furry Kind.

Remember one thing. Your old dog has squatter's rights. Do not make him jealous by fussing and making over your new puppy when your older dog is present. He has first dibs on his own toys and treats unless or until such time as he relinquishes that privilege. To minimize his stress over a new dog in his territory, give him extra individual attention with special things he likes to do — Frisbee games, walks in the woods, obedience routines.

Soup's On! Your Puppy's Dinner Plan

Most puppies come equipped with tummy timers that prompt them to eat on schedule. Give him three meals a day for the first three months and then feed him twice a day for the rest of his life. Sure, lots of dogs eat only once a day. Twice-daily feeding is preferred by most breeders and professional trainers. Smaller meals are more satisfying, promote better weight control, and may prevent bloating, which is a good reason all by itself. Plus, your dog will think it's a big deal getting that food bowl twice a day.

Some folks may tell you that *free feeding,* also called *free choice,* is more convenient, and that it surely is. But it's a lot harder to housebreak a free choice puppy — what goes in at odd times will come out when you least expect it. It's also harder to monitor the amount your puppy eats, which is important in fast-growing breeds like Goldens. And down the golden road, you may have some health problem that requires a stringent feeding protocol.

Food is also a primary reinforcer. A puppy who is dependent on you for his basic needs will be less independent and more likely to consider you his leader. If he has food available at all times, he will not think he needs you for this basic need.

Feed your puppy at 6 to 7 a.m., again about noon, and dinner no later than 5 or 6 p.m. For easier house training, don't feed him after 6 p.m. and don't give him water after 7 p.m. Give him an ice cube to chew on if he gets thirsty. A 10 p.m. trip outside should carry him through the night. (See Chapter 7 for more on housebreaking.)

He will need three meals a day for a few weeks. Start feeding twice a day when he's about 11 or 12 weeks old. Meal size will vary with each pup, but the average Golden puppy at 7 weeks is polishing off about ⅓ to ½ cup of dry food at each meal. Feed it dry with water available on the side. Feeding dry will help prevent plaque and tartar build-up on his teeth, most important after his adult teeth are in.

Some puppies almost inhale their food as if it were their last meal on earth. To slow the eating process to a healthier pace, you can place a large round rock in the center of his food pan. That will force him to eat around it and slow down.

You should not give your puppy any supplements. A quality food provides the correct proportion of nutrients that a growing puppy needs. Adding vitamins, especially calcium and phosphorous or other minerals, will upset that delicate balance and can actually create structural and growth problems. Veterinary nutritionists are emphatic about no additives. If your vet recommends vitamins, either ignore that advice or find another vet.

Feed your puppy in the same place every day with no distractions like kids and cats so that he can concentrate on the business of eating. Allow about 20 to 30 minutes for each meal. If he doesn't finish during that time, pick up his food and offer the same amount of food at each meal; don't add the leftover kibble from the prior meal to the next.

When should you increase his food allotment? When he's finishing every kibble at two out of three meals, bump up his portions just a tad. I suggest going from a level ⅓ cup to a heaping ⅓ cup at first, then increase to a scant ½ cup, then a level ½ cup, a heaping cup, and up the food ladder according to your puppy's appetite.

Some pups are voracious eaters and gobble up their food like it's their last meal, and others are more finicky and just seem to nibble at their food. Some puppies also go through eating spurts and will eat with more or less vigor at certain times. Not to worry. Your only real concern should be an overweight puppy. Keep him lean.

Making the Most of Mealtime

Use your puppy's meal time to lay the groundwork for other good behaviors. Once he's learned the "Sit" command (see Chapter 9), make him sit before he gets his food dish. At first make it a quickie sit and then hold it a bit longer as he gets more proficient. He'll learn that all good things come from this new human leader who also gives food and hugs and kisses along with his commands and dinner bowl.

Once a day, wiggle your fingers in his food pan while he eats. Occasionally remove his food midmeal, praise him, and return his food. Occasionally, stroke and pet your puppy for a moment as he eats and then leave him alone to eat in peace. Have the children do so as well — supervised, of course. Your puppy must learn to accept your presence at his dinner table and the removal of food and other objects from his mouth. Food guarding is a common habit in dominant or fearful dogs and can lead to biting (see Chapter 16). Proper conditioning at this tender age will prevent that.

The noise factor

Equate your puppy to an infant. He should hear all the normal household noises. You don't want any sudden or unexpected moves to frighten him, but you can still clatter the pans and vacuum at a distance to condition him to the sounds of daily life and insurance against noise sensitivity.

To accustom your puppy to loud noises gradually, once a day drop a heavy book on the floor in the next room while he's eating. Gradually move closer each time until you're across the room. If he shows fear or anxiety, move farther away until he gets used to the sound and then move closer more slowly. He should show normal curiosity, maybe stop eating and look about. You can also substitute other similar loud noises. This is especially important if you plan to hunt with your Golden. It will condition him to sharp sounds, so he'll be ready for the training pistol or a shotgun.

Use this take-it-and-give-it-back routine with his toys as well, saying "Thank you" sweetly when you take them and then return them with "Good boy" praise. Practice this frequently before he develops dangerous habits. It can be rather intimidating if your adorable puppy suddenly decides to keep his rawhide and bares his little teeth at you. Whoops! This exercise is for his benefit as well as yours because someday you may have to remove a fish hook or chicken or fish bones from his greedy gullet. As with all training at this age, it's easier to teach a 15-pound pup who has no bad habits (yet!) than to deal with possessive or aggressive behavior in a 60-plus pound adult Golden.

Continue these mini-lessons frequently throughout your Golden's lifetime. (Put a permanent flag on this chapter!) Dogs develop dominance tendencies at various stages in their life (see Chapter 8). These measures are simple reminders of your leadership and will ward off guarding tendencies and also warn you of impending problems you might overlook.

Why is this dominance thing so important? If your dog is to grow up well behaved, he must respect you as his pack leader. The ideal time to establish yourself in this lofty position is when he's young and manageable. If you wait too long, he may start thinking of himself as your leader ("Me boss-dog, you under-dog") and will consider your attempts to train him as a challenge.

Discovering Puppy Antics

Playing with your puppy is important. Before your puppy left his mom, he spent most of his day frolicking with his littermates, chasing and wrestling until they all fell asleep from pure exhaustion (see Figure 6-5). What happens to all that excess energy now that he's home with you?

Figure 6-5:
Before you entered his life, your puppy spent his day frolicking with his siblings.

Exercise is as essential to his well-being as his food and water. If he doesn't get enough, he may act hyper, refuse to calm down, and would redirect his excess energy into destructive activities like chewing up your house.

Adopt a reasonable puppy schedule and modify it as your puppy matures. Use the activities in Chapter 17 and invent your own to keep him properly exercised. This is a busy time for both of you. Goldens are smart pups, but they won't play *safely* without your help.

Conducting a Body Search

Your puppy must learn to submit to handling his body parts. He'll need it for grooming, nail trimming, ear cleaning, vet exams, and doggie times like wiping muddy paws. Start as soon as possible. If you wait until he's 3 or 4 months old and approaching adolescence, he'll be bigger, stronger willed, and less accustomed to hands-on body games.

Hold brief daily body exams. You can make a game of them, but insist that he cooperate. Lay him down and grasp and rub his paws and touch between his toes. "Ooooohh, what pretty feet!"

When he's on his back, rub his tummy and softly whisper pretty-puppy talk. He won't care what you say. It's your voice and touch that matter. I've never met a puppy that didn't love to have his tummy rubbed. My last puppy was so conditioned to our tummy sessions that she instantly rolled over onto her back if I as much as whispered to her or reached down to touch her thigh!

Look in his ears and raise his lips and touch his teeth and rub his gums and tongue. Put your hand over his muzzle and gently hold it there for just a few seconds. Slowly run your hands along his body. Use a soft brush for a few brush strokes to create more pleasant associations. Using a brush during these exercises will also prepare him for longer and more detailed grooming sessions later (see Chapter 13). If you begin these exercises early and continue them, your puppy will learn to cooperate and enjoy the process. You can occasionally perform these exercises on your lap. You can also add tasty tidbits to these body sessions to make them even more pleasant for your puppy.

Nipping Puppy's Nails

The puppy stage is the ideal age to introduce the nail clippers. He'll need those pedicures all his life, so get him used to it now before he gains another 40 pounds.

Using a standard canine nail clipper, remove just the tip or the curved end of the nail (see Figure 6-6). At first, you might succeed in doing only one or two nails before you throw your hands up in despair. (A sleeping or very tired puppy is easiest to work on!)

Keep at it several times a day (or all week), and you'll get all four paws done sooner than later. Dog nails grow quickly and become difficult to trim if they're neglected because the *quick* (the pink vein inside the nail) grows too long inside the nail. If you accidentally nip the quick and the nail bleeds, don't panic. Check out remedies in Chapter 13 on grooming.

Puppy treats are excellent lures for manicures. One friend of mine has done such a good job of this with his three Goldens, that whenever they see the nail clippers in his hands, they automatically roll over onto their backs and hold their four paws in the air to get their nails done because they know they'll get a milk bone when he's done. Now that's positive reinforcement at it's finest!

Figure 6-6:
Start nail
clipping
at an
early age.

Socializing Your Puppy

Socialization is a puppy's introduction to the human world. From birth to 7 weeks, he's been learning proper canine behavior from his mom and litter-mates. Now at 7 weeks, he's old enough to make the switch from dogs to humans. Years of research have shown that 7 weeks is the best age for a puppy to begin forming social bonds with people. He's now emotionally mature enough to adjust to lifestyle changes and begin learning new behaviors.

That same research has also proven that your puppy's brain is like a sponge and that everything that happens during his first 20 weeks of life will perm-anently imprint on that little brain. Both positive and negative experiences will have a lasting effect on everything he learns later in life and the adult dog he becomes.

Heed this message! The time and quality of the time you invest in your Golden puppy now will directly affect the quality of the adult Golden you will live with for the next 10 to 13 years! Make the most of this critical growth phase. Never again will you have this supreme chance to mold his personal-ity and behavior. Your puppy could become a 14-karat wonder dog, a common gold-plated canine, or a tarnished, garden-variety scamp.

An unsocialized dog will grow up to be spooky, shy, and fearful of people, other dogs, and strange places, and possibly aggressive towards humans and other animals. He'll be one unhappy fellow. Rehabilitation is rarely possible; you can't turn back the clock.

Overcoming social golden butterflies

A quiet, placid household without noise and people, especially children, is developmentally dangerous for your puppy. Make your house an active, puppy-friendly place. If you don't have children, invite relatives or the neighbor kids for puppy parties to play with him (supervised, of course). He has to interact regularly and often with children of all ages, or he will be uncomfortable with them later on. That's how dog bites happen.

Your puppy also has to interact with other dogs so that he learns to respect and enjoy their company. Without other canine experiences, he may grow up to be fearful or aggressive around other animals. After he's safely immunized, arrange brief, supervised play with friendly dogs once or twice a week. A puppy class also offers great puppy party times.

Building confidence

Your puppy is especially impressionable during what is known as the 8- to 10-week fear period. This is a fragile time when object associations can leave indelible imprints. It's vital that he have only positive experiences with people, other animals, and places during this critical period.

It's equally important to *avoid* painful or scary experiences until after 11 weeks of age. That means you and your puppy are in effect limited to home and very safe places for the next three weeks. Just concentrate on making home a happy dog house.

Some situations can't be avoided, like going to the vet. But if you've chosen your vet wisely, you can turn the visit into a happy experience where your pup is praised and petted. Your vet will understand, and the two of you can happy up the exam and/or puppy shot with praise and laughter and puppy treats. If your pup shows fear or apprehension, do not offer sympathy or soothing reassurance; you'll just convince your puppy that things must be pretty awful and that it's okay to cower and act scared. He will respond to your reactions, so keep them upbeat and positive. See Chapter 11 for more details on vet visitation.

Puppies frequently spook at some object they perceive as strange — a lawn mower, vacuum cleaner, a large box. Don't sympathize or force him to confront the "bad guy." Instead go to the object, pet it, laugh a bit, and talk happily to encourage him. Let him sniff and investigate it on his own.

Making the world his oyster

Once your puppy is past the fear period and your vet tells you he's safely immunized, commit to two or three away-from-home trips every week to expose him to new people, sounds, and smells. The more he sees of his new human world, the more confident he'll grow up to be. Start slowly with a neighbor's yard, a local grocery store, or friendly place where you can both relax and browse. Carry him if you think strange dogs have soiled the area. Car rides are always great fun.

Gradually add shopping malls and/or other busy places to your pup's agenda. Puppies should be exposed to all sorts of new and different situations such as stairs, elevators, different types of vehicles, people in uniform, delivery trucks — the list is endless. Hang out in front of grocery stores where he'll encounter shoppers with noisy shopping carts. On city streets, walk over the sewer grates. If, however, your puppy is worried or shows signs of fear or apprehension, be enthusiastic but don't force him. Back off and try again later. Avoid extremes and condition him gradually to the unusual. Follow his cues and plan accordingly.

Experienced puppy raisers often set people goals to socialize their puppies, declaring that every pup should meet 100 people in a variety of settings before it reaches 4 months of age. That type of social whirl is the key to a confident puppy and adult.

Creating that golden bond

Bonding is the process of becoming your puppy's No. 1 priority and takes a lot of one-on-one time between just the two of you. Like children, puppies need someone to love and respect, to learn from and depend on. Until now, that someone was his birth mother. Now it's you. And you begin the day you bring your puppy home.

Turn these first weeks at home into a special golden bonding time. Take walks together around the yard or some other quiet place, such as a field or park that is safe from road hazards, crowds, and other animals. Take advantage of his dependence on you. Chat with him to keep him close and call him to you for a treat or a hug. He's learning how much he needs you for security.

Tethering is an excellent way to enhance this one-on-one relationship. Put him on his 4- or 6-foot leash and tie or clip the other end to your belt loop. It must be long enough for him to sit or lie down comfortably, but not long enough to allow him to wander several feet away from you. Make sure that he's had an outside trip before you start so that you won't be interrupted by an accident. (If it happens, learn from it and forget it.) And make sure that he's been introduced to his leash.

For about 15 or 20 minutes every day, tether yourself to your puppy while you go about the normal, every day business of your house. Chat with your puppy a bit to keep him happy to be with you, but don't give any commands. Do not confuse bonding time with training. If he jumps up or bites, give a swift tug downward on the leash and tell him "No!"

The plain truth is . . . everything you do with or for your puppy, from cuddling right into training, will enhance the bonding process. What better reason to devote these next few months exclusively to him?

Golden Designations

Your puppy's name is more than just a cute or clever moniker. It's the word that should snap him to attention, change his focus, and make him look at you.

Make a point of using your dog's name only when you praise him or give him a command. If he gets praise or goodies when he hears his name, it will become a thing of value, and he'll respond quick as a wink. However, if you use his name too casually or frequently in normal conversation, it will lose its impact, and he'll soon ignore it.

If you talk to and about your dog often, substitute a handful of nicknames rather than his "call" name so that he doesn't become so used to his name that he tunes it out. If you use the nicknames often enough, it will become a habit. Our 10-year-old male Golden, Apache, is known around here as the Patchman, our Patchpie, the Big Man, and a few other names that are too silly to repeat here. When I say Apache, he knows I either want to tell him to do something or treat him. Either way, he has an "Okay, what's up, boss?" attitude when he hears his name.

Minimizing the "No" Word

Another no-no involves using the correction word "No." Because you want your dog to love his name and respond to it like magic, don't connect it to negative words like "No." "No" does not mean pay attention or do something as in a command word. "No" means stop doing something now. Puppies learn by doing, so "No" is a tough word for puppies and young dogs because it doesn't tell them *what to* do.

The word "No" is often overused or used improperly (with kids, too!). Just as overusing a dog's name will teach him to tune it out, so, too, will he ignore "No" if he hears it all the time. Too many dogs think "No" is the first or second half of their name!

Save "No!" for the big-time errors, like snacking in your cat's litter box or stealing food from countertops. (You can bet your boots he'll try those things.) In early puppy training, it's more positive — and comprehensive for the dog — to redirect his behavior by giving an alternate behavior you can praise. He picks up a shoe to chew. Tell him "Drop" and give a chewy toy instead. He puts his paws up on the sofa, and you know what he's thinking now. Tell him "Off!" and do the chew toy bit again.

Chapter 7

Crate Training and Housetraining

. . . .

In This Chapter

▶ Using the three Ps of puppy training

▶ Practicing your best puppy voice

▶ Crate conditioning your puppy

▶ Mastering housetraining

. . . .

*F*ast forward into puppy mode. Most Golden puppies adjust quickly to their new human families. They are happy souls by nature and will bond to anyone who dispenses love and gentle handling and explains the rules of the new household in terms that are canine-logical.

This chapter gives you three golden *P* rules you will use for life. If necessary tattoo them on your hand, or at least post them on your refrigerator door so that you won't forget them. You also can read about the joys of crate training and why your Golden can't live without one. And you find out how to teach your puppy elimination skills, more commonly called *housetraining*. This is one chapter you don't want to skip!

Puppy Training and the Three Golden Ps

Praise, Patience, and Practice are the three *Ps* of puppy training. You'll need a generous supply of all three starting the moment you and your puppy leave his mom and littermates.

 ✔ **Praise:** Goldens thrive on praise. Like candy to a baby, your puppy will respond to praise as if it were a can of Mighty Dog. Praise is one tool you'll use for his entire life.

 ✔ **Patience:** Stock up now before you run into puppy disasters that will test your golden mettle. You will need to save a bunch of it to use periodically during your golden life.

✔ **Practice:** Hang in there and keep doing the good things you're learning from this book. You may feel like ten thumbs now, but all things golden get easier with time. The more you practice handling your dog, training and communicating properly, the better you'll both be down that golden road. When things get a little sloppy at times in your adult Golden's life, practicing will come in handy.

The Message in Your Voice

When you're teaching or otherwise interacting with your dog, you need to use your best dog voice. How you say something means as much as what you say. Give commands in a firm, commanding voice.

A lower voice is more compelling, which may explain why some dogs respond more to men. What dog in his right mind would give credence to a weak and pleading voice that's whining like a littermate? Now you also know why puppies don't respect a child's high-pitched, squeaky voice. It sounds just like another animal.

That low, stern voice can also have the opposite effect. A heavy sounding voice (especially male) can be so intimidating it prevents a happy working attitude. "Good dog!" in a ferocious baritone will not make your dog feel happy and successful. You'll need a positive, upbeat tone to get positive, upbeat results. The right inflection in your voice can set the tone for success or failure.

Always use normal volume when you give commands. Don't shout or raise your voice. If you start out with maximum volume, you'll have nowhere to go when you want to add a little oomph to your message.

Whispering is a very effective way to hold your pup's attention if you start it early. Use a soft, whispery voice when you rub his tummy or pet his ears. Whisper lots of sweet talk nose to nose, and he'll make sweet associations with your whisper voice. Think of the advantages of whispered dog talk.

Introducing the Crate

For the first two or three months, you should confine your puppy to just one or two rooms, ideally the kitchen and/or a room with access to an outside door. Use a baby gate so that he's contained but won't feel isolated. This gate will limit his space and play areas until he learns which exit to use for potty trips. It will also limit puppy accidents all over the house and your frustration over damaged furniture and carpets. Keep his crate in the area of confinement.

Timeout!

Crates are also good for puppy time-outs when he has to cool it for a while, like when your prissy aunt comes to visit and you know how she hates dog breath. Just send him to his crate so that his feelings won't be hurt. The crate also serves as a dual-purpose security system, providing confinement for your pup and protection for your house and furniture (think antique chair legs). With puppy safely crated in his little castle, he can't get into mischief when you leave the house, work in the yard, or clean the basement. A cruel prison? No. Peace of mind? You bet!

In your pup's opinion, his crate is his little hide-out, his own house within your house. If you're lucky, your puppy learned about crate life at the breeder's (although that's not very likely). Regardless, you need to start the crating process right away. Show your puppy his crate by tossing in a treat to make the den inviting and praise him when he enters on his own. You can also offer his first one or two meals in the crate (with the door open) so that he'll think it's a pretty fine place (holy cow, a restaurant *and* a hotel!)

 Never use the crate for punishment or crate your puppy immediately after a scolding. It's okay to use the crate as a disciplinary tool — just make sure that *he* doesn't realize it. You want to create only pleasant and positive associations with his room.

Pick a crate command like "Kennel" (or "House," both make sense) and use it consistently as an entry word. Toss in his treat and when he enters, use the K word. Then tell him "Good boy, Kennel!" Use that phrase consistently each time you crate him, and he'll quickly learn it through word association.

 You can choose any word you like to teach a specific behavior as long as you use the same word consistently. If you said "Howdy" every time you crated your Golden, he would learn to recognize that word. The words mean more to you than to the dog.

Crating on the road

Crates add a dimension of safety when traveling with your Golden. If he's safely crated, he can't leap into the front seat while you're speeding down the interstate. (You've heard the one about the motorist who told the officer he was speeding because his dog was licking his ear?)

Many motels also welcome crated pets, and your dog will have his own room within your room wherever you stay.

For more on choosing a crate, see Chapter 5.

Dealing with crate accidents

Accidents happen. Your puppy will wet his crate a time or two, which will be your fault and not his. His puppy mat will absorb the urine and keep him dry and clean. It's easier to wash the mat than bathe the pup.

If you put newspaper in his crate, it will leave newsprint on his fur, and you'll have a gray-looking smelly pup. And because newspaper is associated with traditional housebreaking, keep it out of the picture entirely. You don't want him to piddle on the morning paper that lies next to your easy chair.

Crating adult dogs

I'm almost as crazy about crates as I am about Goldens. I use mine forever. But that probably won't be your bent. Still, six months' minimum use is a must, and the first year is even better. Fussy housekeepers and decorator moms can't wait to run out and buy one of those cute doggie beds at the pet store and ditch their crate furniture. But if you travel or vacation with your Golden, remember those crate advantages and motel restrictions. And should any problem behavior crop up in the future, you can always return to the crate routine, and your dog won't object. So it's best to keep your adult dog conditioned to his crate.

Home, sweet home

Your dog's crate should be large enough for an adult Golden to lie down and turn around, but he doesn't need to stretch to his full body height or lay down stretched out like a rubber band. I suggest putting the crate in a people area of the house so that he doesn't feel isolated. (Also, make sure that it's not too far from the door where he goes out for potty stops — of course, you know why.) Don't leave food or water in the crate, but do provide a few safe chew toys to keep him occupied and happy. Leave the crate door open when he's not in it so that he can enter and leave it at will.

Don't crate him during his first day at home. Just do the treat-toss and the first meal or two as a crate incentive. Bedtime will be soon enough. It's a good idea to move the crate into your bedroom at night (actually — it's a great idea!) and next to your bed for the first few weeks so that he won't feel left alone. Knowing you're close by will also feed the bonding process. If you're lucky and own two crates, just leave one in the bedroom all the time. Another plus to having the crate in your room — you'll hear him if he whimpers during the night to relieve himself.

Bed sharing is risky business

To a dog and lesser pack member, sleeping on the bed means equal. Bed sharing is a luxury he gains only with permission, and he earns it only by recognizing you as Leader. That goes for your kids' beds also.

I don't mean to dash your dreams of someday curling up in bed with your Golden, especially when I sleep with several of them myself. A few miles down the training road we might let your adult Golden into bed with you. But that choice is best made later in the dog's life when you know whether he can handle bed sharing without becoming possessive or territorial over it. You risk a dog bite if that happens.

Cover the top and sides of your puppy's crate loosely with a large towel or blanket so that he can still see out and get air. Drop the covering at night for sleeping (and for naps if he takes to howling during his midday crate times). It will enhance the denlike environment and signal him it's time to rest.

Remember that puppy towel his littermates dragged around? Put it in the crate with him, or use an old bath rug or other towel. You'll have to use good judgment here. If your puppy chews these things up, thus rendering them useless, remove them and don't replace them.

Lights out!

When it's bedtime, drop your puppy's crate curtain (carefully away from the crate sides) so that he knows it's time for sleeping. (It's that cozy den thing again.) If he whines and you know he just pottied and doesn't have to go again, you can just wiggle your fingers in the crate to comfort him a bit. (No chewing on those fingers!) If the noise continues, just be patient that first night and ignore it. He's not resisting the crate itself. It's his first night away from Mom and family, and he's adjusting to the controls of a new and unfamiliar environment.

Sometimes a softly ticking alarm clock, soft music, or a humming fan will soothe a restless pup. It may work for you, too, if his whimpering keeps you awake!

If the whining persists past that first night, proceed to Crate Plan B . . . with the crate still covered, when he complains, slap the kennel lightly with your hand and tell him "Quiet." Repeat as necessary. The noise should intimidate him to be quiet.

Crate Plan C is more extreme and only if his whining gets really nutso for a few days. Again, with the crate covered, jiggle a shaker can and repeat "Quiet." Repeat, if necessary.

Most properly raised Golden puppies settle quickly into their new sleeping quarters. If your pup is the exception and continues fussing night after night, just move the crate to a nearby area so that you can get some sleep. Do not, as a last resort, invite him into your bed for consolation. He'll make the natural connection that if he whines or cries, he gets released and hugged. He'll also figure out that it's okay to be on your bed, which is not a good idea this early in your relationship. Bed privileges must be earned, and you have not yet taught him you're the privilege-maker (see the sidebar "Bed sharing is risky business").

Here are some other important crate rules to remember:

- ✔ **Do not ever call your puppy to come to you and promptly send him to his crate.** Puppies learn by association, and if he thinks his reward for coming to you is confinement, he may decide not to come at all. It's far better to simply carry him or walk him to the crate.

- ✔ **Establish a daily crate routine right away.** Crate your puppy for one- to two-hour intervals during the day according to his personal nap schedule. If he falls asleep under the table or curled up at your feet, just put him in his crate and close the door. If you leave the crate door open, the obvious will happen. He'll wake up, toddle out to piddle, and then hop on over to say, "Hi!" A closed door will force him to let you know he has to go. At this tender age, puppies have tiny bladders, which they have to empty often. So don't ignore his message, or he'll adjust his housekeeping habits accordingly.

- ✔ **Keep the crate door open whenever he's not in it.** In short order, he should be curling up in there on his own for naps and quiet time. (Don't forget to close that door gently after he goes in there!) Make sure that the kids don't disturb his down time or reach in and pull him out. Instruct them to call him gently to come out on his own.

Don't overuse your crate

Crate use can be overdone. For the first ten weeks, never leave a pup unattended in a crate for more than two hours at a time (unless he's sleeping). Pups 3 months old can be in a crate for three hours. You can go four hours for the 4- and 5-month old, and no more than six hours for dogs 6 months and older. If you can't be home to tend the pup, have a relative or neighbor come in to let him out and feed him or hire a trustworthy dog sitter.

If a crate won't work for you at all (I can't imagine why not, but just in case), you can use an indoor exercise pen at least 4 feet by 4 feet square. Make sure that it's sturdy enough to stand alone or secure it so that it won't fall if the puppy jumps up on the sides. Make it large enough to allow a corner for elimination and another one for play and sleeping. Cover the floor area with newspapers. When you determine which part of the pen area he has chosen to relieve himself, you can limit the papers to that corner or area. You will still need a companion to visit him at least once during the day.

Some owners use a backyard chain link kennel or dog run to give their Golden a change of scenery and give themselves a doggy break. These work well for short periods, but their convenience makes them easy to abuse. You can't just put your puppy or dog outside in a pen and forget about him. He will be bored and lonely, and untrained and wild when he's released. If you have an outdoor kennel, be sure to use it only as an outdoor break for brief periods of time. Quality house time is essential to your Golden puppy's mental and emotional well being. Goldens do not thrive if they are raised separated from their human families.

Don't rely on baby gates to contain him if he's unsupervised for lengthy periods. Most Golden puppies master them within a week and will scale them like a mountain goat.

Decide how you're going to handle your puppy's maximum confinement periods before you bring him home. Remember that raising a puppy without people is like raising a child in a closet. If he's merely confined without proper supervision and training, he will not learn people rules, good manners, or correct canine behavior. He won't grow up to be a Golden companion; he'll just be a dog.

If you are unable or unwilling to make appropriate arrangements for a puppy, don't despair. You can still live the Golden life. Consider an adult or older Golden, a rescue Golden, or a retiree from a breeder. See Chapter 3 for details. Cats and ferrets also make good pets who do well without a lot of human interaction or attention.

Housetraining Routines

Like wolves in the wild, dogs don't like to soil their sleeping space, which is your biggest asset in teaching him to eliminate outdoors. It's the main ingredient in housebreaking. This doesn't mean he will never soil his crate. He probably will. If that happens, just clean it up, be patient, and be more vigilant. It's a rare Golden who doesn't give you a clue that he has to go.

Canines of all ages learn best and thrive on a routine that meets their daily needs. Puppies especially need a schedule to keep their body clocks in tip-top working order. Routines and consistency are your best tools for teaching your new Golden puppy the rules of the world outside the whelping box. His little brain sponge is just waiting to soak up information. Housetraining (which is a better term than house "breaking") is his first important lesson.

Bladder control varies with each puppy, and he may piddle as often as every half hour that first week or two. I set my oven timer to remind me — a half hour whizzes by so fast. Pups between 7 and 12 weeks of age will need eight

Odor neutralizers

Those accident spots have to be deodorized. Goldens have a "nose brain" that can identify odors that are ages old and in amazingly tiny amounts. (Didn't you ever wonder about fire hydrants?)

First, blot up the moisture with paper toweling or an absorbent sponge designed to sop up liquids. Clean with a crystallizing carpet cleaner. (Dish detergents will leave soap residue that attract and hold dirt.) Then generously spray with an odor neutralizer (available through pet suppliers) to remove the smell. (Some owners use a four-to-one water-vinegar solution with good results.) Soak the area with the odor treatment, cover with a clean, nonstaining towel, and top with a heavy book for 24 hours. (Tell your friends you're teaching your puppy how to read.) Try both and see what works best for you.

to ten trips outside each day. From 13 to 20 weeks, he'll need seven or eight trips a day for walks and elimination stops. Adult Goldens should always go outside at least four times a day.

Always take your puppy outside the first thing in the morning, every time he wakes up or leaves the crate, within 5 to 20 minutes after eating, before you bed him for the night, and many times in between!

If your puppy does have an accident, never use ammonia to clean it up. Dog urine contains ammonia, so you'll just make the spot a good reminder to "pee here." (See the sidebar "Odor neutralizers" for more cleanup tips.)

Create good elimination habits:

- **Start teaching him "Outside" right away.** When he leaves his crate, just tell him "Outside" and take him to the door. Use it every time, and he'll soon learn that "Outside" means the door, the one he'll use to do his job. Smart owner, smart puppy, right?

- **Use the same area in your yard or other appointed spot for his outside trips.** He'll learn to associate the area for that purpose, and the odor from previous outings will help stimulate him to go. (The fire hydrant principle again.)

- **These potty trips are business trips, not time for play.** If he wants to romp or visit, just ignore him until he does his job. Once he's finished, praise him and go back inside. Reward him with his walk or other playing after he has gone.

- **Teach an elimination word.** Teach your puppy an elimination command and use it every time he goes. My personal favorites are "Hurry Up" and "Get Busy" (although I confess to also using "Go Potty," "Peeps," and "Poopers" in the past). As soon as puppy squats to urinate or move his bowels, use your chosen command (softly, or he'll become too excited to finish the job) and offer praise. "Hurry up. Good boy, hurry up."

Give brief praise while he's actually going. You don't want a lot of conversation, and you don't want to praise him if he's merely squatting. (I've seen puppies simply squat and not go when they heard the magic word just to get the praise!) He'll soon recognize his key word and understand the purpose of those little trips outside. You can praise more heartily when he's done and even give a tidbit treat once in a while.

- ✔ **Don't talk or praise your puppy before he does his business.** Puppies get distracted easily — by your voice, a blowing leaf, or a daffodil. Start praising softly while he's going.

- ✔ **Be sure to use the same door or exit for his business trips.** Within a few days, you should see him go to the door on his own.

- ✔ **Teach elimination skills one room at a time.** Goldens are pretty smart pups, but even a genius Golden won't know how to find his bathroom exit if he's upstairs or several rooms away. That's the beauty of baby gates (see Chapter 5). When a puppy owner tells me her little one always has an accident in their upstairs bedroom while she's making the kids' beds, guess what my answer is? Why is he there, for heaven's sake?

After a week or two, you'll find that he may not always "go" as soon as he goes outside. There'll be irresistible sights and sounds that will distract him from the job at hand. That's okay! He just discovering the world you take for granted. Be *patient* and enjoy the moment with him. Like children, puppies grow up all too soon!

In addition, resign yourself that you just can't just pop your puppy out the door to go. You must go with him on each trip to teach the word and give the praise. You also need to check his stools for signs of diarrhea, blood, or parasites. Rain, shine, or 2 a.m., you have to make sure that he does his job and gets his praise.

Every dog develops his own signal system. Some whine at the door, a few may paw at it, others simply stare at the door, while some just sniff the floor in circles. At this age, one pass at the door is all you'll probably get before he lets it fly, so be alert! Eventually he'll be more persistent. My own Goldens never bark to go outside. They simply come and stare at me, leave the room, and then come back again and stare.

When your puppy squats indoors — or starts to squat — quickly clap your hands and use a firm "No!" or sharp "Aahh, aahh, aahh!" (no shrieking, please) and then scoop him up and carry him outside. The sharp sounds may even startle him to stop going. Take him out even if he doesn't go again and offer praise for completing his job if and when he does.

If puppy makes a mistake indoors when you're not looking or if you find it later, just forget it and try harder next time. You have to catch him *in the act* to show him that indoors is not acceptable; even seconds later is too late. Puppies — in fact, dogs of any age — cannot connect a correction with something they did a heartbeat earlier. (Burn that in your brain. That truism applies to everything a canine does throughout his lifetime.)

Rain, rain, go away

Some puppies don't like to go out in rainy weather. For starters, use a big umbrella as a weather shield. Then wait for a nice, easy shower to gently introduce puppy to the joys of playing and eliminating in the rain. It will make future trips outdoors much easier. The opposite is true of snow. He won't want to come back in!

Never use a newspaper (or your hand or foot) to hit your dog and never rub his nose in his "mistakes." These are pointless punishments he will not understand at all. Rather, he will only learn to fear the newspaper or your hand. If you miss his duty call, it's your mistake, not his. Punish yourself instead for not being vigilant when your puppy had to go!

One survey by the National Council on Pet Population Study and Policy found that 34 percent of people who surrendered their dogs to shelters thought rubbing the animals' noses in their feces would help housetrain them. It is, in fact, disgusting and counterproductive. The reality is that only praise and reinforcing positive behavior are effective.

Chapter 8

Canine Communication and Growing Pains

*T*ry to think like your dog! Tough, huh? Humans do not think naturally in canine terms. What's clear to you is seldom clear to the dog. (I will say this often, so bear with me!) Given that axiom, it's also obvious that a dog will rarely understand what seems so logical to his human master. Animals enter this world as creatures of instincts and heredity, and you need to remember that *(always)* and start thinking like your dog in order to successfully teach him the rules of his new world.

Puppies are little learning machines. Everything a puppy does or encounters teaches it something, either positive or negative. That's why early intervention and structured learning situations are so important in raising a well-adjusted dog. Goldens are bright students with a strong propensity to please, which is a plus in their education process.

This chapter gets inside your puppy's head and explains how and why he reacts to situations and learns from them. Then it explains the correct way to handle those responses and turn your little guy into a model citizen.

Welcome to Puppy Preschool

Your puppy started canine grammar (dog talk) school the day you brought him home. Just like children, puppies learn best through repetition (remember those multiplication tables?) and "Good Dog!" rewards.

Everything your puppy does is motivated by his instincts until you teach him otherwise. Your Golden puppy spent the past seven or eight weeks learning from his mother how to be a proper dog. He knows nothing about human standards of behavior. During these next important learning stages, it's best to keep his life as simple as possible and his space uncluttered with temptation.

The most successful obedience methods today rely on positive reinforcement instead of older negative and cruel corrections such as jerking, hitting, and other forms of punishment. Your Golden must learn what's right before you can correct him for being wrong. With positive reinforcements such as praise and food rewards, correct behavior is rewarded. That makes the dog feel good so naturally he wants to repeat the behavior.

This is true of any canine behavior, even if you are not involved in the reward process. If your dog gets away with *anything* that makes him feel good, like sleeping on the sofa or snatching food from the kitchen counter, you can bet he will repeat that misdeed. He doesn't know he did something wrong; it's only incorrect behavior in people terms.

Dogs also learn behaviors only in the present tense. Take the best (and worst!) example — piddling in the house. You have to catch your puppy in the act. Timing is so critical that even seconds later is too late. A correction after the puddle, or any other undesirable behavior, even when he's been told before, will not be understandable to the dog. (See Chapter 7 for more on housetraining.)

The better your timing, the clearer message you send the dog. In some cases, you don't even have to wait for him to actually get into mischief. Say that he lingers near the table peeking at the meat that you've set out for dinner, and you recognize that "Should I?" look. Use a sharp "Aaahh, aaahh!" to stop him in his tracks. You've just redirected his behavior without his suffering the consequences of a correction. This kind of mind-reading technique avoids the use of harsher negatives and creates a more confident attitude in your pup.

Never punish your Golden for something he did hours or even minutes earlier. Punishment must be dispensed within three to five seconds after the behavior, or your dog won't understand it. The same is true of praise.

Consistency Counts

When working with your puppy, use the same word for the same behavior every time. Add food lures and lots of "Good boy!" praise to make the action pleasant. Puppies, being greedy creatures, will be enticed to perform the action when they hear the word.

Memorize these important guidelines to successful puppy training:

✔ **Be clear and consistent.** It's not okay to allow your Golden on the couch with you and then scold him when he jumps up beside your visiting Aunt Agnes. Rules apply all the time.

✔ **Use simple one- or two-word commands such as "Buster, Sit," or "Buster, Quiet."** Don't nag with a long lecture he won't understand. ("Buster, why don't you ever sit down when I tell you to, for goodness sake!")

✔ **Dispense a correction only if your dog doesn't do what he was told to do.** Use appropriate discipline or corrections that are not excessive and do so immediately.

✔ **Always praise as soon as he complies.** For two important reasons. You want to praise the act of stopping the undesirable behavior. And you want him to know that you are pleased that he performed a particular behavior. You're capitalizing on his desire to please you.

✔ **Never strike your dog with your hand, foot, newspaper, or other object.** I cannot emphasize this enough. It's hard to believe that in this enlightened era some people still think they should use newspapers to swat their dog and believe that a good cuff across his nose is an okay thing to do. Cuffing any dog could not only hurt the dog; it will also provoke fear and cringing and sets the dog up for violent responses at some later time. Corrections are not random acts of violence.

✔ **Never call the dog to you for a correction.** That's the quickest way to turn "Come" into "Go away fast!" The dog will associate coming to you with the discipline and not the behavior that warranted the correction. (Present tense, remember?) Go and get the dog instead. And remember, by the time you reach him, he will not remember what he did moments earlier, so a correction is not appropriate.

✔ **Use common dog sense.** The best way to keep your Golden out of the trash is to put the trash away.

✔ **Never discipline your Golden for something he did hours or even minutes earlier.** The punishment (or praise) must occur within three to five seconds of the behavior, or he won't associate the discipline with the act.

Your Voice Says It All

How you talk to your puppy or dog is as important as what you say. Your tone of voice relays your message as much as the words you use. In "doggese," a low-pitched heavy sound tells him he's pushing things too far. A high-pitched voice means all is well, and it's time to play. When issuing warnings or corrections, use a lower voice and keep it short, sharp, and simple. No dragged out sounds like Nooooooo and never plead or whine. Use your high-pitched, happy voice for praise and during training sessions to tell your puppy what a smart guy he is.

Human anger and your Golden

Given that puppies, in fact all dogs, respond so strongly to tone of voice, you should also understand they will become scared and confused in the middle of a family feud. Canines do not understand human anger. Conflict within their pack or human family frightens them. It doesn't matter if you're yelling at the kids or spouting at your spouse, the dog is sure you're mad at him. Just watch him dive under the sofa when the tempers flare. When parents fight, the child believes he is somehow responsible for their anger. Dogs, too. After all, he's just a kid at heart. Make yours a happy dog house. No arguing or fighting in front of the dog. The kids will love it, too!

Voice pitch and inflection can be difficult for some to master. Practice using your best doggie voices to see (hear?) how you sound to your dog. Would you think obedience was fun if your boss thundered, "Ruffy, Heel!" in a deep intimidating voice? Would you hop right to it if she said, "Drop it" in a high-pitched tone that dripped with sugar?

Discipline Is Not a Four-Letter Word

Of course, in all puppies' lives there comes a time for discipline. *Discipline* simply means dispensing appropriate corrections to teach the dog correct behavior.

Do not confuse discipline with punishment. Punishment (as a physical tool of force or worse) is not appropriate and will, in fact, cause behavior problems like aggression rather than correct them. Corrections, on the other hand, are humane disciplinary tools that help your puppy understand what he did wrong and what he should do instead.

Discipline should be mild and minimal. Goldens are smart, sensitive little guys, and you can encourage correct behavior by distracting him as soon as you see him "think about" getting into mischief (which in a puppy's mind is merely play). A sharp "Aaah, aaah, aaah" or a sharp hand clap can startle him and shift his attention from his mischief (pawing at the trash bin, chewing on the rug). Always praise him profusely when he stops and give him a toy or treat for a reward.

Timing is always critical. All discipline must occur while he's actually performing the misdeed, and the discipline should fit the act or misbehavior.

When your pup displeased his mother weeks ago, it took but a single snarl or snap from Mom to make him sit up and take notice. As his new pack leader, you can use the same type of tactic as a means of correcting misbehavior.

If he still persists in his misbehavior after a verbal correction, you can add a collar shake just like Mom did in the whelping box. Keep your short collar tab attached to your puppy's collar. Just give him a quick shake and tell him, "Aah!" or "No!". I'm not talking rough house here — just a quick and gentle shake on his collar or collar tab. Use your firmest voice and maintain brief eye contact but don't turn this into a stare down session. Dominant canines consider that a threat and may challenge you with an aggressive response. That's normal for a dog, and you want to keep that eventuality out of your training picture.

Join a Super Puppy class

In times past, it was believed that puppies were not prepared to learn or handle a classroom atmosphere until they were at least 6 months old. Not so today. The 21st century puppy's education starts the day you bring him home and is enhanced by early group training (see Figure 8-1). These programs are casual and fun and designed to allow the pups to interact with other pups and people as well as learn.

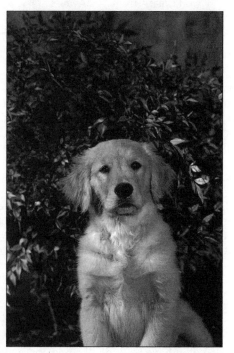

Figure 8-1:
Your dog's education starts when he's a puppy, not when he's 6 months old.

Close Encounters of the Furry Kind.

Calculating your Golden's age

Think of your puppy as a not-quite-2-year-old. Even though some experts maintain that an adult dog can achieve the comprehension of a 5-year-old child, living with a fully grown canine is more like living with a 3-year-old who never grows up. No matter how well trained, he will always chase a squirrel into the street. He will never resist the chicken bones in your trash. You wouldn't allow your toddler outside to play unsupervised. The message here is clear.

In the past, a dog's age was multiplied by seven to calculate canine development in comparison to human age. Today, more sophisticated methods are used, incorporating factors such as size, breed, and temperament when evaluating age.

Small dogs mature more quickly than large-breed dogs, which may take as long as two to three years to fully mature. After age 2, each year of dog life is equal to only four years of human life. Once they have reached maturity, large dogs, such as Goldens, age more rapidly than small ones, which is why smaller dogs tend to live longer than the big guys.

Puppy Age	Human Age
2 months	2 to 3 years
4 months	5 to 7 years
6 months	10 to 12 years
1 year	15 years
2 years	24 years
3 years	28 years
6 years	40 years
12 years	64 years

Puppy kindergarten classes such as Super Puppy can help speed up the social learning process. The age of enrollment varies with each class. Wait until he's 11 or 12 weeks old and has completed his first two or three shots (or whatever your vet recommends). These are fun classes that will get you started on a good canine communication system. They're not structured lessons or rigid obedience. They are designed to teach your puppy how to learn, and show you, the owner, how to teach. It's the beginning of an attitude.

All dogs, even super-dogs like Goldens, go through predictable rebellious stages on their journey from puppyhood into grown-up dog (see Figure 8-2). Research on a dog's maturation process reads almost like a canine Dr. Spock. These are trying times that will add an extra dimension of challenge to your first Golden year, but forewarned is forearmed, which can make these periods less difficult and even fun.

Even though most people think of their Goldens as little kids dressed in furry coats, the fact is that dogs are not little people, and they sure don't think in childlike terms, so their behavior has to be examined differently. Conclusion: If you want a well-behaved dog, you have to think like one and make sure that you're always one dog thought ahead of him.

Close Encounters of the Furry Kind.

Figure 8-2:
As your puppy matures into an adult, he will go through predictable rebellious stages.

Ages 3 to 6 months

Your puppy's 3- to 6-month pre-adolescent period is complicated (or enhanced, depending on how well you handle it!) by his gradual increase of independence and confidence. Your little guy will venture further and further from your side, following his nose and curiosity with grand new feelings of confidence about his human world. If you're planning to spay or neuter your Golden (and only serious breeders keep their dogs intact), do it by 6 months of age, or as near that age as your vet recommends. Those disruptive hormonal swings will only add to the complications of his adolescence.

Through his first 12 weeks, it was instinctive for your puppy to stick close to his leader (you) and his den (your house). But suddenly the big, scary world isn't so scary any more and off he goes. About this time, obedience instructors often hear puppy owners complain, "My puppy was so good until this week. He never left the yard, and now I have to chase him down the street."

Your pup is entering the terrible twos of puppyhood. It's time for greater supervision, your 20- or 30-foot long line, and a basic puppy obedience class. Basic obedience is a step up from Super Puppy class. Those first classes offered social exposure and taught your puppy how to pay attention, which was a huge step forward for a little fellow. These next basic classes will teach specific exercises to help you mold and control his behavior — very important with a spunky Golden pup!

A smart owner will continue obedience training during these difficult growing-up periods when he most needs that training. The value is in the class itself as well as the lessons learned: the multiple-dog atmosphere, assistance from an experienced instructor who will tackle your puppy's unique problems, the incentive to teach your puppy every day so that you won't look like a jerk when you go to class. And there's nothing like a little group therapy to give you moral support when your puppy's antics move from normal and reasonable to you-won't-believe-what-he-did-last-night!

Puppy FRAPS

At about 4 or 5 months of age, puppies enter a period some experts call the "puppy crazies," the "zooms," or puppy "FRAPS."

Fortunately, it's not contagious! *FRAP* stands for Frenetic Random Activity Period, a wild time in his young life when for no apparent reason he'll run like a demon possessed, through the house and over the furniture, spin around in circles, and zoom back and forth across the yard for five or ten minutes once or twice a day. He may even growl at imaginary beasts that exist only in his fuzzy madpup head.

This nutty behavior happens out of the blue, often just when your puppy starts showing encouraging little signs of maturity. I often get calls from puppy families who think their adorable puppy just popped a screw loose and that they did something to cause his absurd behavior.

Don't worry or try to discourage that behavior, as long as he isn't being destructive. It may last two or three months, and he'll outgrow it along with his puppy teeth, although some dogs never seem to totally outgrow it. My 9-year-old Golden still loves to do huge zooms around our property.

During this pain-in-the-ankle stage, it's often tempting to keep your puppy outdoors in the yard or in his kennel run. Don't! This is a vital developmental stage, and your puppy must spend quality time with you indoors learning proper house manners and how to settle down when you insist on it. Golden puppies are such eager students at this age. Prime that learning pump while it's at its peak.

The terrible teens

Did you know puppies go through a teenage puppy adolescence period during their first 2 years just like kids do? This stage begins anywhere from 6 to 9 months of age, often after that cute puppy stage, and unfortunately, just when you think his silly puppy behavior should be over. He's entering sexual maturity, and as those big-man hormones start pumping through his puppy veins, he will discover independence, confidence, and even arrogance, all of which will probably be directed at you, the loving owner he's supposed to please.

The symptoms of adolescence can be sudden and inexplicable. Suddenly your once-adoring Golden challenges your authority (I don't want to do that today, thank you!), jumps on furniture, and forgets commands he once responded to. He digs, barks, jumps, nips, becomes possessive and demanding, mounts your leg, and marks his territory. (Females just stare at you and then squat and wet the rug.) The teen period can last for several months and beyond, sometimes until the dog is 2 years old. (Dig out that P for Patient!) But if you can tough it out, you'll have a wonderful companion for the next 10 or 15 years. Sound like a teenager you used to know and love?

Your Golden's needs for stimulation, companionship, and activity during his adolescence are very high, and his tolerance for boredom and inactivity are low. Now there's a golden opportunity for you! Your challenge is to channel his energies in positive directions. Use exercise and games that appeal to and tax both his mind and body and don't forget those daily walks (or jogs if you're up to it).

Provide plenty of safe opportunities for vigorous play and exercise, and safe toys to occupy his teeth and mind. Use jogging, Frisbee and ball chasing, swimming, and other energetic ways to entertain him and wear him out. (See Chapter 10 on exercise.) Avoid situations in which his occasional lapses in obedience could lead to disaster, such as off-leash work or play in open or unsecured areas.

The best safeguard against these adolescent problems is, of course, a good foundation in obedience to fall back on during such difficult times (see Chapter 9). Think of it as stockpiling supplies in your behavior bomb shelter. Although most teen-dog challenges can't be avoided, with lots of patience and persistence, they can be managed if the dog knows you're the boss *before* his hormones slide into overdrive. A daily Sit-Stay or Down-Stay can go a long way in controlling adolescent antics (see Figure 8-3). Use those obedience tools to insist that he obey, even if it he does it in slow motion. Never encourage aggressive play or behavior and don't give him free run of the house when you're not home. As in all canine life stages, this, too, will pass.

Your year-old Golden is still a puppy even though he looks grown up. Large breeds like Golden Retrievers are not fully mature until about 2 years of age. Make appropriate allowances and adjust your behavior expectations accordingly.

Twelve to 18 months

At some point during this period, your Golden will reach emotional maturity. Dogs with tendencies toward dominance will begin to assert themselves at this time, hoping to raise their status in the "pack" (your household!). This behavior usually occurs within a structure of familiar relationships and surfaces only when the dog is approaching emotional maturity.

Figure 8-3:
A daily Sit-Stay or Down-Stay can keep your dog in line.

Living with a dominant dog does not mean you must "conquer" the dog, but obedience challenges must be recognized immediately and taken seriously. He must, in no uncertain terms, accept you as his leader. Punishment or discipline is not the appropriate method of dealing with early dominance and is likely to provoke a dangerous response. You should instead demand *rigid* obedience compliance — that means "always" with no ifs or buts. If serious signs appear, like growling or baring teeth, consult a qualified behaviorist.

The problem with most problem behaviors is that most of it is normal canine behavior; it's *your* problem, not the dog's! Nevertheless, it's your job to reshape that behavior to acceptable human standards. That's most easily accomplished when a dog is very (as in *very*) young. Otherwise, you have a secondary problem — you're working with bad habits while you try to teach the dog.

To Chew or Not to Chew

Golden puppies love to chew. So do adult Goldens. It's in their job description. It's a natural and healthy canine habit that goes way back to their wolf ancestors who gnawed their way around the den. Chewing on bones will satisfy your dog's emotional needs as well as certain physical needs that are important to his health. From a human perspective, it's *what* they chew on that presents a problem (see Figure 8-4).

The dog grudge myth

"He's just plain spiteful. He knew what he did wrong."

You've heard that one before. Maybe you've even said it yourself. The dog knew he was naughty because he had this guilty look on his muzzle every time his owner found a pile of feces or shredded Kleenex on the floor. Naturally the owner snarled at the dog, maybe even dragged him over to the crime scene to remind him just how bad he was. And naturally, the dog cringed and tucked his tail. His owner is enraged, but intelligent people like yourself understand that he's reacting to the anger, not the mess in the living room.

Your dog does not do destructive things to "get even" with you. He is incapable of those human emotions. Dogs are naughty because they get lonely, tired, or bored and simply act out of canine instinct. It's up to you to teach him manners and make his environment canine-friendly.

Dogs learn by repetition. Hereafter, whenever the dog sees the shredded tissue in the same room with his owner, he knows the boss is going to go bonkers. He will never understand it's because he tore up those tissues a few hours earlier. It's just another case of what's obvious to humans is not clear to the dog.

What should also be perfectly clear is that if you remove the tissue source, you will remove the problem. Move the wastebasket, for goodness' sake! These are grin-and-bear-it times. If you're not at home to supervise your dog, you can't discipline him for his mischief in your absence, but you *can* prevent future accidents from happening. Remove temptation, take him for an extra walk, and crate him when you're gone.

Illustrating the unfortunate conflict between the human and canine mind, one survey of 3,772 pet owners by the National Council on Pet Population found that 53 percent of people who surrendered their dogs to animal shelters incorrectly believed animals behave out of spite. Dogs are incapable of that kind of rationalization. Hopefully, those same folks understand their kids better than they do their dogs!

Mouthing and chewing are the most normal of Golden puppy problems. It's how curious puppies learn about their environment. It's a stress reliever. It feels good. And it's one of the hardest habits to correct.

The pros of chewing

Believe it or not, chewing does have its positive sides. In puppies, chewing on hard objects stimulates the growth of their adult teeth. Chewing hard bones helps scrape away the plaque, which causes bad breath and serious dental problems. Just as in people, plaque can damage the gums and ultimately allow bacteria to enter the bloodstream. People use dental floss. Dogs chew bones. Simple analogy. (Forget the fact that a puppy who is chewing on a bone is not chewing on your shoe or table leg!)

Figure 8-4:
Chewing is only natural; it's what your Golden chews on that's a problem. Garden hoses are an obvious no-no.

Close Encounters of the Furry Kind.

My veterinarian is always amazed at the healthy condition of my Goldens' teeth and gums. The credit belongs to the vast numbers of hard bones and Nylabones that litter their crates, kennel runs, and my living room floor.

Chewing is also good therapy for loneliness. Dogs who are left alone during the day can get lonely, depressed, or anxious, and maybe all of those. Your Golden most likely waits all day to hear your key turn in the door, and a good bone or two helps a lonesome fellow pass the time away. No bones to chew? How about the sofa pillows or the antique butter churn?

Chewing also releases pent-up energy, so dogs who don't get enough exercise will do what? Chew! Does your chewer get three or four brisk walks each day? Chase the Frisbee in the yard? Those activities will keep him mentally stimulated and physically too tired to chew.

Prevention power

To best prevent destructive chewing, you have to understand why it happens in the first place. Dogs don't chew because it's good for their teeth. They chew because it *feels* good to chew. Chewing relieves boredom and a host of other stressors. Just like kids (and even some adults), dogs who have nothing to do get bored and eventually get into mischief. Chewing is quite simply something to do with idle time.

Because Golden puppies are famous for their chewing exploits, you'll have to dig deep into your bag of Puppy Patience. It will take time to teach him what he may and may not chew or carry in his mouth.

Chew solutions are three-dimensional, involving the usual ounce of prevention, a dash of distraction and direction, and a dose of correction when all else fails.

- ✓ **Keep your people stuff out of your puppy's reach.** That means no shoes or slippers on the floor, no open wastebaskets to tip over, or dish towels hanging within puppy range (think jumping puppy!). A good rule is to keep anything you value in high places — above puppy level. That will prevent him from chewing on forbidden objects and keep him focused on his puppy toys. He can't destroy what he can't sink his teeth into.

- ✓ **Give him a variety of chewies to satisfy his urge to chew.** Not too many, though, or he'll be overwhelmed and bored. Keep two or three in his toy bucket and rotate them every couple of days to keep them stimulating. Add new toys occasionally to keep them interesting. Dozens of newfangled canine toys will captivate your pup — and you! So go ahead and indulge yourself!

- ✓ **Notice what forbidden objects he takes a liking to and spritz them with Bitter Apple or Tabasco sauce.** If he chews a no-no anyway, it's too late. Do *not* scold or holler at the pup. You've already lost this round. Go to the puppy, say "Drop" or "Leave it" (your choice, but stick with one), praise him for releasing it, and offer him a substitute toy.

- ✓ **Distract and redirect.** When he decides to nibble on a no-no, remember this: He does not know better. Just remove the object from his mouth with your command word "Drop," give him an enticing, legal substitute to chew on, and praise him when he takes that toy.

If he refuses to release his prize, grab his collar or collar tab, give him a gental shake and a verbal "No," and take the toy. If this refusal happens frequently, examine your relationship with the dog or pup. He's on his way to mutiny, and you need to re-establish your position as his leader with less cuddle stuff and more obedience.

- ✓ **Crate him when you can't watch him.** Despite rawhides, Nylabones, hard bones, carrot bones, woolly toys, and squeaky toys, a puppy will still dismantle your woodwork or cabinet corners if he's left alone too long. Crating is your *guaranteed* ounce of prevention.

You won't cure the chewing habit overnight. Your puppy will need many, many lessons and reminders before he's fully chew-conditioned. After all, the Golden Retriever was bred to retrieve and carry something in his mouth. It's hard to battle Mother Nature; the wiser course is to work with her instead.

Match the bone to the dog

Bones can entertain your dog for hours and keep his mind stimulated, which is especially good for older dogs who are less active or who are physically handicapped.

Select bones that match your dog's chewing needs and habits. A bone that softens more easily will satisfy the gentle chewer who has a softer bite, although not too many Goldens qualify in that department. Aggressive chewers will enjoy the harder bones, like sterile real bones, which also last longer. No meat bones for your dog of any age. Cooked steak, chicken, and pork bones splinter easily and can cause nasty internal problems.

Some of the newer model dog bones soften in the microwave and thus satisfy both gentle and aggressive chewers. Some bones are even made with tasty flavors that become intensified in the microwave.

Biting the Hand That Feeds

Biting and mouthing are different war games from chewing, although like chewing, both are natural behaviors that started in the whelping box. When your puppy wrestled and chewed on his littermates in play-fighting, he learned valuable lessons in canine communication and etiquette. When another puppy yelped in pain, it meant "Time out, I won't play with you any more." He learned to bite more gently or his playmate would say, "Adios!"

His mother also taught those lessons when she snarled or nipped him when he got too rough. Now that you're walking in his mother's pawprints, you have to round out his education to include his human family.

Biting involves anything from playful mouthing and nipping to curling back the lips to taking a chunk out of your arm. When your puppy tugs your pants leg or nips your fingertips, he's just being playful. When he shows those tiny canines, he has other thoughts.

With mouthing and play biting, you need to teach him "bite inhibition" in the same way his mother did. Your puppy has to learn that human flesh is just as tender as his siblings' ears, and he's not allowed to hurt it.

Whenever your puppy nips or attempts to bite your hand, do not pull it away. It's a natural canine instinct to view your hand or foot as a toy or prey and start nipping even more enthusiastically. The key is to hold your hand perfectly still (grit your teeth), bend toward your puppy, and issue a single, sharp command such as "No bite!" or a loud "Ouch!" This should startle him to stop biting or to release the pressure on your hand. Remove your hand and immediately reward him with soft praise and offer him a chew toy.

Ignoring your puppy can also be effective because it deprives him of your attention, which he dearly wants and needs. When your puppy nips your fingertips, shout "Oouuuch!" in a loud voice, and when he stops, immediately turn away and fold your arms. Wait just a minute and then return to normal, but do not praise or pet the pup. Speak to him quietly but firmly. More nips, more isolation. Goldens are social butterflies, and this method can work wonders. You will probably have to do this repeatedly for a while. Goldens are notoriously oral creatures.

Some owners use a glove to teach a puppy gentle mouthing and not to bite. With a glove you can protect your hand and keep it in his mouth while telling him "Easy" or "Gentle," which is a secondary No-Bite command that will allow you to put your hand in his mouth without his biting down.

Praise softly as soon as he stops biting, pet him gently, and offer him an alternate chew object: a woolly toy or other favorite chewie. Be consistent and make sure that the entire family does the same. Your puppy will discover who and what he may and may not chew on. If the kids don't follow these same rules, they will remain fair chomping game.

If your puppy bares his teeth during any of these maneuvers, hold his collar or collar tab and give him a shake or tug with an obedience command like "Sit." That will defuse his attitude and remind him you're in charge. If such incidents continue, take a good long look at your relationship. You need to follow a more rigid training program. This is one problem that *will* escalate from minor to major if you don't do your own nipping in the early stages.

Do not get physical with your pup; tough tactics only stimulate and encourage aggressive behavior. Instead use obedience reinforcements that will remind your puppy that you're the alpha dog who gives the orders.

By the time your puppy is 3 or 4 months old, he should have his play biting under control with perhaps just an occasional nip here and there. If the habit goes beyond that age, even a submissive dog may be tempted to take over as top dog. Now you're entering the danger zone. Reassert your authority with consistent leadership exercises.

Obedience is the best nonconfrontational way to remind him you're his boss and master. Make him earn his meals and treats and play activities by obeying those commands. He'll be less apt to sink his teeth into his leader's arm!

If he bites or tries to bite when you correct him or take his food away, his behavior is dominant-aggressive, and he's challenging your leadership. That behavior is more threatening and hints at future problems, so it must be dealt with more firmly and immediately. Consult a professional trainer or behaviorist for advice on how to deal with it. There are also several good books on canine aggression that will help you understand and correct your dog's behavior.

Chapter 9

Home Schooling Your Golden Puppy

*I*f there's one principle that applies to all dogs regardless of breed, size, or color, it's this: The quality of your adult dog is in direct proportion to the quality and amount of time you invest in *training him as a pup*. You'll both be glad you did.

In this chapter, I focus on how to teach your puppy basic obedience commands, like walking on a leash, coming when called, and sitting and lying down when told. You don't need much to start: a happy voice, a pocketful of goodies, a 6-foot leash, and a 20-foot long line. Proper training collars will come later.

The Cookie Principle

To treat or not to treat. That's the $64 question. Proponents walk on both sides of the food fence, but both pro and con trainers suggest using treats for first-time puppy lessons because it produces an immediate and positive response and then gradually weaning off the food rewards. Of course, you can't use food forever. Imagine offering a tidbit to a 90-pound Rottweiler who's charging you with his pearlies bared!

Food is just one of several positive motivators for *behavior enhancement*, which is just a fancy term for obedient behavior or plain old-fashioned good manners. Eventually the trainer phases out the food in favor of other rewards like verbal praise, hands-on petting and hugs, squeaky toys, and balls to chase and find. You can use all these delightful tools to teach and stimulate your puppy as well as your adult dog.

Research shows that any behavior that is rewarded will increase in frequency. So before you begin any training exercise, stockpile an arsenal of the preceding reward systems.

Begin by stuffing your pockets with tiny pieces of soft puppy treats or dried liver treats (find them at your pet store). Tiny slices of hot dogs (cheap ones) work, too, but they won't store well in the pockets of your shirts and jackets.

In fact, keep treats in all your pockets all the time. Every day loads of training opportunities seem to fall from the sky, and you have to be prepared to meet them with a goodie. Get used to soggy dog biscuits in your laundry tub.

Keep your treats small enough so that he won't have to stop to chew them up, yet big enough to make them tantalizing. A crunchy puppy-size milkbone easily breaks up into three tiny pieces. You don't want to offer so much food that it affects his appetite or dramatically increases his food intake.

The entire family should understand the basics of your puppy's education, but only one person should do the actual training exercises. Your puppy needs the consistency of one message from one messenger. Just make sure that everyone in the household does nothing to conflict with what he's learning. You need consistency, consistency, and then more consistency.

Choosing a Release Word

Before you begin training your dog, you need to choose a release command like Free or Okay. Many professional trainers prefer Free because Okay is too commonly used in conversation. I use Okay because it's easier to remember, and I've never had a problem with it. I go with Okay for this book, but the choice is yours.

Use your release word to free your puppy from the Sit position (or whatever stationary position you have put him in). Say it in a happy tone but not so cheery as to send your pup into a frenzy. You want to keep him in a trainable frame of mind.

Mastering the Don'ts

Just as important as those things you do to teach your dog to come are things you should *not* do:

These are training absolutes, when never means *absolutely* never!

- ✔ **Never discipline your puppy or adult dog after he comes to you.** That's the fastest way to turn "Come" into "Stay away" or "Catch me."

- ✔ **Never call your dog to you for something unpleasant like bathing, giving pills, crating, or kenneling.** (This does not infer that crating is negative, but it can become so if he ends up crated every time you call him.) Go and get the dog instead. If you're too busy or too lazy to go get him, give him lots of hugs and kisses when he comes on his own and then, after a minute or two, do your dirty work.

- ✔ **Never call your puppy when he's distracted or preoccupied.** Call him only when you're sure that he will respond. Start indoors because there are too many fun distractions outdoors. An older trained dog should respond to "Come" regardless of distractions.

- ✔ **Never train your puppy or adult dog when you're in a sour mood.** Your Golden will sense your irritation and feel like he's displeasing you, which creates a negative attitude toward training. Keep your training sessions positive . . . for *both* of you.

- ✔ **Never repeat any command.** Say it only once. These are not three or four-word commands. He has to learn just like any smart toddler or adolescent that he must Come or Sit or Down the first time you say the word (unlike your teenager!). There are, however, some exceptions to this rule.

- ✔ **Never scold your puppy when he breaks his Sit to come to you.** Just use a firm "No" and return him to the Sit position. Scolding will just confuse him and create a negative attitude toward training.

Introducing Puppy to His Leash

Introduce the leash within a few days of coming home. Just attach it to his buckle collar and let him drag it around the room or play area to get used to it. If he tries to chew the leash, as he surely will, spray his end with Bitter Apple. Toss a few toys to distract him from the trailing leash and use your best praise voice. After he knows how to sit when told, have him sit before you attach his leash. You're laying the foundation for your leadership.

Taking your first walk

Once he accepts the leash, put yourself on the other end and take your first walk together in the yard. Your goal during these outings is to have your puppy simply accept control and not resist walking when leashed. (Think 10 pounds compared to 30 or 40 pounds straining at the other end!) As with all other puppy exercises, fill your pockets with puppy treats before you start. Use your happy voice for encouragement and just talk to him along the way.

Restraint is a new experience for your puppy, and he may resist walking with you with every inch of his tiny puppy frame. He may freeze in his tracks, spin, and whirl like a roped young calf, or tug and pull with all his might. Give him a moment to settle down, but don't go to him to offer reassurance because that would reward his resistance. (It's that connection thing again.) Instead, bend down to coax him to come to you, and when he does, of course, reward him with a treat.

Now try taking a few steps with a treat lure held at your left side at nose height where he can see and smell it. Pat your knee and use a lot of happy talk to entice him to walk near your left knee.

Leash walking is not heeling; that comes much later in basic obedience class. Leash walking is incremental puppy training . . . a few steps, a treat, a few more steps, another goodie. This shouldn't be a difficult process. If it becomes a daily battle, seek the help of a professional obedience instructor now or as soon as you can find a class.

After your puppy has accepted the leash, your goal is to teach him to simply walk near you like a little gentleman without tugging on his leash or yanking your arm out of its socket. Fill your pockets with puppy treats and start walking.

1. **Design your walking area.**

   Draw a mental circle around yourself about 3 feet in diameter. This is your puppy's walking space. Now memorize the walking words, "This way" and "Easy." The usual "Good boy" is a given.

2. **Move forward with "Let's Go" and start walking briskly around your yard or driveway.**

   Show him the treat to get him looking at you and moving next to you. All you're looking for is a few good steps. Walk briskly for just 10 or 20 successful paces, then stop with an okay, and praise him big-time.

3. **As he follows and looks up, praise him and give him the treat.**

4. **Keep him within that 3-foot circle with "Easy" and "Let's Go."**

   If he wanders ahead of you outside that invisible circle, tell him "Easy" and gently tug him back, saying "Good boy" whenever he's at your side. If he lags behind, repeat "Let's go" and gently pop him forward (no dragging please, just a quick and gentle tug and quick release of the leash.) If he looks away, chat sweetly to regain his attention and give a treat when he's at your side and looking at you. Be sure to praise each time he's at your side (and *only* at your side.) and praise every time he looks at you.

Your second goal is to teach your pup to look at you when you walk. Most Goldens are natural "watchers" and easily tune in on this walking business.

 ✔ **Praise only when he's near your side or when he's looking at you.**
   Your happy praise should make him look up at you. Don't give praise if he's lagging or pulling ahead on his leash. (Association, remember?)

✔ **Never scold or nag.** After all, he doesn't have a clue about what you want him to do. As with all his other exercises, you're trying to create an attitude that says, "Let's do this some more!"

✔ **Walk straight ahead.** Walk in a straight line at first, turning in very wide arcs or circles with no sharp or 90-degree turns.

✔ **Make 90-degree turns.** After a few days of walking in wide circles, add some challenge and occasionally make a corner turn and go in another direction. Give a tug if you must to get him to turn as well, saying, "This way," when you turn and tug. As soon as he joins up with you (don't go too abruptly or too fast), give a treat and big-time praise.

✔ **Once he gets the hang of it, increase your walking time to no more than half-a-minute in one stretch, but you can do several stretches in one session with brief play in between.** That doesn't sound like much, but count to 30 slowly. That's a long time for a puppy. Your objective is to keep his interest peaked and prevent boredom.

✔ **Progress slowly.** Don't move ahead to formal heeling until you start obedience class. Your goal for now is a pleasant (for both of you) walk together.

During all this puppy training, you're going to run into roadblocks — the leash will tangle around your feet, your puppy may jump and jump some more, and he may sabotage your best efforts. This is where a good puppy class comes in handy. A good instructor can work wonders!

Your Golden's leash on life

The last thing you want is a Golden who runs off to visit your neighbors or other dogs or who refuses to come when he's outdoors. How to accomplish that? Simple! Don't let your dog run free. A loose dog is in danger from automobiles, from other animals, and from unsavory people. These considerations far outweigh the pleasure any dog gets from running free.

Your neighbors also deserve your consideration. A loose dog may be (and probably is) digging in their compost heap or flower bed, leaving doggie deposits on their lawn, and impregnating their female dogs.

A loose dog may react defensively if he is teased or threatened. A random bite can send him to dog jail for ten days, raise your homeowner insurance rates, and even risk your right to own a dog.

On-leash walks are the obvious solution. It also strengthens the human-animal bond and offers you and your puppy or dog improved cardiovascular fitness. Give your dog his own leash on life and don't let him run free. He won't know what he's missing, and you won't end up missing him.

The All-Important Come Command

Coming *reliably* when called is the most difficult command to teach, yet it is the most important. This is one exercise you'll need to work on all his life to keep him dependable. As your dog grows older and more confident, and you detect a slower response to coming when called, give him a short reminder course for several days. It could someday save your dog's life. Get real — do you *honestly* believe your dog would never chase a rabbit or a squirrel across the street?

Teaching Come starts the first day you bring your puppy home. Every time you see your puppy start to come to you, tell him "Puppy, Come!" in your twinkliest, happy voice. Vary your body posture at times to keep it interesting and unpredictable, squat down on one knee, open your arms wide, clap your hands, pat the front of your legs, pat the floor, and act just like a silly fool every time he comes to you. Remember to praise him while he's in the process of coming, not just when he gets to you. Use the same word and happy tone of voice every time you call your dog.

Here are a few Come reinforcements:

- ✔ **Use his meal times as reinforcement sessions by calling your pup to Come every time you feed him.** Rattle his food pan and tell him "Come" in a happy, lively tone of voice. That tasty kibble is a great reward for coming when he's called.

- ✔ **Try different places.** Practice Come in different areas of the house and vary the rewards between hands-on praise, tidbits, or a squeaky toy.

- ✔ **Add distractions.** Once your puppy is responding well, continue to work indoors, but add distractions. Wait until he's preoccupied to call him to you. If he doesn't come immediately, it's no big deal. Simply go *to* the pup, clap your hands to get his attention, and call him once again. Time then for a treat reward. Spend several days indoors before you move outside into the yard (see the next section).

The Come command outdoors

Your primary rule outdoors is to never allow your puppy to run free without a long line anywhere outside, in your yard or elsewhere, until he's completely trained and has proven himself reliable under very distracting circumstances (see Figure 9-1). In most cases, that will take about a year. (If you think you've accomplished it in six months or less, you're either deluding yourself, or you don't need this book!) My young Goldens usually wear a long line outdoors for their first year of life. That way I always have my "weapons" handy, and I never position myself for failure.

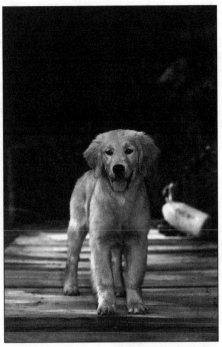

Figure 9-1:
Never allow
your puppy
to run free
until he's
completely
trained —
usually
at about
a year.

Close Encounters of the Furry Kind.

Outdoors, with your puppy on his 20-foot-long line and you on the other end, walk away and call him. Once. Lay on the praise as soon as he starts coming to you and kneel down to encourage him. Give him a food reward when he reaches you. If he hesitates when you first call him, give a firm tug on the line and run backwards saying, "Come" with each tug. No pulling or dragging him toward you. Act like a nut and use lots of happy talk while running backwards and shower him with the usual praise and treat when he arrives. Follow this yard routine for about a week.

Now mix it up with some complications. Add the leash with the long line. Walk with your puppy and drop the leash but not the line. When he starts moving away from you, give the Come command and if he doesn't come running right away, give a sharp tug on the line and say, "Come." Do this for another week and then add distractions in the yard. Put a favorite toy in your walking path, a food dish or a ball, and call him when he starts toward the distraction object. Don't forget the praise and treats.

Never progress to the next phase of training until your puppy is reasonably reliable on the exercise you're working on. This principle applies to all aspects of dog training.

As he improves, switch to your 50-foot-long line and repeat the process. As you progress, gradually eliminate the food rewards (first every other time, then every third, and so on) while continuing the praise and hands-on petting each and every time he comes.

Continue this process beyond when you feel your puppy is reliable. History shows that puppies *will* do the unexpected, especially at certain stages in their lives. The more conditioned your puppy is to "Come," the better he'll respond when faced with irresistible temptations.

Hit the road!

Take your puppy on the road. Practice in different locations . . . a park, a neighbor's yard, a retail parking lot. Expect a setback each time you move. In truth, you should back up your training when you switch to a new place. Backing up means using the long line only, but no distractions, or whatever was the process in your next-to-last lesson. Then add each new element individually just as you do in your own yard.

The Sit Command

The Sit command is a breeze. Stand in front of your puppy and hold a bit of treat or hot dog in front of and just above his nose. Slowly move it backward (not too high) over his head. As he tips backward for the treat, his rear end should slide down toward the floor into sit position. (If he tips up off his front feet, the treat is probably too high.) As soon as his behind hits the floor, tell him "Sit, good dog, sit," and dispense his treat. When you give the treat, be sure to praise profusely and pet or rub his ear with your other hand as preparation for that later time when you will wean him off the treat and onto strictly praise rewards. Now give a release word to let him know this Sit is done.

If he resists setting his rump down or jumps up and paws your hand, just be patient and enjoy his puppy antics. He's merely problem-solving. Your pup is one smart fella. He wants that treat, and he'll soon figure out how to get it. Just take a few steps and move about and then repeat the exercise. Your puppy should master this one by the second or third bite! Repeat about ten times once a day (or twice daily if you're a truly golden person). As he becomes more proficient, wait just a moment longer before you give the treat.

Once he's sitting reliably, give the Sit command from a few feet away (see Figure 9-2). Make Sit a happy fun command, almost like a trick.

Figure 9-2:
Try giving
your dog
the Sit
command
from a few
feet away.

Close Encounters of the Furry Kind.

You have countless opportunities to master Sit. Make him sit at meal times for his food dish. Make him sit at the door when he comes in from the yard and then give him a treat. Soon he'll be sitting every time he comes inside. You'll love this habit when he comes in with wet or muddy paws to wipe.

Wait as a Command

The Wait command is a close relative of Sit (see the preceding section). Use it for going in and out of doors or cars or other openings. He doesn't have to sit; he just stands patiently, waits for you to proceed first, and then follows with permission. This exercise also reinforces your alpha persona, reminding him that leaders always go first. (See Chapter 8 for more on alpha.)

With your dog on leash, approach any doorway in your house, from the inside going out first, and then do the reverse. Tell him to wait, put the palm of one hand in front of his nose, and with your other hand hold him back with the leash while you go through first. Give your release command and allow him to pass through. And, of course, praise him for his expertise. Do a few run-throughs on this every day. If he already knows Sit, he'll understand the difference, and this one will be a snap.

The Down Command

Down is a great multipurpose command. This command is a normal extension of Sit, but it's a bit handier because it places your dog in a position where he can just relax, maybe even take a little snooze. It's also a submissive position that reinforces your top dog position every time you use it, which should be at least once a day. It controls your dog at home, when you eat, work at your computer, or watch TV, and when you have guests and you want him to behave. It also controls him in public places like your vet's office and takes him out of harm's way. There are dozens more reasons why Down is another big gun in your dog talk arsenal. It's one command you'll want to work on and perfect.

To teach the Down command:

1. **Begin by placing your puppy in the sit position without using the Sit command.**

   You don't want to confuse him with two commands in the same exercise.

2. **Now hold your treat lure in front of his nose and slowly lower it to the floor, pushing it away from you and toward his front feet and body.**

   He should slide down in a backward motion to follow the treat.

3. **The moment his elbows completely touch the floor, say "Down. Good boy. Down" and give him the reward.**

   Be sure to follow up with praise and petting.

4. **After the praise, give him your release word to break position and another hug; then take a few steps and begin again.**

As with Sit, you may have to experiment a bit and try this once or twice to master the correct maneuver. A bit of wiggling at first won't mess him up. Just be patient and keep trying. Once he's doing the Down exercise without hesitation, wait a bit longer before offering the food reward and a bit longer before releasing him. You're conditioning him to Stay. Do at least ten repetitions once or twice a day. Do them in various locations around the house and add distractions once he's solid and reliable. Gradually phase out the food treats (see the section "The Cookie Principle" earlier in this chapter).

Advancing to Sit-Stay and Down-Stay

Your puppy must be proficient on the commands described earlier in this chapter before you progress to Stay. You'll need your 6-foot leash. The procedure is basically the same for both:

1. **With the dog on leash and in front of you, give the command for the desired position, Sit or Down.**

2. **With the dog in correct position, place the palm of your hand in front of his nose and then give the Stay command.**

   If he attempts to move, use a quick leash pop (upwards for sitting or downwards for the down) to keep him in position and say a sharp "Ah!" or "No!".

3. **Wait just 5 or 10 seconds and then release him with a soft Okay (or your chosen release word) and a big hug.**

   Dance a few steps together and then settle him down for a rerun.

4. **Do five or six repetitions.**

Gradually increase the Stay time in short 10-second increments. Always vary the length of time for each command, 30 seconds one time, 10 seconds, or 1 minute on the next, to keep his attention peaked and to make sure that he doesn't start anticipating his release. Even puppies are smart enough to figure out what you'll do next.

And remember that he's just a puppy with a limited attention span and lots of energy. Long stays beyond a minute or two are not reasonable for a very young pup.

Practice Sit-Stays and Down-Stays after your puppy has blown off most of his energy and he's ready to settle down. A fully rested, wide-awake puppy plus a Stay exercise equals a recipe for failure.

It's hard to keep a dog happy and willing during static exercises (ones in which he doesn't move) because it places the dog in a submissive posture or position. So don't do more than ten in a row and *be sure* to do fun "happy-ups" in between. It's worth the effort. A dog who stays in one place is a joy to live with!

Establish gold medal goals on your puppy's obedience exercises. By the time he's 6 months old, he should do a 15-minute Down-Stay without a fuss, and double that length of time by 9 months of age.

The Drop It or Give Command

You'll have lots of opportunities to work on the Drop or Give command, considering how often your Golden will have something in his mouth! Your early fetching games should have laid the foundation for this command (see Figure 9-3).

It's important for him to believe in his heart of hearts that he *must* give you anything you ask him for. That means his toys, his food, and any object you don't want him to have, which includes things that could injure him or make him ill.

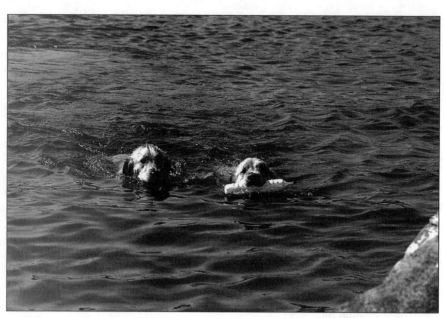

Close Encounters of the Furry Kind.

If your dog won't release the item willingly when you say your chosen command word, try this technique:

1. **Press his flews (lips) against his teeth and gums while saying the command.**
2. **Remove the object from his mouth.**
3. **Give him a substitute object or a treat.**

Be sure to praise. If he resists, you can add a little emphasis: Grasp his collar or collar tab, firmly tell him "Aah, aah," and repeat the command.

Drop is one lesson that requires an A+. A dog who won't give up his toys or bones or food is a potential biter and will challenge you in other sinister ways as he grows into those 65 pounds of muscle. Think Hulk Hogan with sharp teeth. (See Chapter 16 for more on problem behavior.)

There's one more way to make your dog drop something in his mouth. Place your fingers inside either hind leg and press hard upwards into his abdominal area. For reasons known only to the dog and possibly the professional retriever trainer who taught me that one, it works. I don't know if it enhances your alpha spot, but it surely convinces the dog you mean it. You may have to practice this one a few times to find the exact spot and the amount of pressure.

Teaching the Off Command

Use the "Off" word to discourage jumping up. (Don't use Down because that will only confuse him with that command.) Jumping is natural puppy behavior that started in the whelping box.

To teach the Off command:

1. **Put your puppy on a leash or a short cord, a line that you can tug to make your point.**

   This allows you to demonstrate what you want without physically touching the dog.

2. **When he begins to jump, command "Off" and tug downward with the lead.**

3. **When he's got all four feet planted once again, tell him to Sit and then praise your brilliant dog.**

   Be alert if he thinks about trying it again. You can step on the lead just as he starts and force him to abort the jump. Praise him when he settles down.

If you have a predictable jumper, you can also use a shaker can as reinforcement (see Chapter 5). When he begins to jump, shake the can loudly behind your back and tell him "Off!" If that doesn't work, on his next attempt toss the can to land on the floor *near* him (never on him) and command "Off!" When he gets down, be sure to praise and have him sit. He has to understand getting off makes him a good boy.

If neither of these methods works, refer to Chapter 16 for more jumping corrections.

When the Message Is Enough!

"Enough" is a handy word to let your dog know that the game is over or that he has to stop doing whatever it is he's doing at that moment. It's especially useful when your dog's play becomes a bit rowdy or escalates into more than you feel up to at the moment.

You teach Enough simply by using the word every time you stop playing or when you end a game. Of course, use it also when he gets a little out of hand. Say it in a low firm voice. If he doesn't stop his roughhousing or nonsense, just turn your back, which in effect deprives him of your presence and attention. Or you can grab his collar or collar tab and give a little shake while saying, "Enough" as a gentle reminder that you mean business. Always praise when he stops, but do so quietly so that he doesn't get all revved up again.

Attending a Puppy Class

Your puppy does not have to be obedient to attend a puppy class. Super Puppy classes or other puppy kindergartens begin as early as 11 or 12 weeks of age after your puppy has been safely immunized. These are not formal obedience classes where all the dogs walk around in circles. Rather they are structured playtimes to jump start puppy's learning process. This early group environment helps speed up the social learning process and will complement any obedience training you already do at home. *Do not wait* until you have mastered basic home obedience to attend a class.

But hear this! Don't stop at puppy class. Continue your Golden's obedience training at least through the novice level. It's bonding as well as training, so you'll become a better team in body and in spirit. (Your neighbors will be so envious of your dog's devotion *and* behavior!) You both need the practice this early in your relationship.

When you advance to the next level of obedience, novice or beyond, you'll need to change from puppy's clip or buckle collar to the chain or prong-type collar, which are designed *for training use only* after 4 or 5 months of age. They can be used separately or together, depending on how well you and your dog are mastering your techniques.

The chain or "choke" training collar

A chain collar must be the right type and size collar *and* put on the dog the correct way in order to be effective. Select a wide-link collar because the larger links are more gentle on the neck and will make a clinking noise that helps communicate your commands to the dog. Remember the pop and release you use when working on his leash walking skills? The click of the chain link collar adds one more dimension to the message in the leash.

Determine the right size by measuring the widest part of your dog's head just in front of his ears and add two inches to that dimension. Collars come only in even sizes, so if you measure an odd number, move up an inch to round it out.

The collar must be put on correctly to work properly. That can be tricky for the novice dog owner, so don't feel badly if you goof this up at first. My 4-H dog obedience class members learned how to put the collar on their dogs by using the letter P as their guideline.

1. **Begin by dropping the chain through one of the end rings — either one will do.**

2. **Hold the collar so that it forms the letter P around your hand or fist.**

3. **Using that position, face your dog and slip the collar over your dog's head.**

4. Now clip your lead to the active ring.

The active ring is the one that allows the collar to tighten or go slack.

The secret behind the collar's use is a slack leash and the timing (ah timing, as in all things canine) of the collar correction. Your leash must be loose or slack to create the snap-and-release effect that sends signals to the dog.

When using the collar during walking or beginning heeling, follow the same principles: Always use a slack lead (which seems to be tough to master for most novices), a snappy pop and release, and praise, praise. The leash does the correcting, and your voice says you're the good guy.

The prong collar

With all those nasty hooks that could dig into your poor dog's flesh, the prong collar looks like something from a medieval torture rack. The happy truth is that the prong collar is actually more humane than the chain collar, which can choke your dog to death or damage his trachea if used improperly or used with a heavy hand. The prong collar is self-limiting and cannot tighten indefinitely around the neck. The prongs (which are not sharp or pointed, by the way) pinch the neck when you tug lightly on the leash, creating immediate discomfort, which the dog will try hard to avoid. These collars are quite effective on strong and strong-willed dogs. Face it. A 90-pound woman would have one heck of a time leash popping a 100-pound Rottweiler. Most prong collars come in three sizes with the smallest at 17 inches and therefore are not intended for puppy use.

I often use both collars on a dog at once, switching from one to the other as I need them. I include the choke collar as a precaution because I've had prong collars pop loose — not a safe happening if you're walking on a busy street or if your Golden is the type who might run off.

The head collar

If you're appalled at the idea of a collar pinching your dog's neck or if you are physically unable, undisciplined, or too discombobulated to use a choke collar effectively, consider using a head collar. Head collars look like horse halters and lead in the same fashion that halters lead the horse (who would not respond at all to a single collar around his neck). The Halti collar is available through pet suppliers, and the Gentle Leader and the Promise collar — used in guide and assistance dog training — can be purchased through veterinarians. Both control the dog by controlling his head and require little physical strength from the handler, which is a blessing for youngsters and small adults. The collars come with instructions on how to introduce it to the dog, how to put it on, and how to use it — all are very simple for the human at the other end.

Part III
Keeping Your Pal Healthy and Happy

The 5th Wave   By Rich Tennant

"Oh Martin—I told you never to leave the dog unsupervised in the backyard!"

In this part . . .

You don't just want your Golden Retriever to survive; you want him to thrive. In this part, you discover the secrets of a healthy dog — proper nutrition, daily exercise, preventive care, and a regular grooming routine — as well as how to care for your dog if he gets in to anything as deadly as poisons. You also find out the special treatment you need to give your older Golden.

Don't fall in love with the first pretty face you see. You need to make sure that your pet is right for your personality and lifestyle (see Chapter 1).

When you visit a breeder, resist the temptation to take two pups instead of one. The pups will bond naturally to each other and grow up to be dog-dogs instead of people dogs. (See Chapter 4.)

Golden Retriever puppies are adorable when small. But without proper training, they will be unruly and difficult to control when fully grown. See Part II for training tips.

Golden Retrievers and children under 3 don't always mix (see Chapter 1). As you can see from this photo, they both enjoy the same toys!

The Golden Retriever is famous for its grand looks and friendly disposition. To find out more about the breed standard, see Chapter 2.

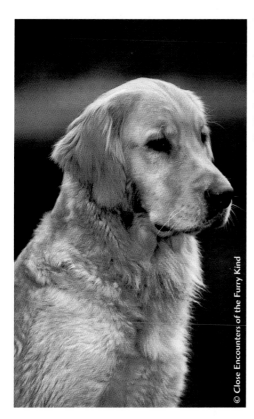

© Close Encounters of the Furry Kind

© Close Encounters of the Furry Kind

If you're not sure about the future color of your pup, check out his ears. The ears are a good indicator of the adult dog's coat color.

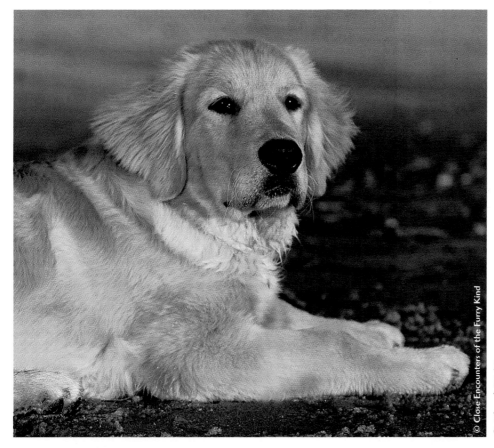

© Close Encounters of the Furry Kind

Some Goldens are more laid-back than others. To find a dog that suits your personality, check out Chapter 4.

There's more to owning a puppy than puppy chow and hugs. Preventive care is a key element of pet ownership. (See Chapter 11.)

Pet owners should be well versed in basic canine health care. Here, an owner applies ointment to her Golden's eyes. (See Chapter 11.)

Toys are important for dogs of all ages. Without them, they will invent their own fun. (See Chapter 5 for toy ideas.)

A healthy dog enjoys everyday activity. For other signs of good and poor health, see Chapter 11.

Even puppies need a rest. For more on your dog's needs, see Chapter 10.

When you envision your Golden Retriever's life, do you think about fun outdoor activities? Or would you prefer cuddling on the couch? See Chapter 1 for tips on selecting the perfect-fit pup.

Socialization should begin with the breeder and continue when your pup comes home. For more on proper socialization, see Chapter 6.

True to their name, Golden Retrievers love to retrieve, although some love it more than others. Find out how to test your pup's natural retrieving ability. (See Chapter 4)

Chew toys are a big part of every Golden puppy's life. Never give your puppy an old shoe or sock to chew and play with; you'll regret it later! (See Chapter 5.)

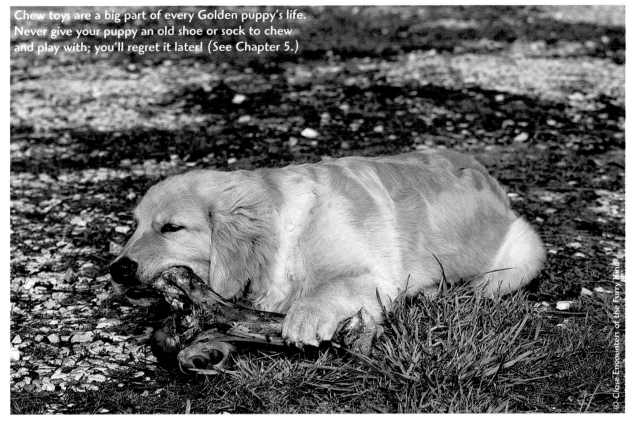

Make sure that your Golden has access to fresh water at all times. (See Chapter 10.)

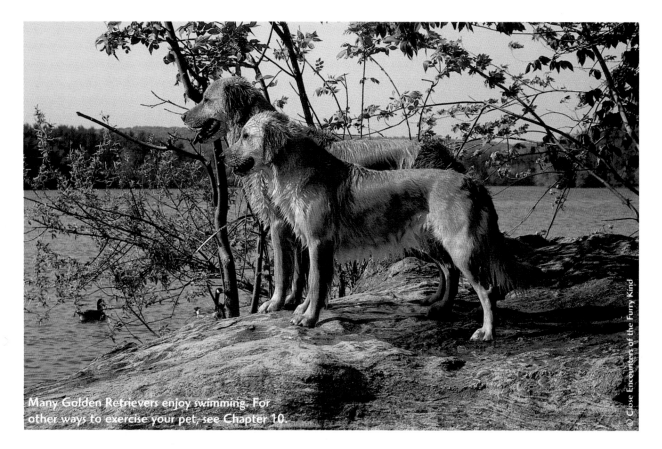

Many Golden Retrievers enjoy swimming. For other ways to exercise your pet, see Chapter 10.

Even dogs enjoy a day at the beach. For more on exercise, see Chapter 10.

Don't fall in love with the first pretty face you see. You need to make sure that your pet is right for your personality and lifestyle (see Chapter 1).

When you visit a breeder, resist the temptation to take two pups instead of one. The pups will bond naturally to each other and grow up to be dog-dogs instead of people dogs. (See Chapter 4.)

Golden Retriever puppies are adorable when small. But without proper training, they will be unruly and difficult to control when fully grown. See Part II for training tips.

Golden Retrievers and children under 3 don't always mix (see Chapter 1). As you can see from this photo, they both enjoy the same toys!

The Golden Retriever is famous for its grand looks and friendly disposition. To find out more about the breed standard, see Chapter 2.

If you're not sure about the future color of your pup, check out his ears. The ears are a good indicator of the adult dog's coat color.

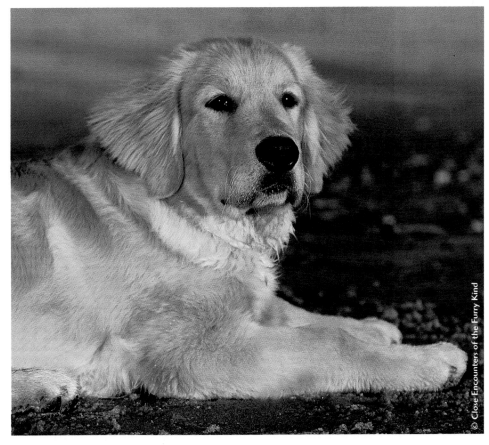

Some Goldens are more laid-back than others. To find a dog that suits your personality, check out Chapter 4.

There's more to owning a puppy than puppy chow and hugs. Preventive care is a key element of pet ownership. (See Chapter 11.)

Pet owners should be well versed in basic canine health care. Here, an owner applies ointment to her Golden's eyes. (See Chapter 11.)

Toys are important for dogs of all ages. Without them, they will invent their own fun. (See Chapter 5 for toy ideas.)

A healthy dog enjoys everyday activity. For other signs of good and poor health, see Chapter 11.

Ron Kimball

Even puppies need a rest. For more on your dog's needs, see Chapter 10.

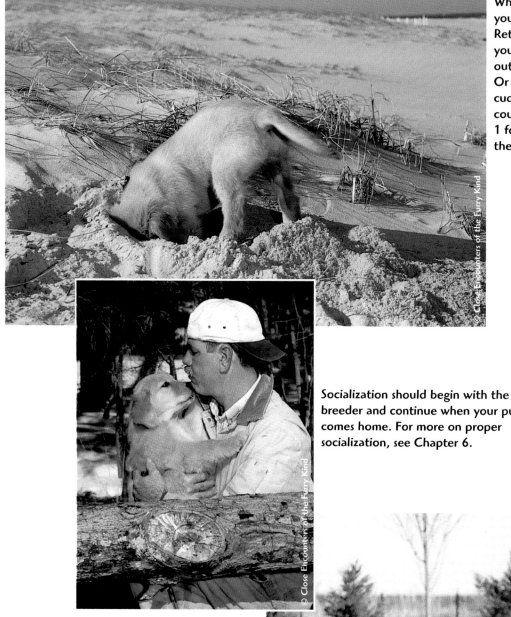

When you envision your Golden Retriever's life, do you think about fun outdoor activities? Or would you prefer cuddling on the couch? See Chapter 1 for tips on selecting the perfect-fit pup.

Socialization should begin with the breeder and continue when your pup comes home. For more on proper socialization, see Chapter 6.

True to their name, Golden Retrievers love to retrieve, although some love it more than others. Find out how to test your pup's natural retrieving ability. (See Chapter 4)

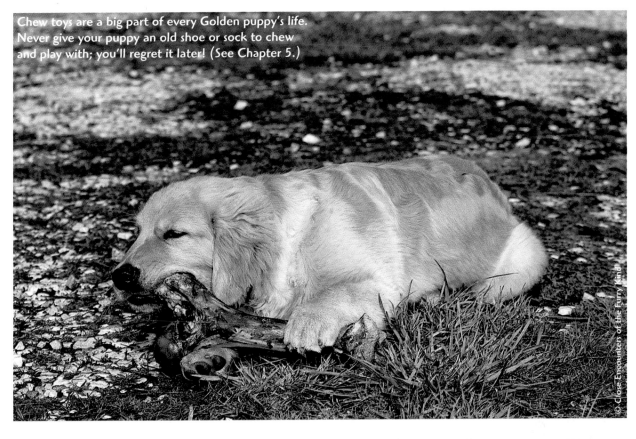

Chew toys are a big part of every Golden puppy's life. Never give your puppy an old shoe or sock to chew and play with; you'll regret it later! (See Chapter 5.)

Make sure that your Golden has access to fresh water at all times. (See Chapter 10.)

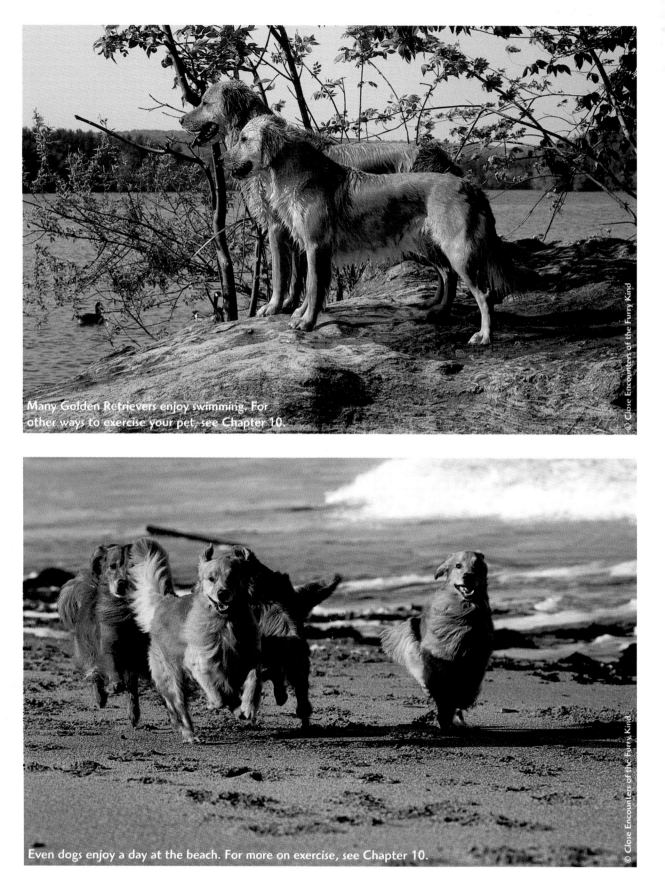

Many Golden Retrievers enjoy swimming. For other ways to exercise your pet, see Chapter 10.

Even dogs enjoy a day at the beach. For more on exercise, see Chapter 10.

Chapter 10

Healthy Habits: Nutrition and Exercise

. . . .

In This Chapter

▶ Dishing the real scoop on dog food

▶ Analyzing the ingredients

▶ Handling the burden of obesity

▶ Exercising for health and happiness

▶ Spaying or neutering for good health

. . . .

*F*eeding your Golden is like putting gas in your car. You can't use watered down fuel and expect good maintenance or peak performance. Likewise, you can't feed your dog substandard dog food and expect to have a healthy, active animal who will live to a ripe old age. So what's a captive consumer to do? Get smart. Know the proper way to fill your Golden's nutritional gas tank.

But good health means more than just good nutrition. Without proper exercise, even a well-fed dog will not be healthy or content. In this chapter, I provide information on quality dog food and explain why diet and daily exercise are essential to your dog's longevity and quality of life.

Cheaper Is Not Better

Pet food means big bucks in these United States. In 1999, Americans spent over $9 billion (yes, that's "B" as in *billions!*) on dog and cat food compared to $6 billion on baby food. And get this. Studies show that there is greater profit in pet food than in human food.

When you're planning a recipe for your Golden's happy meals, remember this. If you want to save money on dog food, don't spend less. Cheaper is not economical in the long run. It costs less to use a premium dog food than an economy brand because of the nutritional power packed in the better food. Countless studies have proven that you have to feed much larger quantities of cheap food to get the same nutritional benefits of the premium foods. Additionally, your dog can end up with dermatitis-skin problems from a lack of the vitamins and minerals he needs to support healthy skin and coat. Even if the food bag doesn't say generic on the label, if it's an off-beat brand, beware.

Dogs do not need a change in diet to keep them interested in food. Your dog actually looks forward to the same food each day (see Figure 10-1). Unless some health condition requires it, frequent changes in his diet are not good for him. So once you find a quality dog food he enjoys and thrives on, stick with it.

Figure 10-1:
Your dog needs a quality dog food to maintain good health

Checking Out Food Labels

When you read the information on your dog's food bags (of course, you do!) the first thing you should check out are the *labels,* the panels on the side or back of the bag that contain the nutrition information. Look for these important food facts.

- ✔ **Ingredients:** Labels list the ingredients in descending order of weight or amount in the food. You should find meat or its byproducts among the first three ingredients. (See the section on dog food ingredients, later in this chapter, to find out why.)

- ✔ **Guaranteed analysis:** This list breaks down the minimum percentage of protein and fat, and the maximum percentage of fiber and moisture in the food in its present form. By law, if the food label *on the front* says it is beef, chicken, or meat, it must contain at least 95 percent of that product. (This refers to canned foods.) If it states, "beef formula, beef dinner, or chicken platter" it must contain a minimum of 25 percent of that meat. "With chicken" means at least 3 percent, and "chicken flavored" is up to the taster.

- ✔ **Byproducts:** Now here's a term to watch. What's a byproduct anyway? Byproducts are things other than meaty muscle tissue, including, but not limited to, lungs, spleen, brains, blood, bone, hair, hooves, beaks, feathers, and other "hmmmm" ingredients.

- ✔ **Manufacturer information:** These lines should include a toll-free number to call for more information. A reliable company will be glad to send you literature on its products and will help you select a food that meets the nutritional needs of your dog's life stage. Check out the company to make sure that it conducts ongoing pet feeding nutrition studies.

- ✔ **Nutritional guarantee:** This will include the AAFCO statement. AAFCO stand for the Association of American Feed Control Officials, and this organization runs animal feeding tests. This dual purpose advisory organization dictates uniform definitions and regulations with regard to the production, labeling, distribution, and sale of animal feeds in the multibillion dollar pet food industry. This nutritional adequacy statement specifies which life stage the food is formulated for (growth, all life stages, maintenance, and so on). As a pet owner, you want the production manufacturing process and labeling to conform to AAFCO guidelines.

Digging into the Dog Food Bag

The guaranteed analysis section of a dog food label tells you what's in the food you're feeding your dog. The following sections dissect the basic and most common food ingredients.

Protein

Protein is the big gun in your dog's food bowl because about 50 percent of the dry matter in a dog's body is made up of protein, which is an essential component of his cell structure.

Protein contains amino acids (another word you often hear a lot in canine nutrition), which are critical to his bodily functions like digesting food, fighting off infections, and carrying oxygen in his blood. The absence of quality protein can result in poor growth, weight loss, poor hair coat, impaired immune function, depressed appetite, energy loss, irregular *estrus* (female heat cycles), and poor reproductive performance — just to name a few! We serve our dogs "higher protein" and "all-meat protein" and hope we're dishing out a better meal.

Meat, poultry, and their byproducts and grains like corn and soy are the most common protein sources in most dog foods. The difference lies in the balance of protein in each product. For example, beef is a higher quality protein source than corn because it contains a better balance of amino acids.

Beef, chicken, and lamb are the most frequently utilized meat protein sources, and if the label states "beef meal," it means it has no added byproducts like those listed in the section "Checking Out Food Labels," earlier in this chapter. "Chicken" as an ingredient is better than "poultry," which could include a whole variety of birds: turkey, duck, geese, chickens, whatever. The more specific the ingredient description, the better the quality.

Protein requirements change throughout a dog's life just as they do in humans. The animal's size and age, his individual energy demands, and daily stressors vary from dog to dog. Optimum protein intake is more crucial at certain times in most dogs' lives.

During off seasons, hunting and hard-working dogs' energy requirements decrease, and they should eat less nutrient-dense (the term refers to protein) food or less of the higher calorie food.

At one time, the high levels of protein in growth foods were thought to contribute to structural problems like hip dysplasia and other skeletal disorders like OCD. Current research holds that calories primarily from fat, not protein intake, are the likely culprit.

Large breeds like Golden Retrievers just naturally grow fast, which puts a big strain on young and fragile joints. A high-fat puppy diet promotes even more rapid growth, thus increasing the risk of hip and elbow dysplasia and other skeletal problems. While the average dog owner may think you need to feed, feed, and feed to keep that growing body growing, research has shown that overfeeding actually contributes to poor joint development.

At least two major dog food manufacturers have developed growth foods for the various breed sizes with a lower fat and protein content to meet a large-breed puppy's restricted caloric needs. The object is to keep the puppy lean during his major growth phase of three to eight months.

Here's another protein myth — high-protein diets cause kidney disease in older dogs. Not so. Although an already damaged kidney cannot properly metabolize protein, the protein itself will not cause the problem.

That said, most dog food manufacturers do offer a somewhat lower protein food for senior canines — in large breeds, defined as dogs over 7 years old.

Because the amount of protein is restricted, the quality of the protein becomes vitally important. Healthy older dogs still require adequate quality protein to maintain lean body mass and help support their immune system.

The two faces of high fat

Fat calories have their place. Dogs need fat for healthy skin and coats and to prevent constipation. An adult dog food should contain 10 to 15 percent fat to keep a healthy animal healthy. Although animal fats are more palatable, fats derived from vegetable oils are better sources of the fatty acids they need to lubricate their outsides (see the sidebar "Good and bad fats").

Fat also contains more than twice the metabolizable energy of protein, so a Golden who hunts or works at other strenuous activities will need extra fat more than extra protein, to maintain his energy and stamina. Watch for terms like "calorie-dense" or "high-caloric density" in performance food because they refer to the fat content of the food.

Preservatives

Dog foods require preservatives because they contain fats, which will spoil when exposed to heat and air (a process called *oxidation*).

Manufacturers use antioxidant materials to prevent oxidation. The antioxidants used may extend the fat life, but some add dangers worse than rancidity to the food. One preservative sometimes used is called *ethoxyquin,* which is a recognized cancer-causing agent, as are two others known as BHA and BHT.

The preservative used will be listed on the label and may be shown on the front of the bag as well. Many quality dog foods today are preserved safely with vitamin E, or you can purchase natural foods with no preservatives from specialized dealers. Ask your vet about those products if they interest you. You can also find information on natural dog foods on the Internet.

Good and bad fats

Although animal fat is a real yummy for dogs (bacon grease or meat fat), vegetable fat is better for his skin and coat. A dog with a dull coat or flaky skin may benefit from a tablespoon of safflower or canola oil added to his food. More is not better. Feeding larger amounts can make him fat.

Artificial coloring

Because dogs don't see most colors, any color added to their food is for the owner's benefit. Red dye has been used for years and is known to cause allergies in canines, yet some manufacturers still sneak it in. Check your dog food label.

Vitamins and minerals

If you had one dog food rule to follow, it should be no vitamin supplements. A quality dog food (the key word being quality) should be complete with no supplements necessary to meet the life stages of the pet. In fact, supplementation can create toxicity problems, causing poor growth, abnormal eye conditions, and impaired reproductive performance.

Supplementation is especially dangerous for puppies. If extra calcium, phosphorous, or vitamin D is added to a puppy's diet, it can cause skeletal disorders. Normal tooth and bone development require

✔ Adequate and balanced levels of calcium, phosphorous, and vitamin D.

✔ A proper ratio of calcium and phosphorous of 1.2 to 1.

A quality growth food contains a correct balance of easily metabolized sources of these nutrients.

Feeding Wet or Dry

Adding water to dry food is optional. Feeding dry is recommended as a dental plus because it helps prevent plaque and tartar buildup. However, a dog who gulps his food like it's his last meal may inhale the dry particles or choke on them and may do better with a generous splash of water in his food. It's also thought that adding water helps reduce the risk of bloat. I add about a half to one cup of water to each dog food pan immediately before offering it. The food is still crunchy enough to preserve dental benefits, and the water releases flavor and adds to palatability (although eating slowly has never been my dogs' problem). Some foods *require* the addition of water to release the digestive enzymes in the food.

Always have fresh water available for your dog, even if you add water to his food (see Figure 10-2).

Figure 10-2:
Your dog should always have access to fresh water — but it should always be from a bowl and not an outdoor faucet!

The Real Skinny on Obesity

Studies indicate that obesity is the No. 1 nutritional disorder in dogs and that a large percentage of pet dogs seen by veterinarians in this country are overweight. An extra 10 pounds on your should-be-65-pound Golden would be comparable to an extra 20 pounds on a woman who should weigh 120.

Just like people, every Golden is an individual with different metabolic needs. The same "food X exercise" ratio that keeps one dog lean and physically fit may lead to obesity in another. You have to know your Golden.

Your dog should have an hour-glass figure when viewed from above, with a *defined* waistline behind his rib cage and in front of his hind legs. Put your hands on his back with your fingers curled around his ribcage. You should be able to feel his ribs easily with very slight pressure.

Obesity is simply excess consumption — too many calories in and too few calories used — and is no healthier in dogs than it is in humans. It can lead to diabetes and skin problems and will aggravate orthopedic problems, heart conditions, and nervous disorders. It *will* shorten your Golden's life. Either cut back on food portions and/or the type of food, or increase his exercise. Doing both is better.

To keep your Golden slim and trim:

✔ See your veterinarian before you put him on a diet.

✔ If he's overweight, switch to a quality food with less fat and higher fiber. Fat delivers twice the calories per gram as carbohydrates and protein. More fiber provides more bulk with fewer calories, making the dog feel full.

✔ Eliminate all table scraps and check the contents of his biscuit treats. (See "Scrap those table scraps," later in this chapter.) Many are very high in fat and sugars.

✔ Always feed him twice a day. He'll have more to look forward to and will feel more satisfied.

✔ Step up his exercise. Every day walk farther, throw more Frisbees, take him swimming, and expend more energy. (You'll probably look better, too, even without a diet!)

Scrap those table scraps!

Dog owners love to gooey up their dog's food. It's another way of lavishing attention. Bad idea. It usually makes the dog fat and possibly unhealthy. Table scraps are no big deal if given in moderation (as in not-much-not-often!). A bit of fruit, vegetable, or potato won't hurt most dogs occasionally. (Raw carrots are great for his teeth!) Although it adds extra calories, a taste or two shouldn't upset the nutritional balance of a good commercial diet.

Feeding table scraps carries another subtle danger: the finicky eater. If a dog gets used to goodies in his food bowl, he might refuse to eat his normal diet. Offer him a veggie treat separate from his dinner time.

Never feed your dog old or moldy leftovers, especially aging cheeses, nuts, or other similar food. He could become ill and later recycle the food on your bed or pillow. Not a healthy idea.

Using diet to deal with allergies

Because allergies top the golden list of health problems, diet can have a major impact on their overall well-being — and *your* mental health as well! Natural foods and hypoallergenic diets use less common protein sources such as lamb, rice, fish, or potatoes that are less irritating to the dog.

Some highly allergic dogs do well on homemade diets. Homemade may help your dog, but it's also lots of work and requires a firm commitment from the owner to follow a strict dietary regimen.

If your dog has food allergies, work with your vet or a canine nutrition specialist (find one through your veterinarian, kennel club, or a veterinary teaching institution) to develop a diet he can tolerate.

Pure chocolate is toxic in doses that are proportionate to the dog's weight. (About 2½ ounces of unsweetened chocolate can be fatal for a 25-pound dog, and a 2-pound bag of chocolate chips can kill a 50-pound dog.)

Onions are also highly toxic to dogs. The vegetable contains an alkaloid that ruptures the red blood cells, causing fever, darkened urine, and death. Cooking does not eliminate the danger.

The raw food debate

The big news in the dog food world today focuses on feeding strategies that use raw and natural ingredients. Claims abound about such diets that have conquered lifelong allergies and other chronic ailments in Goldens as well as other breeds. Although this is a highly volatile subject among breeders and trainers as well as pet owners, it's worth investigating. Ask your vet, check with your breeder, surf the Internet, and, of course, *read*. You can find several good books on alternative feeding methods.

Exercising Your Dog

Exercise is more than a good health habit. It's as essential to your Golden's overall well-being as food and water. It's also important to your own mental health, because a Golden who is not exercised will redirect his energy into creative mischief and destruction. You'll swear Hurricane Andrew came ashore.

If you think dogs will exercise by themselves, you'd better think again. Most dogs, including Goldens, are just like you and me. They only move about if they have a reason to do so. A fenced backyard will not provide physical stimulation for your Golden. *You* are your dog's motivation to run, play, and get physical.

Whatever your exercise pleasure, keep your Golden on a leash! There are dozens of doggie temptations that could turn your morning mile into a nightmare chase scene. Even the most reliable dog can defy his owner and zip off after a squirrel, often across a busy street. A leashed dog is seldom a statistic.

Golden energizers

Your Golden needs high-energy retrieving games like Frisbee toss and fetch-the-tennis-ball. Capitalize on your Golden's natural instincts and throw canvas or plastic bumpers for him to retrieve. If he doesn't bring them back, run in the opposite direction to entice him to chase you. This retrieving business is in his genes; he'll catch on fast. A 15-minute (minimum) backyard retrieving session every day will help keep the average dog in shape.

> # Street salt is bad for the paws
>
> The street salt used on roads and sidewalks during the winter can burn your dog's paws. Be sure to clean his paws after a walk outdoors.
>
> It's best to wash, not just wipe, because wiping may actually rub the salt into cracks on and between the toes and do more damage.

Your dog also needs his daily walk. How far and how long depends on the individual dog, so just make sure that he can keep up with you (and vice versa!) without undue stress (on you, too!) and don't push beyond his endurance level. Many dogs don't know what's best for them and will extend themselves beyond their limits. Goldens are notorious for that.

Is your Golden still a growing pup? Young bones should not be unduly stressed because the growth plates are still forming. Puppies need more frequent, shorter walks. Your vet can tell you how much walking a young dog can handle without injury. A healthy adult will enjoy, indeed thrive on, a longer, faster pace. If he's a senior citizen, slow down and watch for signs of weakness or aching muscles the next day. (See Chapter 14 for more on caring for your older dog.)

Try to find a park, field, forest preserve, or beach where there are no traffic hazards and plan a hike or bicycle outing once or twice a week. You don't have to be creative. Just get him outdoors for exercise.

Check the forecast

On warm days, walk during cooler mornings and evenings and rest if you notice that your Golden is panting excessively. He can become overheated very easily. Hang a water canteen on your belt and stop occasionally for a drink. In extremely cold weather, walk at midday when it's warmer.

Examine his footpads frequently, and if cracks or bleeding occur, clean them and apply petroleum jelly to soften and soothe. In winter, check his toes for ice buildup after a run in the snow and wipe his paws to remove any salt and chemicals he may have stepped in.

On summer walks, stay off hot cement or tarred and blacktop surfaces, which could burn your Golden's footpads. If you can't walk barefoot on the pavement, neither should your dog. Blacktop is especially dangerous because he can also get the hot gooey tar on his feet. If he accidentally steps on hot tar and it sticks, don't put his paws in cold water and then peel it off because that will also remove healthy tissue and make the damage worse. Instead, rub his paws generously with vegetable oil and apply a bandage. The tar should wash off the next morning.

If your dog is exposed to extended periods of summer sun during exercise or on long summer walks, protect his nose with a sunscreen formulated especially for dogs. Check your pet supply house or catalog for approved products.

Hit the jogging trail

If you're a jogger, your athletic adult Golden Retriever is a perfect running partner. He not only loves to run, he'll inspire you to stay the course, and you'll both benefit from the emotional bond that will grow from running together.

Before you decide to do the three-minute-mile with your Golden, a quick health check with your vet is a good precaution. Then start out slowly. Out-of-shape dogs will gladly run themselves into exhaustion and then collapse. Make sure that he can hang in there before you up your speed.

If your dog licks his feet after running through a field, he may have picked up tiny pointed grass and weed seeds, which wedge themselves into the foot tissue. If not removed at once, the seeds can become painfully embedded and infected, which means another trip to your friend, the veterinarian. Always check his feet after an outdoor jaunt.

Spaying or Neutering Your Dog

Spay/neuter is another preventative health-care no-brainer.

A female spayed before her first estrus has a 90 percent less risk of cancer of the uterus and/or mammary glands. Males neutered before their male hormones shift into high gear equally reduce their risk of testicular and prostate cancers.

Everyone knows spay/neuter helps prevent pet overpopulation. Each year more than 12,000,000 dogs, cats, puppies, and kittens are left at animal shelters. Sadly, nearly 8,000,000 of those animals have to be euthanized because there aren't enough homes for all of them. It doesn't take a genius to figure out that spay/neuter is the obvious solution.

Beyond statistics, your Golden is the ultimate winner. Consider Chelsea, a gentle little blond who should have lived her normal life expectancy, but was euthanized at 9 years old. Her owners didn't get around to spaying her until they found her first breast tumor when she was 7. She was spayed at the same time the tumor was removed, but by then the seeds of cancer had already started to spread throughout her body.

How about Katie, a tiny Golden bitch who was spayed at 3 years old because of a raging uterine infection? The surgery cost four times what a routine spay would cost.

And there's Max, a rangy male Golden treated for ugly and painful tumors in his testicles, never neutered because his owners thought it would be "cruel to take away his manhood."

Arthur wasn't as fortunate as Max. The big red Golden was euthanized at 2 years old. Never neutered, he had become aggressive, and his owner became afraid of him.

If those sad stories don't make you think twice, consider this:

Spayed females have a reduced risk of breast cancer, cystic endometrial pyometra, false pregnancies, mastitis, venereal sarcoma, ovarian and uterine tumors, cystic ovaries, chronic endometriosis, vaginal prolapse, and uterine torsion or uterine prolapse. Your darling female will no longer drip estrus fluids all over the house (or wear those goofy pads for dogs in heat), nor will you have to chase those Romeos who come courting at all hours.

Males benefit from a reduced risk of testicular cancer, benign prostatic hyperplasia, acute prostatic abscess, tumors around the anus, infection of the testicles, anal hernias, and venereal tumors. He will also hang closer to home and will not become macho with other male visitors. You, on the other hand, will also benefit thanks to absolute birth control for life and relief from hormone-induced aggression toward other dogs, especially males, territorialism at home, wanderlust in search of romance, urine marking at home and in new places, dominant and overt sexual behavior such as riding or mounting your leg or your mother's, licking and arousal, and your own frustration when intact male dogs feel their hormones and resist doing what they're told.

Most importantly, altered animals are less likely to bite or exhibit temperament problems that would affect your family and neighbors. Surgical alteration will not affect your dog's true personality. He or she will still be the funny, fun-loving Golden critter you know and love.

Chapter 11

Golden Health Care 101

Choosing a veterinarian is a major dog decision. You're selecting your Golden's HMO. He'll be there for you through sickness and health, hopefully more of the latter than the former. This chapter helps you understand all his ministrations, poking, prodding, and advice.

Choosing a Veterinarian

Finding a veterinarian in most U.S. cities is easy. Finding a *good* veterinarian will take a little more time and research. It's worth the extra effort.

Today's veterinarians wear a dozen hats. Many specialize in specific areas of canine health — orthopedics, ophthalmology, oncology, cardiology, nutrition, dermatology, reproduction, internal medicine, acupuncture, or holistic medicine, for example. Even the general practitioner vet often has some special area of expertise.

Ask your dog friends where they go for veterinary care. Ask your breeder or call the secretary of the local kennel club or area Golden Retriever club. If you can, find a veterinary clinic with at least two doctors, more if possible. In an emergency or the onset of some mysterious ailment, several vet heads are better than one.

Your Puppy's First Visit

Select your veterinarian well before your pup's arrival and make his first appointment within his first two or three days of coming home. He may not be due for a shot, but you'll want a health check anyway, especially if his breeder gave a health guarantee. (Most breeders guarantee a puppy's health for three days to a week.) Bring his health record of all shots and wormings to date, a fresh stool sample in a small clean container, and a pocketful of puppy treats. This veterinary visit is your one exception to "no outings during your puppy's early fear period," so make it a pleasant one.

You and your puppy should wait in the car until the vet can see your pup, and his little paws should not touch the clinic floor. There are too many things lurking there that could infect your puppy. Carry him into the office, place him directly onto the table in the exam room, and pet him lavishly so that he's not scared.

If you've chosen wisely, your vet will gush over your puppy to make this visit a positive experience. If your pup is apprehensive, don't coddle or console him; that will only encourage his anxiety. Stay happy and relaxed, and he'll think it's pretty neat to get all this extra hands-on attention.

With gentle hands, the vet should examine all your puppy's usual body parts — eyes, ears, throat and glands, genitalia (especially to make sure the testicles have dropped), skin and coat for fleas or flakiness, heart sounds for irregularities, temperature, and palpate for swollen glands and hernias.

Use your dog radar during this first visit. Does the vet's hands-on manner put your pup (and you) at ease? Does he come across as a caring and capable professional? Does he encourage you to ask questions or call him any time? If not, keep looking until you find a vet you're comfortable with.

Wait in the car

Regardless of my dogs' ages, I always wait in my truck and take them directly into the examining room when it's available. The last dog who waited there may have had fleas or parasites, a virus, or contagious illness. Who needs those problems?

Your Puppy's Health Agenda

Your puppy's initial health program should include a series of shots and pills. Most vaccination schedules consist of a series of injections given at 3 to 4 weeks and intervals from 6 or 7 weeks of age through 16 to 20 weeks. He will receive a booster shot on most of these at one year of age and annually thereafter, depending on the current recommendation from the American Veterinary Medical Association (AVMA). A few vaccines that were routinely given are no longer recommended except for those dogs that are at risk due to individual exposure or lifestyle. The rabies shot may given every three years, with the first rabies shot given at the time mandated by local public health laws.

These early shots are critical to your puppy's long-term resistance to canine infection and disease. Puppies are born with an umbrella of antibodies (gifts from their mother) and receive more natural antibodies from the colostrum in her milk. These immunities last through very early puppyhood and gradually wear off. Because no accurate test can confirm when those immunities are completely gone, puppy shots are scheduled about every three weeks to provide maximum protection. This is a vulnerable period, because those maternal antibodies may be strong enough to override the vaccine, putting a pup at great risk during his first 10 to 12 weeks of life.

In recent years, the veterinary profession has offered a vaccine that overrides the natural immunities passed from the dam. These shots are given at three-week intervals after 6 weeks of age. Be sure to ask your vet whether your puppy's shots gave him that protection.

Your vet will also prescribe a *heartworm preventive,* a daily or monthly pill to protect your little guy against heartworm disease. Heartworm is found today in all 50 states, and all dogs are at risk. In warm regions, dogs must take the preventive all year long. In colder climates, the medication is given only during mosquito season. If your vet doesn't offer it, be sure to ask. (See Chapter 12 for more on heartworms.)

The Puppy Vaccine Puzzle

Vaccine protocol varies from veterinarian to veterinarian. One may give a single injection that combines five or up to eight vaccines and covers all the bases. Others prefer separate vaccinations, perhaps giving distemper-parvovirus as separate injections or giving the lepto and Lyme vaccines in the last shot series, to minimize the shock to a weak or immature immune system.

That, of course, means a few more visits for each shot. But consider this: Just as today's medical world believes humans have overdosed on antibiotics and weakened their own immunities, a large segment of the canine medical camp subscribes to that same theory, especially given the increase in cancers and other autoimmune diseases that were rare in dogs of yore.

I'm of the latter school. I prefer to separate my puppy's shots to allow his little system to recover from each shot.

The following breaks down your puppy's disease prevention program into CORE vaccines (recommended by the AVMA for all dogs due to severity of disease and ease of transmission to other dogs and possibly humans), and NON-CORE (recommended for only those dogs known to be at risk).

CORE vaccines include

- **Rabies:** Viral. Affects central nervous system. Symptoms: Lack of coordination, seizures, aggression. Risk: Fatal. Method of exposure: saliva, found in some species of wild animals — raccoons, skunk, fox, bat, and others. Immunization: One between 12 weeks and 16 weeks, booster every three years. Required by all 50 states, can be transmitted to humans.

- **Canine Distemper Virus (CDV):** Viral upper respiratory disease, highly contagious. Symptoms: Cough, fever, vomiting, diarrhea. Method of exposure: Airborne. Risk: High, usually fatal in puppies. Immunizations: Three between 6 weeks and 16 weeks, annual booster.

- **Canine Parvovirus (CPV):** Viral, attacks lining of the intestines, highly contagious. Symptoms: Bloody or watery diarrhea, fever, vomiting, dehydration, intestinal pain. Method of exposure: Infected feces. Risk: High, usually fatal in puppies. Immunizations: Three between 5 weeks and 16 weeks, annual boosters.

- **Canine Adenovirus (CAV2):** Viral respiratory, part of kennel cough complex, highly contagious. Symptoms: Harsh, spastic cough. Method of exposure: Airborne. Risk: High, possibility of blocked airways and pneumonia, puppies at greatest risk. Immunizations: Three between 6 weeks and 16 weeks, annual booster.

- **Infectious Canine Hepatitis (CA1):** Viral, affects the liver (not related to the hepatitis virus in humans), highly contagious. Symptoms: Fever, appetite loss, vomiting. Method of exposure: Infected urine, saliva, respiratory discharge, contaminated clothing. Risk: High, puppies at greatest risk. Immunizations: Three between 6 weeks and 16 weeks, annual boosters.

NON-CORE vaccines include

- **Canine Parainfluenza:** Viral, respiratory, part of kennel cough complex, highly contagious. Symptoms: Harsh, spastic cough. Method of exposure: Same as Adenovirus. Risk: High, same potential as Adenovirus, puppies at greatest risk. Immunizations: Three between 6 weeks and 16 weeks, annual boosters.

- **Leptospirosis:** Bacterial, affects kidneys and liver, very contagious. Symptoms: Fever, appetite loss, bloody stools, listlessness, vomiting, increased thirst. Method of exposure: Urine of infected animals — cattle, sheep, wild animals, rats. Risk: High in certain areas. Immunizations:

One, vaccine can produce severe side effects. Immunity short-lived, less than 4 months to 6 months. Immunize in high-risk areas and only after 12 weeks of age. Unless there is risk of exposure, many vets do not recommend this vaccine.

✔ **Canine Coronavirus:** Viral, intestinal. Symptoms: Diarrhea, vomiting, persistent fever. Method of exposure: Infected feces. Risk: Moderate. Immunizations: Two between 6 weeks and 16 weeks, booster suggested. Only young pups and elderly dogs are at risk. Many vet schools no longer recommend corona unless there has been an exposure to the disease.

✔ **Bordatella bronchiseptica:** (Canine or kennel cough). Viral, respiratory. Symptoms: Harsh spastic cough, wheezing, fever indicates complications. Method of exposure: Airborne, most common in boarding situations. Risk: High, leads to weakened immune system and secondary bacterial infection. Immunizations: Two intranasal or injection between 6 weeks and 16 weeks, annual booster or whenever there is risk of exposure.

✔ **Lyme (Borreliosis):** Bacterial disease. Affects joints. Symptoms: Lameness, fever, appetite loss, swelling at joints. Risk: High in tick-heavy areas. Method of exposure: Tick bite, at least two species of ticks implicated. Immunization: Controversial at this time, efficacy of vaccine debatable, can produce side effects, use in high-risk areas. Two doses initially, annual booster in high-risk areas. One brand of topical flea preventative also protects against tick bites.

Annual Checkups Are Important

Your Golden should have, at the very least, an annual check-up to update his shots, annual heartworm test and fecal exam, and a hands-on physical exam. Regular visits also help your vet become familiar with your Golden, which is vital to a solid doctor-canine client relationship. If you ask questions and you keep notes, you can transform these visits from simple routine health care into a Golden learning experience.

When you make your dog's appointment, tell the receptionist why you're scheduling this visit — illness or routine visit — so that she can allow enough time to investigate the problem.

Avoid appointments in the early morning and late afternoon during the week because these are prime drop-off and pick-up hours for pets who are boarded or hospitalized. Both you and the vet will be less hurried during the hours in between those times.

If you have questions, write them down before your visit so that you won't forget to ask. Get all pet care instructions in writing and don't leave until you read and understand them. Your vet will appreciate the extra time you take to be careful and follow through. It makes his job easier and your dog healthier in the long run.

Thinking about Holistic Veterinary Medicine

Acupuncture, acupressure, homeopathic remedies, natural foods — all are today available to pets as well as people. Many breeders and pet owners who struggle with a constant plague of health and fertility problems have found relief by using natural foods, herbal remedies, and holistic medicine. They use herbal products to treat everything from allergies, insect bites, bruises, digestive upset, and whelping problems to fleas and internal parasites, and they claim to do so successfully.

Acupuncture and acupressure are often used on dogs (by licensed practitioners) to treat arthritis and arthritic symptoms, seizures and other ailments, and even immune problems. I've seen acupuncture benefits on a couple of my own gimpy Goldens who showed dramatic improvement after just one acupuncture treatment.

Massage therapy, a relative of acupressure, will strengthen the circulation and flow of energy in your dog, and it's something you can do yourself for free. Geriatric dogs especially benefit from a good massage. If you're really into hands-on treatments for your Golden, you can find good books and tapes to help you learn the process.

Proponents of holistic veterinary medicine stress that natural remedies should not replace traditional medical care for serious illnesses, but they definitely have one foot in each medical camp. This is an area of canine care that's worth exploring. Start with a good book on holistic medicine and decide for yourself.

Keeping a Golden Health Calendar

If your pet is ill, even for a day or two, keep written notes on your golden calendar about whatever problems you observe, including changes in eating or elimination habits, appearance, or behavior. Also keep notes of even minor changes like the following:

- ✔ Has he been picking at his food pan lately instead of gobbling it up in his usual slobbery manner?
- ✔ Does he occasionally stumble during your walks or limp once in a while after exercise?
- ✔ Does he take more time than usual to catch his breath after a romp in the park?
- ✔ Is he sleeping more, chewing his rear at night, scooting across the floor on his behind?

✔ Has he been urinating more frequently than usual?

✔ Does he frequently strain when moving his bowels?

✔ Do you notice anything unusual or different in his habits or his attitude?

These observations will help your vet diagnose a condition that may not be apparent during a brief examination. (They are also symptoms that warrant a phone call to your vet when they occur.)

With older dogs, it's especially important to note any changes in their habits or behavior. Even the slightest differences should be noted on your canine calendar. They may signal the start of a problem your vet might not discover for weeks or months ahead, and early intervention could literally save or at least extend his life. Also, if your vet asks you any questions, you can refer back to your calendar notes about when certain symptoms began to occur or when you noticed a specific change.

Always call your vet if:

✔ You find a lump anywhere on your Golden's skin.

✔ Your Golden seems unusually short of breath.

✔ Your Golden has an abrupt change in appetite, up or down.

✔ Your Golden starts losing weight for no apparent reason.

✔ Your Golden drinks more water and urinates more frequently.

✔ Your Golden becomes uncharacteristically fearful or aggressive.

✔ Your Golden has been coughing for more than 24 hours.

Healthy Body Signs

Your Golden should be the picture of perfect health, but what does that look like? From nose to toes, here are your dog's body signs.

✔ **Body temperature:** A dog's normal body temperature is 100.5 to 101.5 degrees. Take his temperature with a rectal thermometer or "instant" digital thermometer that "dings" when done. Dip the bulb into petroleum jelly, lift his tail, and gently insert the bulb into the anus. Be meticulous about your hygiene.

✔ **Heart:** At rest, canines register 90 to 100 beats per minute, with puppies and senior dogs a little faster. You can feel your dog's heartbeat on the inner side of the hind leg, just behind the flex of the front leg. The pulsing action should be easy to locate. A normal pulse can range from 70 to 120 beats per minute.

✔ **Nose:** His nose should be black and smooth, never crusted or cracked. Nose note: A dry, warm, wet, or cold nose is not a dog's health barometer.

✔ **Ears:** Inside the flap and canal should be pink and free of wax and debris. A smelly or waxy substance or discharge indicates ear mites or an infection. See Chapter 13 for ear cleaning instructions.

✔ **Teeth:** Your dog's teeth should be white and free of plaque. Offer hard, sterile bones and Nylabones to chew his way to dental health. See Chapter 13 on dental care.

✔ **Gums:** The gums should be firm and pink with the edges closely applied to the teeth. Some pigmentation or dark spots are normal. A black spot on the tongue is also common. Very pale gums reflect a lowered body temperature and may mean hypothermia or other serious illness or disease. Bright red gums are a sign of elevated body temperature and the onset of heat stroke, which is life-threatening and requires immediate emergency measures. (See the section on heat stroke later in this chapter.)

✔ **Skin and coat:** The skin should be supple without scaling or flaking. The coat should be thick and shiny, although many variations exist in length, texture, and density.

A warm dry nose does not mean your dog is sick. Cold or wet, warm or dry, both conditions can be normal for a canine.

Incidentally, dogs who eat grass are not sick and do not have worms. Even veterinarians don't know whether dogs ingest grass for the moisture content, for a nutritional imbalance, or because of an ancestral instinct. Until research provides an answer, don't worry about it unless it's excessive. Only the dog knows the answer to this one.

Giving Your Dog Medications

Most dog owners dread giving medications because the dog either struggles and wins, or he spits the pill on the floor an hour later. Here's how to make the job easier for both of you. Be firm yet gentle and follow these steps.

1. **Stand behind the dog and grasp the top of his muzzle, placing your thumb and fingers of one hand on each side of his canines (the long tooth on each side).**

2. **Tilt his head back at a 45-degree angle.**

3. **Squeeze gently while pulling the top of his muzzle upward to open his mouth.**

4. **Holding the pill between the thumb and index finger of your free hand, grasp his bottom jaw from underneath with your three remaining fingers and gently lower the jaw.**

5. **Once the mouth is open, place the pill as far back as possible on his tongue and use your index finger to poke it down toward the side of his throat.**

6. **Close his mouth and hold it closed.**

7. **Elevate his nose slightly and gently rub his throat with downward strokes to stimulate swallowing and tell him to "Swallow."**

   Some dogs will also swallow if you blow gently directly into their nose.

Always praise lavishly when he swallows the pill.

If he's too stubborn and refuses to allow you to handle his head or mouth (hmmm, when did *that* happen?), use the old hide-it-in-the-cheese trick or bury it in a dollop of peanut butter or liversausage. (Make sure that the pill is compatible with the bribe.)

You can also try storing pills or capsules in a closed container filled with moist or meaty treats. The pills will absorb the flavor, and you may even fool your dog into thinking it's a treat. At the very least, he'll be more receptive to accepting it.

To give liquid medications, use a syringe base minus the needle, an eye dropper, or turkey baster (no glass, please!). Tilt his head upward, open his mouth, and insert the tool from the side, into the back of the throat. Inject the liquid, hold his mouth shut tightly, and stroke his throat.

Always check the label on liquid medication to see whether it requires refrigeration.

Table 11-1 lists common dosages.

Table 11-1	Medication Dosage Purpose		
Medicine	*Amount*	*Reason*	*Frequency*
Buffered aspirin	8 to 12 mg per lb	Pain relief	Every 12 hours
Benadryl	½ mg per lb	Allergies, itching	Every 8 hours
Hydrogen peroxide	10 mL orally	Induce vomiting	Every 15 minutes
Pepto-Bismol	1 t per 5 lbs	Diarrhea, vomiting	Every 6 hours
Mineral oil	Up to 4 T daily	Constipation	
Kaopectate	1 mL per lb	Diarrhea	Every 2 hours
Tylenol, Ibuprofen	Not recommended for dogs		

Applying Eye Ointments

To apply eye ointments, tilt your dog's head back at a 45-degree angle (see Figure 11-1). Use your thumb or forefinger to roll back the lower lid gently downward and squeeze the ointment into the exposed pocket. Close the eye and gently hold it closed for just a second. Be careful not to allow the tip of the applicator to touch the eye, which could contaminate the medication. If you're using a dropper, hold up his upper eyelid and drip the medication inside the top of the eye. Close the lid _very_ gently.

If you suspect something in the eye, inspect it by gently parting the lids under a bright light. If the eye has been irritated by dust or wind, rinse the surface with all-purpose eye drops using the bottle or an eye dropper.

You can remove small seeds from under the eyelid using a dampened cotton swab to gently slide the seed onto the swab.

Do not attempt to remove other foreign objects. See your veterinarian. Excessive tearing could indicate a blocked tear duct. Again, check with your vet.

Figure 11-1:
Apply eye
ointment
very gently.

Bloat

Everyone's familiar with the human version of bloat. Too much Thanksgiving dinner, too many mashed potatoes. Not quite so with dogs.

Bloat, or GVD (gastric dilation volvulus), is a buildup of gas that can't escape from the dog's stomach. As the gas accumulates, the stomach swells and will quickly twist, blocking food passage in or out of the stomach and blood flow to other internal organs. The dog is in great pain and on the brink of shock and death within the hour.

 Large breeds, like Great Danes, Irish Setters, and retrievers, are most affected, especially dogs who eat large meals, eat once a day, or gulp their food. Symptoms of bloat are sudden discomfort paired with labored breathing, restlessness, roaching (humping) the back, drooling and unproductive vomiting, and abdominal swelling. Tapping the dog's sides will produce a hollow sound. Get veterinary attention ASAP, or your dog will die!

Preventative measures make good common dog sense. Divide your dog's food into two smaller meals a day, and if your dog is a ravenous eater who inhales his food, feed dry kibble with water added. Avoid strenuous exercise for one hour before and two hours after a meal (same as swimmers' rules).

Research at Purdue University shows that underweight, fearful, and nervous dogs are at higher risk for GVD. (Fear, nervousness, and excitement all increase air swallowing in humans.) A happy dog is less likely to get GVD. Message: Keep him happy as a clam!

Diarrhea

There's diarrhea, and then there's *diarrhea!* Loose stools can be due to a dozen things, from a sudden change in diet or drinking water, emotional upset or excitement, to scavenging in the garbage, parasites (see Chapter 12), or other serious problem or disease.

Examine the stool for color, consistency, odor, and frequency and keep a record for your vet. A diarrhea that persists for more than 24 hours, a bloody diarrhea, and diarrhea accompanied by vomiting, fever, or other signs of toxicity should send your dog directly to his doctor. Always take a stool sample with the dog.

You can treat ordinary diarrhea at home. Withhold all food for 24 hours. Offer small amounts of water or ice cubes for his thirst. Give him Kaopectate (same weight dose as humans) or Imodium A-D, one capsule per 25 pounds of dog. Resume feeding with small amounts of a no-fat diet: one part boiled hamburger to two parts cooked rice, cottage cheese, or cooked pasta. Follow for two or three days before going back to regular dog food.

Vomiting

Follow the same protocol as for diarrhea (see preceding section). You need to watch *how* your Golden vomits and notice *what* he vomits. (More notes for your golden calendar!) Most vomiting is due to eating too fast or eating grass or some other tasty indigestible stuff. If you suspect your dog ingested toxic plant material or something equally hazardous, save a sample of the vomitus for your vet.

Secure your outdoor garbage cans with tight lids and keep your compost pile well out of reach. Rotting garbage smells like haute cuisine to most dogs. Your dog can die from eating bacteria-ridden garbage.

If the vomiting is repeated, sporadic with no relationship to meals, bloody, or forceful and projectile, always seek veterinary help. If the vomit contains feces or foreign matter or is accompanied by drooling, whining, or trembling, get to the vet ASAP.

If your Golden swallows something awful like mouse bait, follow the same guidelines as for people (should he vomit or should he not). You should keep a list of vomiting do's and don'ts on your Golden calendar, your refrigerator or taped inside a kitchen cabinet door. Do not induce vomiting if your dog:

- Swallows an acid, a solvent, or other toxic cleaner
- Swallows a petroleum product (gasoline, turpentine, and so on)
- Swallows a sharp object, which can perforate his esophagus or stomach on the way back up
- Is comatose or more than two hours have passed since he ate the poison

You can induce vomiting by giving 3 percent hydrogen peroxide every 10 minutes (1 teaspoon for every 20 pounds of dog). Use a turkey baster poked to the rear of his throat. You can also give syrup of ipecac at 1 teaspoon per 10 pounds of dog.

Some people use table salt to induce vomiting. Don't! Only two grams (less than ½ teaspoon) per pound of body weight is considered lethal to dogs.

Pyometra

Pyometra is generally an "old lady" disease and shows up in unspayed bitches more than 5 years of age. The uterus becomes filled with pus before or after her estrus cycle. Pyometra can be fatal if not caught in time, and spay surgery is usually the only medical solution. In a few cases, a heavy round of antibiotics may help a bitch survive the infection. Obviously, spayed bitches are never at risk — another good reason to have your Golden girl spayed.

Urinary Incontinence

Urinary incontinence is inappropriate passing of urine, usually unintentional, sometimes not. Owners will complain their dog leaks urine when relaxed. It typically occurs in older females, although males can be affected, too. Old age means a weak urethral sphincter muscle. Most cases respond well to drug therapy, but if the underlying cause is renal failure, diabetes, or other abnormality, your vet will have to perform tests to make an accurate diagnosis. (See Chapter 14 for more on aging.)

 Don't confuse incontinence with some male dog's tendency to lift his leg and "sprinkle" every bush even after he's relieved himself. This "marking" system is behavioral and not at all related to his bladder.

Flatulence

Flatulence, or gas, is rarely serious, although it can be annoying. It's more common in older dogs who are less active and experience slower intestinal function.

 If gas is a chronic problem, you might try feeding your dog two or three times a day. Some experts think that gas is created when the dog wolfs or gulps down his food. It may also be a reaction to a certain dog food, so experiment with different (but not lesser quality) foods. (See Chapter 10 for more on choosing a dog food.)

You can also try a new product called Curtail, which is similar to its human counterpart, Beano. If you feel the problem is extreme, it may be caused by digestive upsets, and you should talk to your veterinarian.

Preparing a First Aid kit

Every Golden owner should have a well-planned emergency kit for the home (it can serve double duty for your family) plus a backup kit for the car if your Golden frequently tags along for the ride. Check with your veterinarian for specific items, but these following items should give you a good start.

- First Aid instruction book. Read it cover to cover at least once!
- Gauze (2- and 3-inch pads)
- Adhesive tape
- Vet wrap (a stick-to-itself gauze bandage wrap)
- Cotton swabs
- Hydrogen peroxide and alcohol
- Panalog or other antibiotic ointment
- Syrup of ipecac to induce vomiting
- Kaopectate to control diarrhea, 3-4 teaspoons per 60 pounds. Imodium A-D — one tablet per 25 pounds
- Eye wash
- Rectal thermometer
- Tweezers

- Eye dropper
- Syringe without the needle to give oral medications
- Ascriptin 325 mg — one tablet twice daily. (Tylenol is not good for dogs, ibuprofen is toxic to dogs)
- Tourniquet (a wide rubber band and a pencil will do)
- Muzzle (use a leash, tie or pantyhose)
- Benadryl or Benadryl elixir for allergic reactions (always check first with your veterinarian for the correct dose; generally one tablet for every 25 pounds)
- Towels, one per animal in a vehicle (it can be wet with water or alcohol to cool an overheated dog)
- Blanket (one per vehicle to use as a stretcher or for treating shock)
- Large water container for traveling (an absolute necessity in summer)
- Your veterinarian's office and emergency telephone number.

Your First Aid kit is just a start. You have to be prepared. This is like taking your emergency SATs.

Heatstroke

Dogs overheat more easily than humans do because they aren't blessed with sweat glands. They cool off through their footpads and by panting, neither of which is very efficient. All breeds are vulnerable to heatstroke, but puppies, older dogs, and overweight dogs are more susceptible. Too many people fail to see the risks or recognize the symptoms of heatstroke until their dog is close to death.

Muzzling

An injured dog might easily bite the hand that's helping him. A soft muzzle will prevent you from being hurt along with your dog and make your first aid ministrations more effective.

Using a tie, belt, pantyhose, or strip of cloth, wrap the strip around the dog's nose with a half knot on top. Wind the ends under his muzzle and make another half knot under the jaw.

From under the jaw, bring the strips along each side of his neck and tie a bow behind his ears. Remove the muzzle as soon as possible because dogs perspire through their tongues.

Never leave your Golden in a closed car during warm weather. In spring through early fall, the inside of a car, even with windows cracked several inches on a breezy 75-degree day, can heat up to more than 120 degrees in minutes. A confined animal will suffer heatstroke and die an excruciating death. That extra five minutes in the store may be fatal. Leave your Golden at home!

Symptoms of heatstroke:

- ✔ Excessive panting
- ✔ Drooling
- ✔ Rapid pulse
- ✔ Dark red gums and tongue
- ✔ A frantic, glazed expression
- ✔ Possibly vomiting

Treat the symptoms immediately and then rush your dog to the vet to continue emergency care. Cool him down by immersing him in a pond or a tub of cool water (not cold) or hosing with a garden hose. Put ice around his neck and groin and offer ice cubes to lick but no ice water to drink. A temperature over 106 degrees requires a cold water enema to reduce the body temperature immediately. Immediate follow-up vet care is urgent, because the body temperature can rise again very quickly during the next 48 hours.

The best cure is prevention. Keep your canine cool.

Burns

Electrical shock and burns are most common in puppies who chew on appliance or extension cords, but don't rule out a curious adult Golden. If the burn is severe, the dog will incur tissue damage and retain fluid in his lungs. If he's unconscious and not breathing, give artificial respiration (see the "Choking" section later in this chapter) and get immediate vet attention.

Thermal burns are caused by contact with open flames, boiling water, stoves, or any heated object or surface. First apply ice packs or ice water for 20 to 30 minutes. Follow with a soothing antibiotic ointment twice daily and make sure that he doesn't lick it off.

For a caustic acid or chemical burn, you should flush the area immediately and liberally with cool water. Apply an antibiotic preparation and ice to reduce swelling. Prevent licking the injured area.

Always check with your vet after any type of burn.

Bleeding

Bleeding can be *arterial* (the spurting of bright red blood) or *venous* (oozing of dark red blood) or sometimes both. Both require immediate veterinary attention. Your pet is in danger from shock, coma, and death. Picture your dog's bleeding wound on a child to help determine your emergency situation.

Common cuts and scratches are superficial and should be kept clean and dry to prevent infection. Fresh lacerations over ½-inch deep or long should be sutured to prevent infection and scarring and to speed healing.

There are two *don'ts* to remember. Do not pour peroxide on a fresh wound. That will make the bleeding harder to control. Do not wipe a wound that has stopped bleeding because that may dislodge the blood clot that has formed.

There are three main pressure points on your dog, which, along with direct pressure on the wound, will help control bleeding on the limbs and tail while you rush to the veterinarian:

- ✔ **The upper inside of the front leg.** Pressure here will affect bleeding of the lower forelegs.

- ✔ **The upper inside of the rear leg.** Pressure here will help control bleeding of the lower hind legs.

- ✔ **The underside of the tail.** Pressure here helps control bleeding of the tail.

You may need a tourniquet to control a spurting artery. Apply it to the leg or tail between the wound and the heart.

1. **Loop a strip of towel, a tie, rope, or belt, around the limb.**

2. **Tighten the loop by hand or by inserting and twisting a stick beneath the loop.**

Your dog could lose a leg or his tail if his blood supply is cut off for too long a time. You must loosen the tourniquet every 15 minutes to allow blood flow to the limb. Use direct pressure for three or four minutes and then retighten.

Shock

Shock is the lack of adequate blood flow to support the body's needs. It's caused by a sudden loss of blood, heatstroke, poisoning, dehydration from prolonged vomiting or diarrhea, or severe trauma such as being hit by a car. If not treated quickly, the animal will die.

Symptoms of shock are a drop in body temperature, shivering, listlessness, mental depression, and a weak, faint pulse.

Keep the dog calm and comfortable, cover him lightly with a coat or blanket, and get to the nearest veterinarian immediately.

Dehydration

Dehydration is an excessive loss of body fluids caused by fever, inadequate water intake, and prolonged vomiting and/or diarrhea.

To test your dog for dehydration, gently lift the skin around the top of his neck. It should snap quickly back into place. If the skin hangs loose or remains in a ridge, it means he's dehydrated, an emergency that requires vet attention right away.

You can treat a mild case of dehydration with electrolyte fluids given by mouth. If he won't drink copious amounts of water or electrolyte fluids, your veterinarian will give fluids by syringe.

Frostbite and Hypothermia

Just because your Golden has a long fur coat and loves the snow doesn't mean he's not at risk for either of these serious conditions. Dogs of all breeds can get frostbite just like people do. Dogs exposed to wet or very cold conditions are prime candidates for frozen body parts.

Frostbitten areas will be very cold and pale and may have a bluish cast, followed by redness and swelling. Ears, tails, and genitals are the most susceptible areas.

Gently warm the affected areas without rubbing. (Rubbing can do more damage.) You can use a heating pad on the low setting or try warm — not hot — compresses. See your veterinarian as soon as possible.

Hypothermia is even more dangerous. Prolonged exposure to the cold, especially if the dog is wet, will cause a dangerous drop in body temperature. Your dog will shiver and may appear disoriented or lethargic, even collapse. His rectal temperature will fall below 97 degrees.

If he's wet, give him a quick warm bath and rub vigorously with towels to dry his fur. Slowly rewarm him using a hair dryer on the lowest setting. Offer him a warm drink and warm him under blankets, with your own body heat if possible. You can also apply warm water packs or heating pads to the armpits, chest, and abdomen until his body temperature rises to 100 degrees. Then take him to the veterinarian as soon as possible.

Indoor living does not prepare a dog or his coat for the vagaries of very cold weather. Never clip his long hair in winter. That shaggy fur will keep him warm outside, and regular grooming will keep it healthy for maximum protection.

Ear Hematomas

These soft lumps on the ear flap sometimes come as a surprise as you're scratching your Golden's velvety ears. This thickening is nothing more than a large pocket of blood from a ruptured blood vessel within the flap that popped when your dog was shaking his head or a dog friend punctured it during play. It usually indicates an ear infection as well; that's why he shook his head so hard.

Only your veterinarian can repair a hematoma, so visit him as soon as possible.

Choking

Dogs can swallow anything from chicken bones to balloons. Wrap the dog in a blanket to keep him still. Wedge something sideways between the back teeth on one side of the dog's mouth to keep it open. Use a stick or the handle of a small tool.

Pull out his tongue (cautiously to avoid a dog bite) to check for foreign bodies behind the tongue or in the back of the mouth. Use your fingers or needle-nosed pliers to remove the object. If it won't come out, lift the dog and hold him upside down by the hind legs. Shake him vigorously to try to dislodge the object and clear his airways.

If you're unsuccessful, use the *Heimlich maneuver*. Lay the dog on his side and use your fist or your knee to apply sharp quick pressure to the abdomen at the base of the breastbone. If he stops breathing, give mouth to nose resuscitation — artificial respiration — or CPR.

If your dog has swallowed thread, pantyhose, or something long and stringy, do not attempt to pull it out. You could make things worse. Ditto for his other end. If he is evacuating something long and stringy, let him push it out on his own. If he's unsuccessful at either end, rush him to your veterinarian.

To perform artificial respiration:

1. **Place the dog on his side and extend his neck.**

2. **Open his mouth and check for food or vomit if necessary.**

3. **Hold his muzzle closed and place your mouth over his nose.**

4. **Slowly blow into his nose so that his chest expands.**

5. **Repeat every three seconds.**

To perform CPR:

1. **Place the dog on his side.**

2. **Place both hands, one on top of the other, over his heart (where his elbow meets his rib cage) and apply rapid, downward pressure.**

   Compressions should be about 100 per minute.

3. **Stop every 30 seconds to see whether a heartbeat has returned.**

Hot Spots

If you own a Golden, you probably have or will experience *hot spots* — painful, moist, infected areas on the skin that may develop from repeated scratching or appear out of the blue for no reason at all and enlarge rapidly. One day you brush your Golden, and underneath the long hair on some body part you find an oozing, hairless sore. Hot spots can be horrific. Tackle it immediately before it spreads.

First clip the hair to eliminate the damp undersurface and cleanse it carefully with an antiseptic wash and dilute hydrogen peroxide. Apply one of several topical ointments several times a day. Experienced Golden owners have used the following successfully: Sulfadene or BFI (from your pharmacy), Wonder Dust (a horse powder found in most feed and grain stores and tack shops), and apple cider vinegar (my personal favorite). All are drying agents with healing properties. I know one veterinarian-Golden breeder who swears by Sea Breeze astringent.

You must somehow prevent your dog from licking or gnawing at the hot spot wound. Spray a little Bitter Apple around the wound (never on it!) or use an Elizabethan collar if necessary. If things don't look better in a couple of days, see your vet or you'll soon have a secondary infection to deal with.

Always check your Golden for hot spots and other coat irregularities after a stay at a boarding kennel or if he's been swimming a lot. Some Golden coats take forever to dry, and a constant damp coat provides a perfect host site for a hot spot.

Lick Spots

Officially called *acral lick dermatitis (ALD),* lick sores are born through excessive licking of one spot, usually the front of one or both legs or feet. ALD sometimes starts with a minor injury, a bee sting, splinter, or irritation that the dog licks and chews and then continues licking long after the wound has healed. The resulting aggravation may be due to boredom, stress, or some environmental change known only to the dog.

If you can prevent his licking with anti-chewing sprays, or in desperation with an Elizabethan collar, the spot should heal on its own. A few dogs, however, persist and go back to licking the healed area or start working on a new one. Get creative, keep your Golden busy, and ask your vet for more advice.

Combating Allergies

Golden Retrievers have more than their fair share of health problems common to the breed. (See Chapter 15 for common hereditary problems.) That's in addition to the usual dog illnesses and emergencies that all canines experience. Too bad. But since you can't fight Mother Nature, you have to be smart enough to fight the problems when they arise.

Golden Retrievers are one of several breeds that are highly predisposed to allergies. Some allergies are seasonal, some appear at various life stages, and some skin diseases become lifelong problems requiring frequent or continuous treatment by a veterinarian.

Dogs with allergies don't usually sneeze or get runny noses like people do. (A few do, however.) Instead they itch and scratch, chew, lick, and rub their feet, ears, belly, and any part of their body they can reach. Left untreated, the irritated skin becomes traumatized and damaged and subsequently infected. Allergies are caused by the dog's reaction to various allergens. The most common types of allergens are flea saliva, inhaled substances (pollen, mold, dust), and food ingredients.

✔ **Flea allergies:** The most common and most debilitating is flea allergy dermatitis, which is a hypersensitivity to the protein in flea saliva. It's most commonly diagnosed after age 2, is most severe from midsummer through fall, and always requires veterinary care. In warmer climates, it can be a year-round plague. (For more on fleas, see Chapter 12.)

In flea-allergic dogs, it only takes one tiny flea bite to set a major allergy machine in motion. Flea allergic dogs will scratch and bite themselves raw, with most of the intense itching and biting occurring near the base of the tail.

Your veterinarian will prescribe anti-inflammatory medication, an oral or spot-on flea preventive medication, and also recommend stringent flea control, which includes the environment (house and yard) as well as the dog. Routine grooming, brushing, and thorough body inspections are also vital for flea allergy preventive maintenance.

✔ **Inhalant (also called atopic) allergies:** These are the second most common culprit, with grasses, pollen, molds, danders, and even dust making your dog completely miserable. Atopic dogs rub their faces, muzzles, and eyes, scratch their armpits and ears, bite their feet and legs, and may develop red and swollen patches. Indoor air cleaners, air conditioning, and good environmental sanitation are helpful in keeping indoor inhalants to a minimum. Veterinarians commonly treat inhalant allergies with antihistamines, steroids, and fatty acids, and recommend topical therapy with shampoos and rinses to make the dog more comfortable. Your vet also can refer you to a veterinary dermatologist for allergy skin testing to determine the offending allergen. If your dog is treated with a steroid, you need to know all about side effects and long-term effects to make the best decisions for your dog.

Occasionally, a dog will react to some everyday element in his environment, like carpet fibers, bedding, cleaning agents, plastics, or fertilizers. He may scratch himself hairless, especially in his armpits, lower abdomen, groin and bottom of his feet. Finding the culprit can be difficult, but then at least you can make him comfortable by eliminating it from his life. Keep him off fresh applications of fertilizer (always avoid weed killers and pesticides!), wash his feet after running on freshly mowed grass, and use shampoos that contain healing agents and are free of perfumes and dyes.

✔ **Food allergies:** Although food allergies are uncommon, they also are not seasonal and do not respond to corticosteroids. As with inhalant allergies, food allergies can cause itching, which makes the dog scratch, rub, chew, bite, and lick at his skin. The most common offenders are beef, pork, chicken, milk, eggs, fish, corn, soy, and preservatives. Diagnosis takes time because your vet must remove the dog from all commercially prepared foods and replace it with a two-ingredient diet with adequate supplementation of vitamins and minerals for a period of three to five weeks, then gradually introduce a food to the dog.

I know one retriever who reacts violently to all commercial and people foods and exists solely on a special fish and potato dog food.

Here's another food fact you should know. Food allergy is sometimes confused with food intolerance. *Food intolerance* is an abnormal physiologic response (like intestinal upset) to food, while *food allergy* is an immunological response to an ingested substance.

Topical remedies can provide short-term allergy relief, but don't address the problem. Shampoos and rinses and anti-itch sprays and soaks between baths can help make an itchy dog more comfortable.

Cortisone and other steroids will make your dog feel better, but it's a quick fix that will not make allergies go away. They also have other potentially damaging side effects, so they should never be used long-term. And they only treat the symptoms; the dog is still stuck with the allergy.

Antihistamines can offer relief from certain inhalant allergies. And additives containing omega-3 and omega-6 fatty acids often help because they block the inflammation that causes the itching.

Desensitization is a slow, expensive process, and although a large percentage of dogs improve, there's no guarantee it will work.

In addition to all of the preceding, a number of Golden breeders and owners report success stories about using natural diets to conquer allergies. While such anecdotal evidence is not a substitute for long-term studies, it does provide one more recourse for the frustrated owner and his poor allergic dog.

Is your dog insured?

Along with your home, car, life, and health, you can also now insure your dog. It's not only trendy, it's practical as well. Typical doggy maintenance health care can run well beyond $200 to $300 a year, and more if he gets sick (which is more probable than not).

Doggy health insurance offers a wide range of coverage, from routine health care to ultrasounds and CAT scans. Benefits vary within policies and companies, so do your homework before you sign on the dotted line. Ask the carrier for specifics about its coverage.

✔ Does the policy cover regular checkups and tests, emergency visits and treatment, unusual care (such as ultrasounds and CAT scans) and nonlife-threatening surgeries (such as hip replacements)?

✔ What does the policy *not* cover or specifically exclude — certain illnesses, surgeries, and so on?

✔ Does the policy allow me to use or choose my own veterinarian?

✔ How much is the deductible?

✔ Is there a policy limit on certain procedures or conditions?

✔ Is there an age limit on any part of the policy?

Also ask your veterinarian for more information about policies, his personal experience with dog insurance, and his recommendation on a carrier.

Chapter 12

The Ins and Outs of Bugs and Worms

. . . .

In This Chapter

▶ Knowing the ins and outs of parasites

▶ Preventing heartworm disease

▶ Battling fleas, ticks, and mites

. . . .

*L*ike all beasts furry, your Golden is a natural magnet for an army of nasty little organisms, all determined to create a life of misery for your Golden. Bugs and worms are nasty subjects, but you need to know about the more common parasitic critters that can invade or torment your Golden. In this chapter, I launch a major attack on parasites like fleas and ticks and a bunch of other nasty critters who plague most furry animals.

The Parade of Parasites

A *parasite* is an organism that lives in or on a different organism, a host of another animal, for its own survival. Some of these little devils often travel to the bodies of other dogs, and even to people.

Most parasites are sneaky creatures who will appear the moment you relax your golden guard. To prevent a sudden infestation, keep your dog and dog areas scrupulously clean. Have your veterinarian do twice-yearly fecal exams and call him immediately if your dog shows any of the warning signs — diarrhea, fatigue, vomiting, weight loss, chronic scratching, or bloating. Always consult your vet before using any antiparasite product on your dog or his environment.

Internal parasites

Roundworms and hookworms (see next two sections) account for about 90 percent of all internal parasitic infections.

Roundworms

Roundworms are the most common parasite in dogs (cats, too). They migrate through the lungs, into the bronchial tubes, and then to the intestines where they settle in for the long term. A heavy infestation will cause a pot-bellied appearance, a dull coat, and poor weight gain. A heavy infestation can seriously weaken and even kill a young puppy. Sometimes visible in the stool or vomit, adult roundworms appear as long, spaghettilike strings. They compete for the dog's dinner, robbing him of valuable nutrition and leading to possible starvation even though the animal is eating large amounts of food.

Roundworms are equal opportunity invaders and do not discriminate against humans. In poor sanitary conditions, they can be easily transmitted through fecal contact, especially when people fail to wash their hands after touching or cleaning up stools.

Primary human victims are children under 3 years old who are most apt to eat soil or other contaminated matter.

Most puppies are born with roundworms (toxocara canis). Although most adult bitches (healthy ones, that is) don't have active colonies residing in their pregnant bodies, they can pass along the dormant parasites to the whelp still in the womb or through their milk after the birth. The puppies pass the microscopic eggs in their stools, the bitch cleans it up, and the cycle repeats itself. Most breeders worm their pups routinely after 3 or 4 weeks of age. Your vet will prescribe a safe wormer depending on the types of parasites found in your puppy's stool.

Symptoms of a minor to serious infestation include degrees of the following: dull, dry coat and skin, distended abdomen, loose watery stools, insatiable appetite, dry cough, and abdominal discomfort with whimpering or crying.

Treatment consists of oral medication in two doses, one for the adult roundworm, and a second for the undeveloped larvae.

For prevention, schedule twice-yearly fecal exams, follow careful clean-up procedures, and maintain a consistently clean environment. You can also control roundworms with regular use of the heartworm preventatives Heartgard Plus, Filarabits Plus, or Interceptor.

Hookworms

Although No. 2 on the parasitic popularity scale, hookworms are the most harmful of all canine intestinal parasites, especially in puppies. Like round-worms, they can be passed through the mother, through fecal contact, and can also enter by burrowing into the animal's exposed skin. They take up residence in the dog's intestines, but attach to the intestinal walls to suck blood rather than digesting dog food, resulting in severe anemia and even death in very young pups.

Symptoms include bloody diarrhea, a dull, dry coat, weight loss, weakness, distended abdomen, and insatiable appetite. In otherwise healthy adult dogs, no symptoms may appear.

Treatment consists of oral medication in two doses.

For prevention, schedule twice-yearly fecal exams and keep a strict sanitary environment. You can control hookworms with regular use of the heartworm preventatives Heartgard Plus, Filarabits Plus, or Interceptor.

Tapeworms

Tapeworms come from fleas. Dogs can get one of six types of tapeworms by eating an infected flea or an intermediate host — a rodent, bird, or critter (or part of one) that carries the flea. (Goldens are notorious for gobbling up dead birds and bunny parts.) Tapeworms look like wiggly grains of rice. Many dog owners discover their dog is infected when they see the worm segments in the dog's stool, or in a worst-case scenario, crawling in his anal area. Tapeworm segments can also contaminate rugs and furniture and the dog's bedding.

Symptoms include increased appetite and weight loss, alternating diarrhea and constipation, and chewing at the rectal area. Healthy adult dogs may show no signs other than mild diarrhea.

In my own experience with tapeworm (which is considerable because I live in the country and my Goldens are forever foraging for some dead or rotting animal part), my dogs have never developed diarrhea, but I'm sure that's because I find them *early*; not to brag, but I'm *always* looking at their stools!

Treatment includes oral medication.

For prevention, practice rigid flea control, frequent inspections of fresh stools, and a sanitary dog and people environment. If possible, don't allow your Golden to eat potential host creatures. (Lots of luck!)

Whipworms

Dogs acquire whipworms by ingesting the eggs through either direct fecal contact or microscopic fecal matter on their coat or feet. Whipworms are tough to diagnose and may require more than one fecal exam. They are also very resistant to many disinfectants used to destroy the larvae. (One old-time breeder advises a generous dose of plain old table salt sprinkled generously in the kennel and potty areas. It works, although it is obviously not practical throughout the yard!)

Symptoms include watery, slimy, or bloody diarrhea, which can be intermittent, increased appetite, weight loss, a dull, dry coat, and abdominal pain.

Treatment consists of oral medication.

For prevention, keep the dog's living area clean and dry with good exposure to sunlight. You can also prevent whipworms with the heartworm preventative Interceptor or Filarabits Plus.

Heartworm

This one will kill your dog if not diagnosed and treated. Heartworm occurs when an infective mosquito bites your dog and deposits the heartworm larvae into the animal's bloodstream. The larvae migrate to the body tissues where they spend three or four months maturing into small adult worms. From there, they make their way into a vein, move to the heart, and set up housekeeping in the right side of the heart as sexually mature worms. Of course, they mate inside the heart (must be their idea of romance), and the female can produce up to 5,000 microfilariae in a single day. That colony will sit and wait for the next mosquito bite so that they can hop a ride and continue the same life cycle in another dog.

The adult heartworms will reach lengths of 4 to 12 inches in the heart and arteries of the lungs. The result is obvious — decreased circulation, heart failure, and ultimately, your own heartbreak.

Symptoms of heartworm disease may not appear for up to a year after infection first occurs. The most constant sign is a soft, deep cough, which gets worse with exercise. The dog will become listless and tire easily and lose weight. His coat will become dry and dull, and he may cough up bloody sputum. Treatment is expensive and risky, but without it, the dog will die.

Heartworm medication will prevent the disease. Daily or monthly pills are available through your veterinarian, but the dog must first be tested for the disease before taking the preventive. Why? The medication will kill any heartworms present, and if the dog already has a large colony residing in his heart, they will die there and clog his heart and lungs.

People who live in warm climates where mosquitoes thrive all year should keep their dogs on year-round medication. In North America, heartworm is found in all 50 states.

Your puppy was born heartworm free. He needs to start a daily or monthly puppy-size preventive with your first visit to your vet.

Giardia

Giardia is a one-celled parasite passed through fecal ingestion (eating infected stools) or through drinking infected water in public areas. It attaches to the dog's intestinal wall and can be especially disastrous in very young pups. Giardia is capable of passing from cattle to dogs, dogs to humans, and so on down the contagion chain. Giardia can be fatal in very young pups.

Symptoms include severe watery or persistent diarrhea and dehydration.

Treatment includes long-term medication, and reinfection is not uncommon. The parasite is hard to diagnose because it shrinks after shedding in the stool and may not be present or detectable in every stool sample.

The most effective prevention is through strict sanitation in the dog's living area and by avoiding contact with possible contamination in lakes and ponds frequented by wildlife. For obvious reasons, this is especially important with young puppies.

Coccidia

Coccidia are one-celled organisms that pack a wallop that belies their size. My introduction to coccidia was brutal when three pups in my 4-week-old litter of Goldens suddenly became listless and presented watery yellow diarrhea. After three high-speed runs to my veterinarian, several days of subcutaneous (under the skin) hydration, and round-the-clock neonatal care, we all prevailed triumphant, although I was by then considerably weaker than the pups!

Coccidia is spread through the feces or through contaminated food or water or can be passed from a nursing dam to her whelp. It develops quickly in the dog or pup's intestines. Diagnosis requires fresh stools and special testing procedures designed to reveal this type of parasite.

Symptoms include loose, watery stools, listlessness, vomiting, and weight loss.

Treatment consists of oral medication containing sulfadimethoxine in pill or liquid form. It must be quick and aggressive, but is usually successful.

For prevention, practice conscientious hygiene in a dry, clean living environment with good exposure to sunlight.

External parasites

If it's not bad enough that you and your poor dog may have to deal with creepy crawlers on the inside, there's more. External parasites include fleas, ticks, and other mighty mites.

Fleas

Holding steady as the first and foremost canine adversary, the flea, along with the cockroach, has outmaneuvered all attempts at his extermination. Under the right conditions (warm and humid) one adult flea can produce 25,000 fleas in 30 days.

It's almost guaranteed that you and your dog will encounter fleas at least once during his lifetime. If you hope to wage a winning battle, you first must understand the enemy.

Adult fleas who have had their first blood meal must dine every 24 hours in order to survive. For that reason and their own convenience, most adult fleas will remain on their food source, which is your dog or other warm-blooded animal.

The remaining fleas represent the majority of the flea population:

- ✔ The eggs, which will hatch into first-stage larvae within 21 days
- ✔ The first stage larvae, which will mature into second-stage pupae from nine to 200 days
- ✔ Second-stage pupae, which can become adults in just a few days or take as long as nine months, depending on their food source, and will live in the environment rather than on the dog

Most eggs are laid on the dog and then fall off into your carpet, bedding, furniture, or grass, where they move along in their life cycle.

You can find out if you have fleas in your carpet or house by donning a pair of white socks and walking around the house for a couple of hours. If you end up with black specks on those socks, it's a good bet you have fleas. Double-check by scraping the specks onto white paper and wet with water. If the specks turn red or reddish brown, they're flea droppings filled with blood.

With such huge numbers and so many life stages, flea battle is a tough war with several strategies. Fortunately, flea prevention and eradication has become easier, thanks to modern dog-science. Today, in addition to traditional flea management, several revolutionary new flea weapons put effective flea control in every dog house:

- **Frontline — Fipronil:** Fipronil is a safe *adulticide* (a product that disables the flea's nervous system) marketed under the name of Frontline. It comes in a spray or a spot-on treatment that is applied to the dog's skin between the shoulder blades, providing 100 percent control within 24 hours. The dog, however, must be kept dry for about 48 hours after application. The best part for water dogs like Goldens is that Fipronil is water-friendly, and your dog can swim without reducing its effectiveness.

    Fipronil does not enter the dog's bloodstream; it spreads across the body through the hair follicles and oil glands in the skin, killing fleas within four hours of contact and ticks within 12 hours. (Blessedly, the flea does not have to bite the dog.) One application will control fleas for up to 90 days on dogs and ticks for up to 30 days. It's safe for puppies and provides better protection than the combined use of collar, sprays, and premise treatments. Frontline costs about $10 for one application and is available only through veterinarians.

- **Advantage — Imidacloporid:** Advantage is a safe spot-on treatment applied between the shoulder blades, which quickly spreads, as does Frontline, across the surface of the dog's skin. Also an adulticide, it kills 98 to 100 percent of adult fleas within 24 hours. It is not absorbed into the dog's bloodstream and remains effective for 30 days. No tick prevention here. It's also available only through veterinarians.

- **Program — Lufenuron:** Commonly known as "the monthly flea pill," Lufenuron is an insect growth regulator (IGR) marketed under the name of Program. It prevents the flea eggs from hatching, thus breaking the flea life cycle. Although Program is essentially nontoxic, it does not prevent flea bites, which is a problem for the flea-allergic dog.

Traditional remedies now take a back seat to the popular and less toxic products like Frontline, Advantage, and Program. Nevertheless, they're still out there on the market, and you should know their names and the dangers they pose to your dog.

- **Flea collars:** Insecticides are time-released from the collars and will not control a serious flea infestation. Flea collars may cause allergic reactions due to long-term exposure to low levels of insecticides. Always remove prior to bathing and *never* combine with dips or sprays.

- **Sprays and powders:** Although they're easily applied, they must be used often. They will not penetrate oily or heavy coats and are ineffective in serious infestations.

- **Shampoos:** Shampoos will kill fleas if properly used, but have little residual effect.

- **Dips:** Dips are more effective and offer more residual effect. But because they contain more insecticides, they are also highly toxic. Dips are safest when handled by your veterinarian.

- **Combs:** Flea combs have 32 tiny teeth per inch. Useful for short-term removal, flea combs are difficult to use on heavy or long-coated dogs.

- **Systemics:** These may be oral or topical and may be insecticide or growth regulators, both of which enter the dog's system to kill fleas or prevent maturation of eggs. A few off-the-shelf brands are available at the retail level.

- **Premise sprays:** Sprays applied to the house or yard kill adult fleas or inhibit larvae growth.

- **Foggers:** Foggers are more effective indoors but will not kill adult or pre-adult fleas or flea eggs. You must remove animals and protect food and utensils. Penetration is limited by furniture.

If possible, avoid using pesticide sprays and dips that contain organophosphates and carbamates because they are highly toxic. Products containing natural pyrethins are less toxic (relatively speaking) and therefore a better choice.

In addition, read the label and ask your vet before using carpet sprays or household foggers. Some of those products can cause toxicity problems that are worse than fleas.

What do all those terms mean?

Here are some terms you should know when evaluating traditional flea remedies. Pay special attention to the key word here: *toxic.*

- **Amitraz** is a toxic chemical used in tick collars. It kills ticks, not fleas, and can be used in combination with other flea and tick products. (Many others cannot.)

- **Organophosphates** and **carbamates** are toxic chemicals still used in many flea killing products. They are absorbed into the animal's system and can be fatal, especially if mixed with certain other flea products. Use

with extreme caution. If you don't know what the ingredient is, ask your veterinarian.

- **Pyrethins** are a natural plant extract from the chrysanthemum family found in Africa. It's easily metabolized when taken orally, so it offers lower toxicity to pets.

- **Permethrins** are a synthetic pyrethin with longer residual action, commonly used with quick killing natural pyrethins to control fleas and ticks. Permethrins and pyrethins are faster-acting adult flea killers with low to moderate residual effects (retained in the dog's system).

As a precaution, remember the cardinal rule of fighting fleas. *Always* read labels and directions carefully and *never* combine flea preventives (flea dip with a flea collar, topical flea spray with oral medication, and so on) without first checking with your vet. For example, never place a flea collar on a dog who has been recently bathed, dipped, or sprayed with a pesticide. Some of those chemical combinations can be fatal!

Some dog owners are firm believers in natural remedies such as garlic, brewer's yeast, eucalyptus, citronella, and pennyroyal oil, although no research exists to prove they work. Whether brewer's yeast or garlic actually prevent fleas has never been scientifically established, but both will contribute to good health, so they can't hurt. Some oils, however, can be toxic if ingested or improperly used.

Get the jump on fleas and start prevention before they find your dog. Use a three-pronged attack that covers your dog, your house, and your yard. For your dog, consult your veterinarian and use whatever flea preventative he or she recommends. Groom your dog with a flea comb (dipped in soapy water to snag and drown the fleas) after every trip outdoors and use it at least weekly to check for fleas and flea dirt. If you find suspicious dark specks on his underside between his hind legs or on his back at the base of his tail, rub them with a moist tissue. Flea dirt will turn a reddish-brown color.

In your house, routinely vacuum and clean all floors, furniture, and beds, especially areas where your Golden sleeps, plays, or rests. This simple household chore is more effective than pesticides in controlling fleas.

Drop a two-inch section of a flea collar in the vacuum bag to kill any fleas or larvae you might pick up.

Handling fleas in the yard is harder. Remove any debris and spray with an IGR (Insect Growth Regulator). If you have a serious flea problem and the area's too big to handle on your own, use a lawn service. If you can't afford it, ask your vet for more affordable remedies.

Your personal flea trap

If you suspect fleas in one or more rooms, plant a flea trap. At night, put a small lamp on the floor, place a shallow bowl of soapy water beneath the light wherever you think fleas are hiding, and leave the light on all night. The fleas will jump at the light and fall into the soapy water. They will be unable to climb out of the slippery water and will drown. If you don't find fleas in the morning, move the bowl to different rooms and various areas of large rooms to finish your detective work.

You can buy similar flea traps at your local pet store if you don't want to create your own.

Ticks

Modern science has yet to discover why ticks were created in the first place. These ugly bloodsuckers are everywhere, just waiting for some warm-blooded creature to hop on to.

Ticks are major carriers of disease and must be removed as soon as possible to prevent infection. If you spend time outdoors or in the woods, check your dog (and yourself) twice daily. Tick-borne diseases do not discriminate and affect humans as well as dogs.

Ticks love warm, moist places, so confine your walks and play to open sunny areas. Use a spot-on tick preventive or a spray. Check with your vet before using two tick products at the same time.

Safe tick removal is also important. You want to avoid crushing the tick so that its bloody contents don't spurt out and contaminate you or your dog.

1. **Spray the tick with a bit of flea spray or alcohol to make it loosen its mouth parts that are attached to the skin.**

2. **Use tweezers or tissue to gently pull the tick straight out (not up) from the bite site.**

3. **Drop the body in a jar of alcohol or bleach or flush it down the toilet.**

A clever little gadget called Pro-tick remedy is the easiest and safest means of tick removal. It always (well, almost always) gets the head out, too. You can order one from Safety Consulting Services (SCS) Ltd., P.O. Box 573, Stony Point, NY 10980; 800-PIX-TICK.

Here are some tick-borne diseases:

✔ **Lyme disease (Borrelia Burfdorferi):** Named for the Connecticut city of Lyme where it was first discovered in 1977, Lyme disease is found today in every state. The current vaccine for this disease is still controversial, so the best protection against infection is still prevention.

Spread through at least two species of the tiny deer tick, Lyme's attacks dogs as aggressively as it attacks humans, invading the joints and causing painful swelling, lameness and lethargy. Prolonged exposure can cause permanent damage to the heart and kidneys, so early diagnosis and prompt treatment are important. False positives are common in the testing process, and your vet may have to run two or three titer tests to confirm a diagnosis. Several weeks of the antibiotic tetracycline is the most common treatment.

Lyme arthritis is the most treatable form of the disease, but many affected dogs will have recurring symptoms even after treatment. Cardiac and neurological disorders will respond to antibiotics, but kidney Lyme disease is almost always fatal.

For more information about Lyme disease, contact the Lyme Disease Foundation Inc. at 800-886-LYME, which is a 24-hour hotline.

✔ **Ehrlichiosis:** Similar to Lyme disease, ehrlichiosis is transmitted through the bite of the brown dog tick, with at least one other tick species under suspicion. The disease attacks the blood platelets and may produce Lyme-type symptoms of mild fever, appetite loss, swollen lymph nodes, and abnormal discharge from the eyes and/or nose. The symptoms may come and go, making an accurate diagnosis difficult. Current treatment involves aggressive use of antibiotics, and affected dogs are more prone to reinfection. Erlichia is more common in tick-prone areas, so prompt tick removal is still the best preventive measure.

In 1994, ehrlichiosis was also discovered in humans. It can be fatal in both dogs and people, with advanced stages causing kidney failure and respiratory problems, which makes early diagnosis critical.

✔ **Rocky Mountain Spotted Fever:** Its name implies its origin and where-abouts. Symptoms of RMSF include fever, bloody urine, loose or bloody stools, breathing difficulty and unexplained nose bleeds, and usually show up within two weeks. See your veterinarian for tests to confirm infection. Can be fatal if untreated.

Ear mites

Mites are less visible than ticks but are just as pesky. These microscopic eight-legged parasites love to feast on the various body parts of the dog.

Adult ear mites settle into the lining of the ear canal, causing irritation and extreme itching. Your dog will scratch and dig and try to shove his paw into his ear. He'll shake his head a lot and maybe even walk a little crooked. Mites usually produce a smelly, brownish wax (in the ear — where else?). A veterinarian exam is necessary to diagnose these mites.

A regimen of six to eight weeks of ear drops will squelch the infestation. Mites are transmitted by direct contact and are highly contagious, so they are often shared with other canine family members. If one of your Goldens has ear mites, have everyone in your dog family checked by your vet and give each one a thorough mite-specific shampoo to whack any stray pests that might be wandering around on the dogs. Ear mites are not transmissible to humans.

Mange mites

There are three cousins in the mange mite family, each one rendering its own brand of havoc on your dog.

- **Sarcoptic mange:** Sarcoptes (also known as *scabies*) can be devastating. This crab-shaped mite burrows under the dog's skin to lay its eggs, causing continuous intense itching. The infected animal will be miserable and will scratch, dig, and literally chew himself raw until much of his body is scabby and hairless. The damage is often compounded by secondary bacterial infections resulting from the open sores.

  Scabies mites are microscopic and may require several deep skin scrapings to confirm their presence. Your vet may prescribe a series of dips or injections. Scabies is highly contagious to humans as well as other dogs, so if you develop an itchy rash around your midsection, call your vet before you call your physician.

- **Demodectic mange:** Both localized (confined to parts of the face) and generalized (invades other body parts), this type of mange is considered by some to be the scourge of the mange family. Sometimes called "red mange" or "puppy mange," it is passed to puppies during the nursing process. Demodex usually exists harmlessly in the animal's hair follicles and oil glands. Then for some still unknown reason, one or more pups become stressed for who knows why, and the mites multiply in the coat, causing bare patches around the eyes, face, neck, and front legs. If itching occurs, scratching can lead to secondary bacterial infections of the skin, further stressing the young victim's immature immune system.

  Early diagnosis and treatment are important to keep the demodex under control and localized. That includes superb health care and a stressfree environment to minimize the impact on the pup's immune system.

  Despite an owner's best efforts, about 10 percent of localized demodex progresses into generalized demodex (see sidebar).

- **Chyletiella mites:** These dandruff mites are often called "walking dandruff" because they travel across the surface of the skin, munching lightly as they move along, causing mild itching and flaking on the head and along the back. Your dog will, of course, bite and scratch those areas. Your vet can control the condition with prescription dips and follow-up shampoos or sprays target any leftover mites who escape the treatment.

Generalized demodex

When localized demodex develops into generalized demodex, the hair loss will spread across the puppy's body, causing inflamed and itchy bald patches, secondary infections, and a serious condition called deep pyoderma. Generalized demodex is extremely difficult to control, requiring special bathing, dips, and antibiotics, all while the animal is in great pain due to skin damage from the demodex.

Euthanasia is not ruled out as a last resort. Thank goodness this condition is noninfectious.

Because there is a strong hereditary predisposition for generalized demodex, all dogs with the disease should be sterilized. In fact, some experts recommend that parents and siblings of affected dogs also be removed from breeding programs to protect future generations from the agony of the disease.

Chapter 13

Golden Grooming Basics

• •

In This Chapter

▶ Grooming from the skin out

▶ Lifesaving dental hygiene

• •

Grooming your Golden Retriever is about more than keeping your dog pretty. It's also hygiene and good health. It's all body parts, not just the furry coat. Your own hygiene means more than a shampoo. It's teeth, toes, underarms, and other appendages. Your dog has those same needs, too. In this chapter, I dig out the brush and comb and groom your Golden buddy.

Grooming Is a Year-Round Job

A well-groomed coat is especially important in cold weather. The flow of air through a dog's coat helps regulate his body temperature, and that process is hampered if the coat is matted or full of mud.

Summer grooming is just as important as winter care. Professional groomers tell horror stories about double-coated dogs like Golden Retrievers and Samoyeds that arrive for grooming with their heavy coats hiding inch-deep holes in their flesh from maggot eggs. Flies love to visit unclean dogs and lay their eggs in filthy or badly matted fur. When the larvae mature, they eat into the dog's skin or move up into the rectum. Severe cases can destroy huge areas of flesh and require surgery to correct. There are reported cases of dogs who died because the problem was invisible to the owner who never bothered to brush their dog or look under all that matted fur.

Grooming does more than untangle and remove dead hair. It also stimulates the oil glands, which reduces dander and keeps that Golden fur coat gleaming. It's also a weekly body check for lumps and bumps and critters that hide in the skin and coat. It's weekly ear checks and cleaning whenever necessary. It's weekly dental care and monthly pedicures. If all of this sounds like overkill, remember you're the one who bought this dog!

Your attitude toward grooming can make it fun instead of inconvenient. Most Goldens love the hands-on attention involved in grooming, so think of this as bonding rather than a burden. It's one more aspect of living the Golden life. Your toddler eventually grew up to bathe and shower without help. Your Golden never will.

Your Grooming Tool Kit

You'll need more than that slicker brush you bought when your Golden puppy first came home. You'll also need a steel comb with wide and narrow-spaced teeth, a flea comb, and a mat rake. Some Golden owners use a pin brush. I also have a shedding comb, but I end up using my steel comb-slicker brush combination instead. (I also have one of those grooming gloves that collects loose hair when you pet or rub your dog, but I never use it. I just like the feel of my dog's fur between my fingers!) Pick your breeder's or your groomer's brain for good utensil choices.

Now get out that brush and groom! Brushing will be easier if you follow a pattern on the dog. Always brush with the grain of the coat and start at his rear, working in small sections at a time (see Figure 13-1). Part the coat all the way to the skin as you brush along. Use one hand to hold the hair aside and then brush from the skin outward through the hair. Work in continuous sections, always brushing upwards and forward. Pay special attention to the feathering behind the ears and on the legs and tail as these areas are more prone to matting.

Remove mats and tangles slowly without yanking so that you won't hurt your dog. On larger mats, rub in a few drops of a canine hair conditioner and then work gently with a mat rake. A slicker brush will handle smaller mats. If you must resort to scissors, cut upward into the mat rather than a straight-across angle cut. While you're brushing, check for rashes, hot spots, and other skin problems.

Use your mat rake or slicker brush to work through mats instead of cutting them out. A straight-across scissors cut will leave an unsightly line in the fur. Even if he's not a show dog, you don't want him looking nerdy.

You may not need scissors, but they're handy if you want to keep your Golden neat and trim. The choices are confusing — straight cut, curved, thinning, ear and nose, bent shank, and styling — and some cost more than a designer haircut. Most pet owners don't need elaborate shears to neaten up their Golden. I use a good-quality, medium-priced thinning shears for everything from ears to toes with good results. But then I'm not prepping show dogs. I just want my furries to look tidy.

Figure 13-1:
Always
brush your
puppy's ears
very gently.

Close Encounters of the Furry Kind.

Don't Forget the Paws

Feet and nails are the most neglected home-groomed areas. I see too many Goldens with paws that look like mops, with long hair spraying from between the toes. Can you picture those feet wet or full of mud?

Hairy feet not only look sloppy, but they collect mud, burrs, and ice balls as well — all uncomfortable for the dog. Trimmed and tidy feet also track less mud, snow, and ice into the house.

So when you brush and trim his coat, don't forget his feet (see Figure 13-2). Clip the hair around the foot and between the toes and pads, cutting it level with the bottom of the pads.

You can't work on the feet without tending to the nails. There's great value in 16 well-trimmed nails. They're easier on your furniture and clothing, kids, and grandkids. It's also healthier for the dog because nails that are too long can splinter or tear and cause sore feet. Long nails can also cause the toes to splay and spread apart. In the long term, that will damage the structure of the foot, which eventually affects the dog's legs. It's amazing what a good pedicure can prevent.

Figure 13-2:
Use trimming shears to groom your puppy's feet.

Close Encounters of the Furry Kind.

There's a confusing variety of nail clippers in the dog foot department. Ask your vet which one he recommends and request a demonstration of how to use it properly. It's included in your puppy's visit.

Nail trimming shouldn't be a wrestling match if you began the process when your Golden was a pup. Take your time and be careful not to cut the *quick,* which is the pink vein visible down the center of the nail. Always cut at a 45-degree angle with the clipper facing the same direction as the toes. If you accidentally cut into the quick, it's no big deal. Just apply a few drops of Kwik-Stop Styptic powder or liquid (or use your own shaving styptic) and allow a few minutes to dry. A bleeding nail is not a tragedy, more like a tiny bee sting for some dogs, but it seems to be a nightmare for most dog owners (including this writer!).

Some Goldens have black or very dark nails where the quick is not visible. If you can't see the quick, hold a flashlight beam directly under the nail to reveal the lighter line of the vein. If you're not sure, make small clips in the tip or curved part of the nail.

Trimming a small amount of nail often is better than trying to cut neglected nails that have grown too long. Walking on cement sidewalks or running and playing in concrete kennel runs helps keep nails ground down. Indoor dogs will need more frequent pedicures.

If you handle your Golden's paws frequently during play and petting and give him a food reward during and after trimming so that he associates it with good times, you won't need your boxing gloves. If you dread this chore, have your vet or groomer keep his nails trimmed regularly.

Be a Plaque Attacker

Home dental care is vital to your Golden's long-term health. Plaque and tartar are perfect hosts for bacteria and, if not removed, can cause periodontal disease, which is severe and irreversible. Those gum problems can ultimately lead to tooth loss and systemic health problems that will affect the liver, kidneys, heart, and lungs. Noxious breath is often a good indicator of tooth decay and gum disease.

You don't need a lot of fancy tools to work on your dog's teeth. Cleaning teeth is more elbow grease than gadgetry. You can use a soft-bristled toothbrush and chicken-flavored toothpaste made just for dogs. (People paste will make him sick.) Brush his teeth the same way you would do your own, from the gums down with gentle strokes (see Figure 13-3). If he objects, try wrapping a gauze pad around your index finger and rubbing it across his teeth. If your Golden has learned to accept your hand in his mouth since puppyhood, dental maintenance shouldn't be a struggle.

Obviously, daily brushing would be best. But in the real dog-people world, that's rarely possible. Twice weekly — or at least once a week — is probably a more reachable goal.

If your Golden isn't fond of toothbrushes or gauze pads, try a Finger Brush, which is a toothbrush that fits over your fingers. You can find it in most catalogs and pet stores.

Dry dog foods and plaque-attacker chew products like sterilized hard bones, Nylabones, and floss-ropes will help prevent periodontal disease. Keep his chewie bucket full. Include a dental checkup in your annual visit to the vet. Some dog's teeth may need professional cleaning every year.

Studies show that 80 percent of dogs show early signs of oral disease by age 3. Scary, isn't it? Another survey conducted at one veterinarian congress in Vancouver, B.C., determined that dog owners can literally add three to five years to their dogs' lives simply be providing routine dental care. Isn't that reason enough to preserve that Golden grin?

Figure 13-3:
Use a soft-bristled toothbrush and a toothpaste made for dogs.

Ear Care

Ear problems are easy to prevent. Just pay strict attention to ear hygiene during your weekly grooming sessions. Regular cleansing (weekly or monthly, depending on your dog's ears) with a specially formulated ear cleanser, even if the ears don't look dirty, will help loosen any deep down grime and wax. Squirt several drops into each ear and massage it for 30 seconds. Use a cotton ball to absorb excess moisture and a fresh cotton ball or swab to remove any dirt. The cleansers also act as drying agents (important after *every* swimming session) and will correct the pH environment of the ear, discouraging musty growths, particularly in humid climates.

Flop-eared dogs, especially water-bound critters like retrievers who love to wallow in ponds and puddles, are more prone to dirty ears and recurrent ear infections than those perk-eared little terriers. The long ear flap acts like a terrarium cover that prevents air flow and keeps the ear canal moist and ripe for organism growth.

Infected ears usually emit a foul odor and may have a rancid-smelling discharge. The ear canal will be red and inflamed and/or contain debris or a dark, smelly waxy substance. Often the dog will scratch his head — a *lot* — or tilt his head to the affected side.

Dog owners make two mistakes when fighting ear infections. They postpone going to the vet until the ear has worsened and the bacteria have multiplied into a more severe infection (what they can't see doesn't appear serious), or they stop treatment too soon, before the infection has been killed. If treatment starts as soon as possible, you will avoid secondary problems, and the cure is faster and easier on the dog and your pocketbook. Always continue treatment for the prescribed period, or the problem will surely reoccur (canine law of averages).

Bathing Your Dog

Bathing is an area that's often overdone (in dogs, that is!). Most Goldens need a bath every two or three months, although some fastidious owners have their Goldens professionally groomed and bathed every month. The dogs usually don't need it, but it makes their humans happy and it does help to minimize shedding.

Goldens may need more frequent bathing in the summer if they swim in muddy ponds or have an oily undercoat that tends to smell. Two of my Goldens (who happen to be related) sometimes have an unpleasant body odor that is unique to certain types of skin and coat. (As a result, in the summer our bedroom often smells like you-know-what.)

Your Golden's coat must be brushed and dematted *before* you bathe him. Mats tend to set in like cement when wet, and you'll have one heck of a time getting through them after a good lathering.

The after-bath process is just as important. If his coat is not thoroughly dried and combed out, the damp undercoat can attract fungal and staph infections. Wet is the first half of bathing; drying is the second part.

Wet dogs suds up more easily, so wet the entire dog with lukewarm water (a shower-type sprayer works especially well) and suds the entire body. I prefer a spray bottle to apply shampoo. Some owners bathe their dogs in their personal shower space and claim it is easier on the dog as well as themselves.

Also make sure that you plug his ears with cotton balls and keep his eyes dry. Follow the directions for whatever shampoo you use and be sure to rinse thoroughly. Shampoo residue can irritate his skin. Some owners believe that a warm water rinse will help loosen the dead hair.

Most Goldens are eager movers and shakers, especially after a bath, so wear grubby clothes and be prepared to get a bath yourself. Towel dry and then use your hair dryer to finish the job. If he air-dries in warm weather, just make sure that he dries completely.

Choosing a shampoo

Dog shampoos are as confusing as the human hair-care shelf. Choices include oatmeal, citrus, herbal, protein, tea tree, hypoallergenic, medicated, flea and tick, antibacterial, tearless, lusterizer — the list is endless. Ask your breeder, groomer, or veterinarian for suggestions.

One cleaning product I consider worth its shipping weight is a waterless shampoo. I use it often as a spot treatment when my Goldens roll in something smelly (emphasis on the word *often*). It saves me bending over the bathtub when I'm busy.

Never use human shampoos because they have a different pH formula that can dry or damage your dog's coat and skin. Order your shampoo from a groomer or a pet supply house.

Cleaning the Anal Sacs

You have to make sure that both ends of your Golden are in good working condition. That includes his *anal glands,* which are two scent glands under his skin, one on each side of the anal opening. The gland pockets fill with fecal fluid, and when a dog eliminates, the sacs empty from the pressure of expelled solid matter. Sometimes the fluid collects in the gland, and the dog becomes uncomfortable. That's when you see him scooting his rear end across your carpet doing the proverbial choo-choo — always in front of your nondog guests who will find it absolutely gross.

You should empty these stinky compartments before each bath, or every couple of months if bathing is less frequent. If you don't want to do it, have your veterinarian or groomer do it. Anal glands can become swollen and impacted if not emptied, which can lead to infection and surgical correction, so regular tending is important.

The glands are at 4 o'clock and 8 o'clock on either side of the anus. Using your thumb and two fingers of one hand, press inward and upwards in those spots to express the fluid contents. Place a paper towel over the opening when you squeeze, or you risk a nasty shot in the eyes. Trust me — it's *not* pleasant!

Chapter 14

Caring for Your Senior Golden

. . . .

In This Chapter

▶ Understanding the canine geriatric process

▶ Taking special care of seniors

▶ Saying good-bye

. . . .

*L*arge breeds like Golden Retrievers mark the beginning of their geriatric period at about 8 years of age. Your Golden may still look and act like a puppy, but don't be fooled. He's entering his sunset years.

Of course, you want to make his golden years as healthy as your own, and being a smart dog owner, you know that senior dogs need special care. Besides his checkup once a year, what else can you do to prolong his life and keep him healthy longer? This chapter explains common old age problems and gives you advice on how to add quality and hopefully longevity to your aging Golden's life. For starters, rigid weight control and proper oral hygiene are the two primary canine life extenders.

Slim and Trim

Obesity strains every major system of a canine's body and *will* take years off his life (see Chapters 10 and 11). As your Golden ages, his energy needs will decrease, so you should adjust his food portions accordingly as well as the type of food he eats. Overweight dogs need a higher fiber, lower fat diet. Most dogs over 7 or 8 years old who are not active in competition or working in the field should eat a "senior" diet designed for aging dogs. If you're changing diets, consult with your veterinarian first.

Do a rib check every month. You should be able to feel his ribs with *light* pressure, but you shouldn't see his ribs. Even an extra five pounds puts added stress on older bones and joints.

Healthy Teeth and Gums

Just as important as his weight, good dental hygiene will add healthy years to your dog's life (see Chapter 13). Too many dogs die before their appointed time because of heart, kidney, liver, or respiratory infection and disease, conditions that often start at the gum line and could have been prevented with good dental hygiene. Gums that are loaded with plaque and tartar easily become infected. Left untreated, that bacteria will enter the bloodstream and attack a dog's vital organs.

Studies show that 85 percent of dogs over 6 years of age have some form of periodontal disease, which is an infection in the deep portions of the teeth and gums. If it's not treated promptly, the infection invades the body and can become life-threatening, especially in an older dog with an equally old immune system. The infection will attack his vital organs, resulting in heart, respiratory, kidney or liver disease.

One prominent veterinarian tells of dogs in his practice that have come in for seemingly innocent gum or mouth problems such as an abscessed tooth. The bad tooth has caused a major infection in some vital organ, the owner doesn't even know it, and the dog is in effect dying. If that doesn't make you brush your dog's teeth, nothing will!

An older dog's gums are often more pigmented than when he was a youngster. His teeth should still be white, although some yellowing is normal with age. Very pale or whitish gums are warning signs that say, "Take me to the veterinarian!" They are symptoms of a circulation problem that can be due to any number of serious and life-threatening conditions.

Exercise, Arthritis, and Your Aging Dog

Exercise is important at every life stage, but it is especially important for the senior dog. A senior dog who is sedentary for long periods will grow out of shape more quickly and will take longer bouncing back. However, geriatric exercise should be tailored to fit your dog's age and physical condition.

Walking and running are still the best maintenance workouts (see Figure 14-1). Even the change of scenery will stimulate him mentally, and he'll be extra grateful for the time you spend together. Be careful not to overdo it. Some Goldens have more heart than stamina and will press on even when exhausted. (Sound like someone you know and love?) If he seems to tire quickly or appears to be hurting the next day, slow down and see your vet.

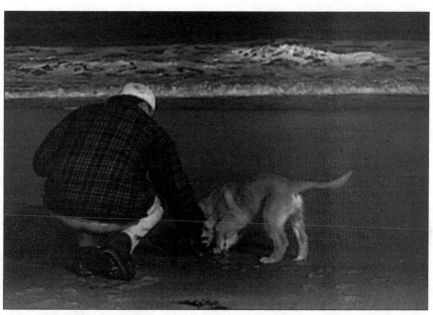

Figure 14-1:
Exercise is a
primary
health
ingredient.

Close Encounters of the Furry Kind.

Be mobility conscious. If your old guy is stiff getting up in the morning or after heavy exercise, he may have arthritis or degenerative joint disease. Your vet should examine him and perhaps take x-rays and prescribe buffered aspirin or drugs to reduce inflammation and ease pain. If steroids are prescribed, ask about side effects and watch for them. Steroids can create a whole new set of problems.

If he has arthritis, make sure that he has a soft, warm place to rest and sleep. If your Golden doesn't already have one (he should!), surprise him with one of the many cushy orthopedic dog beds, and put it in his favorite place and out of drafts. I guarantee he'll sleep like a baby. Ummm, I mean, a puppy. My old Golden has several beds all over the house, so she can be comfy whenever she's with me. For some unspoken reason, my other Goldens never even try to sleep on one of her beds.

Arthritic conditions are significantly more prevalent in obese dogs. Watch that diet!

If your old Golden has trouble getting off or on his couch, bed or favorite spot, treat him to a PawsWay pet ramp. It's available from Pet Care with Love, Inc.

Watch It!

If you notice a change in your senior Golden's eyes or vision, it may be due to cataracts, genetic disease, or simply old age. In many cases, a veterinary ophthalmologist can surgically remove the cataracts and dramatically improve his vision.

Many geriatric dogs develop *lenticular sclerosis,* a hardening of the lens that causes a bluish-gray haze or tint in the eyes. It does not affect vision or require treatment. However, whenever you notice any change in your dog's eyes, see your veterinarian to determine if it is a problem and whether it is treatable.

Hear This!

Some dogs grow deaf with age, while others never do. Try to distinguish between *selective hearing,* when he just wants to ignore you, and actual hearing loss. When my 13-year-old Golden stopped hearing the treat jar open, I knew she wasn't faking it. Like most hearing impaired dogs, she startles easily, so I avoid sudden movements and gently stomp the floor before I touch or pet her so that she doesn't jump. We've developed a communication system of hand signals to say, "Time to come in," "Let's go," "I mean right now!" and other conversational gimmicks.

Beware of hearing loss in a "city" dog. He won't hear a car approaching on the street or in his driveway. I personally know of dogs who have been killed because of their deafness.

Old dog, new tricks?

Yes, you *can* teach an old dog new tricks and good behavior! It may take more time and patience, mostly because you're working around previously learned (and possibly improper) behavior. But if you use logical and practical training methods, your older dog can learn all sorts of good manners as well as fun things to do with you.

Monitoring Lumps and Bumps

Some lumps and bumps are normal, but many are not. While grooming or just petting your Golden (of *any* age), feel his entire body for lumps and bumps. Although skin masses like cysts, warts, and fatty tumors are common in older dogs, you should always have your vet inspect any new growths you find. Cancer in all breeds of dogs has become more common and can attack any organ or body part. Breast and testicular cancers are common in unspayed bitches and intact males. Early spay/neuter is the best prevention.

Skin and Coat

A little gray hair here and there is normal, but overly flaky skin and hair loss can indicate a late onset hormonal problem with the thyroid gland. (A dog's thyroid gland gets tired and wears out just like its human counterpart). Your vet can diagnose hyperthyroidism and treat it with an oral replacement dose of supplemental hormones.

More frequent brushing will help stimulate his oil glands and decrease the extra shedding (see Chapter 13). Your vet may recommend a nutritional supplement to add lubrication to his skin. Senior foods are low in fat and can contribute to dry skin and coat.

Signs of Kidney Disease

Does your dog urinate more frequently? Does he now have accidents in the house or have to urinate in the middle of the night? Does he drink more water than he used to? All are symptoms of kidney or bladder disease or diabetes.

Unfortunately, by the time you see any of these symptoms, there is *already* significant and irreversible damage to his vital organs. His kidneys will be over 50 percent damaged before those signs show up. And if you miss the signs of increased thirst or urination, the dog continues to get worse.

The prevention key in all of these old age diseases is to know your dog and be observant.

Dogs over 7 years of age should have annual blood work and urinalysis to test for kidney and liver function before those visible signs appear. Dogs who are already in kidney failure can be managed with special diets prescribed by the veterinarian to reduce the workload on the kidneys.

Most veterinarians offer a geriatric exam that includes a thorough physical exam, blood work, urinalysis, thyroid profile, and EKG to diagnose problems in the early stages. It's not cheap, but your Golden is worth it. It may save his life.

Detecting Heart Disease

How do you know if and when heart disease occurs? Changes in sleeping habits, restlessness, coughing (especially at night or on first waking in the morning), panting, shortness of breath, and decreased exercise tolerance can indicate cardiovascular problems. If you catch the problem early, you will have greater success in treating it.

Coughing can be serious. It's the most common sign of heart disease in canines. If your Golden has been coughing more than 24 hours, see your veterinarian.

Incontinence

Urinary incontinence is a common problem in older spayed bitches. They start to unconsciously dribble urine. You may be surprised to find wet spots on her bed in the morning. This is one condition that is easily remedied with a supplemental hormone that can improve the muscle tone of the bladder.

Saying Good-bye

Living the good life with a Golden also means the inevitable — you will probably outlive your dog. Despite your best efforts to keep him young and healthy, the time comes when you have to say good-bye. If your Golden friend suffers from cancer or other terminal disease, he will look to you, his caretaker and best friend, for relief from constant pain or inability to function. Euthanasia is the most difficult decision of dog ownership and possibly the most unselfish. After 30 years of living with this magical breed, I've faced that moment many times. Each time it's a brand-new decision, never easier, and always filled with the same gut-wrenching pain. But the sad fact remains, your dog deserves your help when it's time for him to go.

You'll know when it's time. Please believe me, you will know when that moment comes. I learned that again two years ago when one of my older Goldens fell ill, and I knew it would soon be time. But as I heard the bad news in the emergency clinic on a Sunday morning, I didn't have that deep gut feeling that I needed to be sure. We had three more grand days together, he and I. He was comfortable and very loved and spoiled. He left with grace and dignity and died peacefully in his sleep, sparing me for once that dreadful final trip. Fortunately, this time, waiting was the right decision.

Your veterinarian will help you make your decision. Five years ago when my senior female Golden was stricken with a tumor and suffered an exceptionally bad day, my vet assured me it was not yet time and pleaded with me to believe her, that my heart would tell me when. She was right, and a week later, I knew that moment had arrived. I treasure those last days we had together.

Staying with your dog

Most owners elect, as I do, to remain with their dogs to hold and comfort them during their last moments. It's best to stay as calm as possible, but I believe in my own heart that my dog understands why he's there and needs to hear me say, "I love you" one more time. The veterinarian will inject a drug, which takes but a second to make him drowsy and fall asleep, and then his heart will simply stop. If you are unwilling or unable to be with your dog, be sure a family member or a friend he loves stays with him. As difficult as this is, he does not deserve to die alone.

When I began this book, my 14-year-old female Golden napped on her cedar bed next to my desk, my constant companion as I wrote. Sadly, she left us the day after her fifteenth birthday, and I am so grateful she was here to supervise most of these chapters. Now my 11-year-old male has replaced her beside my chair, still in apparent good health. But each day I am reminded that today is one more gift.

Grief is very personal and individual. Some people can't even talk about losing their dog without breaking down completely. Many will cry and grieve for weeks and months before they can move beyond their sorrow and remember the happy times without a tear. That's normal and okay. Your dog's death is a huge personal loss, and you should let your emotions show. There will be those few who claim "It's just a dog" and won't understand why you continue to be upset.

Nondog people just don't get it. Be patient with them but don't let other people tell you how to grieve. Share your grief with other dog lovers who have traveled this lonely road. It's going to take time. All those memories will eventually bring smiles instead of tears.

Adding a new dog to the family

Some people don't want to endure another heartbreak and vow never to get another dog. Some of those will change their minds. Others want a new dog right away. Most of my friends own two or more dogs not only because they love living with a bunch of dogs, but because they won't be without a dog when one dies. I could not deal with losing one of my dear friends if I didn't have a Golden army here to comfort me. But that does not diminish the unique "specialness" of the dog I lose. It just represents my personal consolation zone.

Whether you get a new dog right away or wait until your heart has healed, approach your new dog as a special individual and don't compare him to your last one. None are the same, and each one is your best friend.

Burial

My husband and I have our dogs cremated. For many years, we buried our Goldens in one of their favorite places, up on a hill on our farm under a grove of trees where I walk our dogs each day. Today cremation is available, and we bury their ashes with their Golden brothers and sisters on that hill. Friends may question my sanity, but I always wave a big hello whenever we walk past their spot. I believe they're watching over me.

You may choose to bury your dog or his ashes in your yard or under a tree or bush in some favorite place. You can keep his ashes in a sealed vase or urn on your desk or mantle, or scatter them in your yard or over a pond where he loved to swim. Pet cemeteries offer plots and headstones. Whatever your choice, your Golden will live on in your heart forever.

Children and pet death

The death of the family dog is often a child's first experience with a serious loss. Don't try to trivialize it by saying, "You'll get over it" or "We'll get another dog." Your child doesn't want *another* dog; he wants the one who died.

Be honest with him that your dog is gone forever. Avoid phrases like "putting him to sleep." The child may wonder when he's going to wake up. The words "death" and "died" will not aggravate his grief and will in fact help him face the reality that his pet will not come back.

Share your own grief with your child; it's good therapy for both of you. Knowing you also grieve will help your child understand it's okay to feel sad about the dog. It will also help a shy or quiet child who is reluctant to display his feelings. And if he's angry or feels guilty, it will help him open up to you.

For your child's sake, don't rush out to buy another dog. Doing so may minimize the departed pet's importance in the family scheme. Wait until your child feels better. Children heal differently, and some may be ready for a new dog sooner than others.

If I Die Before You Go . . .

What will happen to your dog if you die before he goes to the Rainbow Bridge? Will your children take him in? Do they even like or want him? You have to make sure that your Golden will be cared for and provided for if you leave this earth before he does. You can do that in your will.

First decide who, besides yourself, loves your dog enough to live with him until he dies. Think about family members, other Golden-owner friends, or maybe your breeder. Are they willing and able to give him the kind of home he needs and deserves? Are you willing or able to provide a yearly stipend for his care (and can you trust them with that money)?

Some people who own a senior Golden believe the dog would be unable to adjust to a new home and prefer that their dog be euthanized after their own death, perhaps have their ashes buried with them. In my personal Golden family, my husband and I have dictated individual wishes for each of our dogs. Our old dogs and those with severe physical limitations are to join us as soon as possible at the Rainbow Bridge, and the younger, healthy ones are to be placed with various family members or friends who adore them and would provide homes we would approve of. Of course, we adjust this as our Goldens leave us or new ones come along.

If you don't have a will, at least draw up a formal statement of your wishes and have it witnessed and notarized. Hopefully, your family will honor your request.

Chapter 15

Hereditary Disease

In This Chapter

▶ Knowing about common hereditary diseases

▶ Interpreting clearances and certification

*A*re you ready for some serious discussion — can we talk? Unfortunately, the very popular Golden Retriever comes with a predisposition to several serious hereditary problems that can shorten its life span or make life difficult or painful. This chapter reveals the not-so-good side of this very special breed.

Hip Dysplasia

The most common and well-known hereditary problem in Golden Retrievers and other large breeds is hip dysplasia. Despite many years of x-ray screening before breeding, hip problems in the breed have not been reduced significantly.

Simply stated, *hip dysplasia* means poor development of the hip joint. It's an inherited disease that's complicated by environmental factors such as over-nutrition, rapid growth, and excessive trauma during developmental growth stages. The condition covers a broad range of severity that includes mild, moderate, and severe levels of dysplasia. A severe case can render a working dog incapable of performance. Even a mild case can cause painful arthritis in a sedentary companion animal, although many dysplastic dogs live normal, active lives. The condition worsens with age, and dysplastic senior dogs can experience great discomfort and very limited mobility.

The only current currently accepted diagnosis is through x-ray. X-rays are evaluated by the Orthopedic Foundation for Animals (OFA), and dogs with "clear" or "clean" hips are issued an OFA number that includes a rating of Excellent, Good, or Fair. OFA certifications issued after the mid-1990s will also appear on the dog's AKC registration papers. Dogs must be at least 2 years old before their joints are eligible for OFA consideration. OFA will evaluate the hips of younger dogs and give a preliminary rating. Breeders often obtain a preliminary rating to screen hips before they embark on a training program with a dog who may not later pass OFA scrutiny.

PennHip evaluation is a second method of detecting HD that was developed at the University of Pennsylvania School of Veterinary Medicine. Known simply as PennHip, it also uses x-rays, but it requires more specific positioning of the hips and examines other hip qualities such as joint laxity and can be used to evaluate dogs as young as 16 weeks of age. Although relatively new, PennHip gains greater acceptance every year, and some breeders now use both methods to screen their dogs.

At this time, only OFA-approved dogs should be used for breeding. A pedigree with a minimum of one or more generations of OFA-certified ancestors is still the best insurance a Golden puppy buyer has for obtaining a Golden who won't be plagued with hip problems early or later in life. Reliable breeders always screen their breeding animals and will proudly produce those OFA clearances on their dogs (see Chapter 3).

Eye Disease

Only a Board-certified veterinary ophthalmologist can determine whether a dog is free of hereditary eye disease. Eyes must be examined annually until 8 years of age because certain forms of cataracts can develop later in life. Dogs who have been properly examined will be issued an ophthalmologist certificate. Clearances can then be registered with the Canine Eye Registry Foundation (CERF). All breeding stock should have eye clearances, and the breeder should produce an ophthalmologist's proof of clearance or a CERF registration certificate. The first three sections require a CERF clearance.

Cataracts

A *cataract* is defined as an opacity of the eye lens, and several types are common in the Golden breed. At least one hereditary type shows up early in life. Some cataracts don't interfere with the dog's vision, while others progress into partial or complete blindness. Cataract surgery is successful in some cases, but it's expensive.

Progressive Retinal Atrophy

A few Goldens are affected with *Progressive Retinal Atrophy (PRA),* which is progressive deterioration of the retina that can result in complete blindness. There is no surgical solution to correct PRA. Although the incidence of PRA is low in Golden Retrievers, afflicted dogs should never be bred.

Retinal dysplasia

Retinal dysplasia (RD) is an inherited defect of the retinal lining and is more common in Goldens than is PRA (see preceding section). Unlike PRA, RD does not result in complete blindness, but it can render a hunting dog worthless in the field or for other working tasks. RD-affected Goldens should be eliminated as candidates for breeding.

Eyelash and eyelid problems

A few hereditary, but less serious, eyelid and eyelash problems affect the breed.

The bluish haze often seen in the eyes of older dogs is a normal aging process and is not hereditary or a breeding problem.

Epilepsy

Epilepsy is a seizure disorder caused by abnormal electrical patterns in the brain. It can be hereditary or caused by a variety of environmental factors, including viral and infectious diseases, trauma, and chemical or nutritional imbalance. Inherited epilepsy usually appears between 6 months and 3 years of age. Some experts believe that epilepsy that occurs in later years may be genetically induced as well. Recurring seizures can be controlled with medication, but long-term medication sometimes causes other health problems. The disease itself doesn't affect a dog's health or longevity.

Although hereditary epilepsy is difficult to diagnose, dogs who suffer recurring seizures should not be bred, and experts familiar with the breed also recommend against breeding parents and siblings of those dogs.

Elbow Dysplasia (ED) and Osteochondritis Dissecans (OCD)

Both of these diseases are developmental irregularities of the elbow and shoulder and are a major cause of front end lameness in many large breed dogs. Both ED and OCD affect young dogs, with typical symptoms of recurring or intermittent lameness usually appearing between 4 and 7 months of age. Radiographs (x-rays) taken of the elbow joint will verify the condition.

In 1990, OFA created an elbow registry to provide a database for dogs who have been x-rayed and certified free of ED and OCD. Although both diseases are believed to be hereditary, nutrition is also thought to be a contributing factor in their development. Feeding diets high in calories, calcium, and protein are suspect, and at least two major dog food manufacturers now produce puppy growth foods that are lower in fat and protein calories and recommended for fast-growing large breed dogs (see Chapter 10).

As with hip dysplasia, Goldens with ED or OCD should not be bred.

Hypothyroidism

Goldens join a long list of other breeds who suffer from the malfunction of the thyroid gland. Symptoms include obesity, lethargy, recurrent infections, and skin or coat problems such as hair loss, dryness, and thinning fur. Treatment consists of daily oral thyroid supplementation, which may continue for the dog's entire life.

Diagnosis can be tricky, and supplementation can be a problem in itself. Get a second opinion before starting thyroid treatment. Early-onset hypothyroidism may be heritable, and dogs so affected should not be bred.

Some holistic veterinarians believe that the huge increase in canine thyroid problems may be due to environmental factors such as overuse of vaccines and exposure to lawn chemicals. If your Golden develops thyroid problems, check with your vet, your breeder, and other experienced Golden breeders before you get into long-term supplementation.

Testing is rather tricky and should be handled by a veterinarian familiar with thyroid problems and this breed. Dogs who are diagnosed with hypothyroidism should be retested annually to continue therapeutic levels of the hormone. Most breed experts agree that dogs with hypothyroidism should not be used for breeding.

Subvalvular Aortic Stenosis (SAS)

This disease is as bad as it sounds. A dog with SAS will simply drop over dead without any other symptoms or a moment's warning. The disease involves a stricture in the left ventricle of the heart, which restricts the blood flow out of the heart, leading to sudden and unexpected death after normal activity or exercise.

As a hereditary disease, there appears to be greater incidence of SAS in certain lines or families of Golden Retrievers. Goldens as young as 8 to 16 weeks of age can be examined for SAS, although they should be re-evaluated at 12 to 24 months before they are considered as breeding candidates. Certification requires examination by a Board-certified veterinary cardiologist.

von Willebrand's disease (vWD)

vWD is the most common hereditary bleeding disorder in canines, wherein puppies inherit a lack of clotting ability from their parents. On certain tragic occasions, it isn't diagnosed until the dog is spayed or neutered and bleeds uncontrollably during surgery. von Willebrand's is sometimes also linked with hypothyroidism, creating a double whammy for those poor affected animals. Fortunately, a reliable blood test exists for vWD, and while the incidence of vWD appears to be low in Goldens, many breeders still test for the disease before breeding their Goldens.

Chapter 16

Problem Behaviors and Aggression

. . . .

In This Chapter

▶ Solving problem behaviors

▶ Recognizing signs of aggression

▶ Preventing aggression

. . . .

*T*he problem with most canine problem behaviors is the human who perceives it. If you were a dog, wouldn't you love to jump into dad's lap or dig in mom's pretty flower bed? These and other objectionable behaviors are fun and/or quite natural to the dog; humans are the ones who have decided that such conduct doesn't conform to the rules of their house or neighborhood.

This chapter deals with the good, the bad and the ugly of your dog's behavior and offers tips on handling the more common canine social misbehaviors. It also shows you how to be the alpha person in your golden home, which will prevent some typical top dog problem behaviors.

Jumping for Joy

Who among you haven't had muddy paw prints on your best white slacks or butted head to canine head when walking in the door? The dog was out-of-his-mind glad to see you, but you can't quite share his rowdy exuberance.

Jumping up is perfectly natural canine behavior. Your puppy has been doing it ever since he was about 3 weeks old. He jumped up to lick his mother's muzzle and started pouncing on his littermates before he left the whelping box and then progressed to jumping on gates or barriers or whatever else stood between him and the person on the other side. What's more, he was such a cutie he was rewarded for that behavior with a scratch behind the ear or even a healthy scoop into loving arms. Talk about reinforcement!

The usual prevent-it-before-it-becomes-a-habit theory is obviously hopeless under these circumstances, considering all that early positive reinforcement. As the "jumpee," your only option is reconditioning and teaching alternate behavior. That's not an impossible task, but it will take time, patience, and the absolute cooperation of your family (especially the kids) and your friends. You may have to run interference for your children on this issue. And if your friends refuse to cooperate, don't invite them over until your dog is 2 years old and fully trained. You might also remind them about those gritty paws on their designer slacks.

Consistency is a key element in correcting jumping. You cannot allow it one day and then correct it the next. Neither can anyone else. Never means never. Everyone means any human being who meets or sees your dog.

Also understand what you should *not* do when your dog or puppy jumps. Never make *his* jumping *your* joy! Your worst response is to pet or hug him. That will only encourage him to jump some more! He's already revved his motor because you came home from the movies or someone came to visit.

The following sections describe jump corrections. The most successful usually involve a leash or a spritzer bottle.

Use the leash

Start with your 4-foot leash on your puppy. When he starts to jump up on you or someone else, grasp the leash about 2 feet from the collar, give a quick snap downwards and sideways (so that you won't injure his young neck and throat), and command him "Off" in a firm voice. Don't use the word "Down" because he'll confuse that word with the obedience exercise. As soon as he has all four feet back on the ground, quietly (quiet is a key word here; he's already too exuberant!) tell him what a good boy he is. If he knows the Sit command, you can then immediately tell him to "Sit." *Now* he has done something you can praise him for. Use soft, easy praise so that he doesn't get excited and jump up again!

A bit of spritz

The spritzer technique works for some dogs. Fill a spray bottle with water. When your puppy starts to jump, tell him "Off" and squirt him with a gentle spritz of water. (You can also add a bit of lemon juice or vinegar.) Now turn your back and leave the room for a minute or so. Do not praise the puppy when you return. Keep the bottle near the front door or wherever jumping most occurs.

Try this for several days until the puppy shows some improvement in jumping situations. Once he demonstrates a little self control, skip the spray and add the Sit command as soon as you think he's tempted to jump up. Follow with the Sit-praise technique as described above.

Turn the other cheek

Isolation sometimes works well without the water spritz. When puppy jumps or starts to jump on you, say "Off!" and quickly turn away with your arms folded in front of you. Keep turned from the dog and refuse to look at him for a couple of minutes. Do not give any praise afterwards; just resume your normal behavior. The puppy should discover that every time he jumps he is deprived of your companionship, which is what the jumping was all about in the first place.

Try a shaker can

Some owners have success using a shaker can as a jump deterrent. Keep one by the front door and rattle it loudly as soon as he begins to jump. Say "Off!" and then praise him when all four feet hit the ground. Next give a Sit command and more praise because he's sitting nicely.

Shake hands

There's yet one more jumping correction if you're caught off guard outdoors and don't have a leash, spritzer bottle, or shaker can handy. (Face it: You can't be prepared *all* the time!) When he jumps up and you suddenly realize that you have no counter-conditioner available, quickly grasp his paws and hold them in the air. Don't squeeze; just grip them firmly, not painfully, and without moving or uttering a word. Eventually, he'll wonder how to get out of this predicament, and he'll start to whine or struggle. Wait a few more seconds and then let go and order him to "Sit" if he has learned that command.

These are jumping no-nos:

- ✔ **Do not bang him in the chest with your knee.** That can harm your puppy or adult dog, and he'll only learn to be afraid of you. Some dogs also view the knee as a game and become even more excited, which is exactly what you're trying to avoid.

- ✔ **Do not step on his back toes with your foot.** It's a clumsy maneuver that may injure his feet if you press on them and hurt both of you if you fail and fall down, as some folks do. And he will only learn to shy away from you rather than *not* jump up.

Jumping corrections for the kids

Training kids to not encourage jumping up is usually like putting water in a sieve. Little folks with their quick movements and squeaky voices stir up memories of the whelping box, and your puppy will instinctively chase or jump on children. In most families, there's usually one child a dog senses he can dominate, and that one becomes his equal, like his littermate. Those situations always call for parental intervention.

Set aside some time during the puppy's play period to work with the child and puppy together to teach him not to jump on his favorite target. With your puppy on a leash or long line and one end attached to your waist or belt to make sure that you have control, have the child move about nearby. When your puppy starts to jump or give chase, tug quickly on the leash, and speak your firmest "Off," then "Sit," and then praise. If he repeats the jump a second time, follow the "Off" and give another leash pop, then release and praise when he finally settles down.

You'll need to repeat this exercise several days in a row (more than once a day if possible), then once a week for a while until you get a solid take. That takes a heap of dedication, but if your child is typical, he'll be running away and screaming every time the puppy jumps. It will be easier to take corrective measures than play referee every time. Fortunately, the kids grow taller and bigger and less enticing for the pup. But do you want to wait that long? Kid-proofing takes time, but in the long run you will *save* precious time extricating your child from puppy misbehavior.

Checking out Counters

Once your puppy has a little leg under him, he will discover there's a whole new world "up there." Tables, counters, dressers . . . gosh, what fun! Your dinner and cosmetics are now at risk. Start preventive measures early before he learns about the joys of counter theft.

Use the old "set up the dog" routine. Place a tempting plate of something yummy near the counter's edge. When pup strolls past, he'll use his golden nose power to investigate the goody. You know what he's up to! When he wanders close and starts to sniff, give him a stern "Aaahh, aaahh!" and then watch him slink away. Use those mind reading techniques often while he's young and impressionable so that he'll grow up to believe you're always one step ahead of him.

If your dog succeeds in stealing tonight's main course or you discover that he's been inspecting counters in your absence, you'll have to set him up for self correction. Make three shaker cans and fasten them together with a length of thread taped to the tops. Tie another thread from the cans to a food lure that is secured to the counter so it won't fall down with the cans. Place the entire booby trap where the dog can grab it, then hide from view. A clattering pile of shaker cans should convince him that the sky has fallen, and he won't try it again. Be quick to pick up any edible food before he can recover from the shock and get rewarded anyway!

On and Off Furniture

If you hate dog hair on your dark wool slacks or in your face when you sleep, promise yourself you will not allow your Golden on your bed or furniture. It only takes one time, one tiny cuddle on the couch or easy chair, and he will believe it's okay all the time. Remember that reinforcement stuff?

If you've laid down firm rules about the furniture and you notice your puppy is tempted to join you on the couch, keep his leash or short collar tab on his collar. When he makes his move, snap his lead and tell him "No!" Repeat several times to reinforce your message.

If you're desperate to sit and snuggle with your puppy while you read or watch TV, just slide down onto the floor beside the couch and enjoy those moments at his level.

You can also offer your Golden his own easy chair and allow him on only that piece of furniture. Just invite him up, and he'll remember. If he tries to climb on something else, snap his lead and take him over to "his" chair and tell him "Up." It's tough sharing your chair with a dog who takes up more room than you do!

Golden Diggers

Some dogs dig, while others never do. Digging holes is a naturally doggie thing to do, but it can drive an avid gardener to his compost pile. If your yard looks like a mini-minefield thanks to your digging Golden, try to identify the reason for his behavior before you despair and pour a concrete lawn.

- **Boredom.** Digging is most often the result of boredom. You own this Golden for companionship. He's figured that out, too. Companions forge their bond through regular play and exercise together. Without that kind of stimulation, your Golden may turn to digging or other creative forms of destructive behavior to alleviate his boredom or malaise.

- **Other misbehavior.** Perhaps his digging is an extension of indoor misbehavior. Any mishaps in the house of late? If so, treat the indoor problem first and then look to resolve the outdoor situation.

- **Air-conditioning.** If you think he's digging because he's hot and wants a cool, damp earth spa to lay his body in during summer weather, set out a small child's swimming pool or move him to a cooler location indoors. Of course, you must do the obvious and make sure that he has access to shade and cool drinking water throughout the day.

- **Pedicure time.** Are his nails trimmed and short? Long, unclipped nails automatically lend themselves to soil-tilling habits. If you don't clip his nails, ask your vet to show you how or have a groomer do it for you.

- **Romance.** Is he digging under fences in search of romance and wild women? Beef up that fence and arrange to have him neutered ASAP.

To stop the digging, you can also booby trap the hole with buried chicken wire, hot pepper, or even the dog's own feces, so he'll scratch into them and become disgusted with his digging site. Puppies are more prone to dig, but take heart! They usually outgrow the habit.

As with most things doggie, the best solution is prevention. If you can't supervise him, keep him indoors and out of holes and pool halls. If your dog could talk, he'd tell you that digging is a natural and self-rewarding behavior and only *you* find it offensive.

Eating Feces

Eating feces is a common problem that usually occurs at some time during many a dog's life. It's called *coprophagia,* and although it's disgusting, it's rarely harmful and it happens in the best of canine families. In the wild, canine scavengers scrounge for their meals and find partially digested food in another animal's feces, yukky as that may be to humans.

Closer to home, your puppy's mom, for example, cleaned up after all her pups because her instincts compelled her to remove evidence of their presence from possible predators. Remember, she didn't know this was the 21st century.

Amid these and other theories that focus on dietary deficiencies, research has failed to produce a single reliable explanation or underlying cause for canine fecal ingestion.

Try a few yard tricks to discourage the habit:

- ✔ **The first, easiest, and most obvious is to pick up the stools at once.** He can't eat what isn't there, and he will probably outgrow the habit.

- ✔ **You can mine the stools with a few drops of Tabasco when the dog isn't looking.** Once he eats it, he should decide it's pretty awful stuff.

- ✔ **Try adding a bit of meat tenderizer to his food, which is supposed to reduce fecal palatability.** Two commercially available products called For-Bid and Distaste work reasonably well for many dogs.

The upside is that puppies who eat their stools seldom continue this practice into adulthood. The flip side is that if they eat another dog's stools, they could become infested with whatever parasites that animal may harbor. So it's worth the effort to eradicate the habit. (Improves dog kissing, too!)

Running Away

Unfortunately, there are no quick fixes for the dog who bolts, whether it's through the open front door or from the yard into the street. I could write volumes on boundary training outdoors and proofing your dog to Come, Sit, Stay, and Down under the most attractive of distractions. But the fact remains — your wonderful Golden buddy is still a dog. He's a creature of unpredictable instincts that can and usually will surface when you least expect them.

Boundary training will not contain your dog forever. The only guarantee in dog life is that your perfectly behaved 6- or 8-year-old dog *will* one day chase a single rabbit, pursue a wayward squirrel, or dash through the open door because he sees something only he finds incredibly tempting. When that happens, there are no second chances. Ask anyone who has ever lost their very beloved and "obedient" Golden under a set of truck tires.

Keep him on a leash. Fence your yard and lock the gate. Build a dog run or install invisible fencing. Do not take chances and don't trust your 5-year-old kid to walk him. This bundle of gold is a precious resource you can't afford to risk.

No Begging!

Begging is so easy to prevent that I say, "Shame on You" if your Golden does it. If you never feed your dog from the table or from your plate during or immediately after a meal, he'll never learn to expect it. Isn't that simple? And no handouts when you're preparing meals or snacking in the kitchen or anywhere else. Hang tough with your kids on this issue, too.

A very young puppy should be crated when the family eats. An older pup who has had some training should do a Down-Stay on his dog mat or away from the table when you eat. You thus eliminate temptation and add one more reminder that you run the ship.

The Scourge of Separation Anxiety

You can avoid the demon of separation distress and anxiety. If you condition your puppy to being left alone in his crate (briefly) from his first days at home, he will automatically learn that your comings and goings are part of his every day routine, and he won't become upset by that. That also further ensures he won't develop the problem when he's older.

Always keep your departures and returns low key. Don't shower him with big displays of attention or affectionate good-byes when you leave the house or come back home. That can create separation distress where none exists! Bear in mind that the dog is a pack animal and, like Adam, was not meant to be alone.

Incremental absences

Start by teaching him to stay in his crate while you're at home, working in another room or in the yard. If he's a crate guy (and he should be), he'll just curl up in his den and take a nap.

Vary the length of time that you're away, 10 minutes one day, a half hour the next.

If you feel (or hear!) that he becomes agitated as soon as you leave, do lots of practice runs. Calmly put on your coat, pick up your car keys, step out the door and close it, come immediately back in, release him from his crate, and give a Down command. When he's down and quiet, calmly praise him. Do this for a week or two and gradually increase and vary the time you stand outside the door.

Do *not* offer sympathy or sweet talk like "Oooohh, did my big baby miss her momma?" Also never punish him for his anxiety. Both techniques will make it worse.

Tasty rewards

To make your departure less stressful for your Golden (only if he's stressed!), try a little peanut butter. Spread a small dab on a Nylabone or press it inside a sterilized hard bone and give it to him just before you leave the house. It will create a pleasant association with your leaving and will keep him happily occupied while you're gone. He should always have a good chewie or two for solitary munching.

Background noise and music

Leave the radio on while you're gone (soothing music please, no heavy metal or hard rock) to keep him company and muffle any outside sounds that might agitate him. A television also works, and of course a night light if you're out after dark.

Enhance his environment

If your dog is uncrated while you're gone (surely not a puppy, though . . .) and you see signs of stress due to your absence, you might try a little "environmental enrichment" to cheer him up.

Environmental enrichment is a lifestyle concept used in zoos and animal parks that may work wonders for your nonstop Golden. Zoo exhibits today have moats and caves and climbing structures to entertain their charges. Modern zookeepers deliberately hide the animals' food in cracks, crevices, trees, and even plastic containers!

Of course, you can't replicate in-the-wild inside your home, and it would be dumb to put his food bowl in a tree. But you can modify these simple methods and offer your dog your own version of environmental enrichment.

A window to the world

The simplest extra is to allow access to a windowsill so that he can survey his "territory" while you're gone.

Be careful about this. You should only give windowsills to well-mannered dogs who have earned full house privileges. Some dogs go bonkers when they see the mailman or another animal outside. You don't need scarred up windowsills or a broken window. Do a few test runs and observe his behavior from a hiding place indoors or outside to see whether he can handle it.

Self-propelled toys

You can provide challenging and stimulating doggie activities with self-propelled "Boomer Balls" that move about randomly and challenge a dog's curiosity and predatory instincts.

If he's a chow hound, try leaving him a sustained-release food device. One commercial gadget called the Buster Cube holds food kibbles or freeze-dried liver. The multichambered cube releases food tidbits one or two pieces at a time as the dog pushes or rolls it with his nose or paw.

Make sure that he's in a room or area where he won't topple the furniture when the chase is on.

Exercise

Exercise, the great canine cure-all, also helps. A dog who is tired mentally and physically is more likely to fall asleep once he accepts your absence. An exercised dog is more content; he's had his bonding time and feels secure again.

Thunderphobia and Noise Sensitivity

If your dog is afraid of loud noises such as thunderstorms or firecrackers, you can try some counter-conditioning to help him overcome those fears. The protocol is a long and delicate process, but worth the effort because of the potential risk and danger to the dog (running away during a storm, injury jumping over a fence) and destruction of property during his fright.

Gradual exposure

Make a recording of the offending noise. Then expose him to the noise by playing it softly at a low level that won't upset him. If he appears tense or uneasy, reduce the sound level until he is calm and relaxed. Conduct the sessions during meal times and petting sessions to create a positive association.

Begin with short sessions, but increase the volume at each one over whatever period of time it takes to relax him with each increased noise volume. Continue very gradually until the dog shows no fear of the noise.

Do not sympathize

Never coddle your dog when he shows signs of fear because that will only encourage the behavior. You should also provide a safe, enclosed place such as a crate with a blanket over it, but don't lock it or confine him in any way. He needs to retain a sense that he can escape if he so chooses. He may choose a dark corner or hide under the bed. Hard as it will be, just ignore his behavior at that time.

Drugs such as Valium and other tranquilizers do not provide a long-term solution to the problem. Sound sensitivity usually gets worse with age, so treat the signs as soon as they appear.

In extreme cases, however, you can discuss the use of tranquilizers with your vet.

Holiday noises

With a thunderphobic dog you need to be especially careful on holidays like New Year's Eve and July 4th. Loud fireworks nearby could send him over the edge. Stay with him in a quiet room, play a radio with soothing music to block the noise, and never allow him outdoors during a noisy celebration.

You can purchase a tape recording made for the very purpose of counter conditioning to thunder and other loud noises such as gunfire, traffic, sirens and crowd noises.

Food Guarding

Food guarding doesn't happen overnight. Your puppy will give you warning signs, and if you ignore them, he'll get wolflike and protect his toys as well as his food.

Look back in time. Does he occasionally stop chewing when you approach him while he's eating, maybe just keep his head tucked in the bowl and kind of freeze in place without munching? Does he ever, even once, grumble at the kids or you during his meal? That's a growl, plain and simple, and it's not necessary or acceptable.

Reprogram his meal time. Start by placing his food bowl in an open area. If he eats in a corner, it will encourage him to expect privacy and will allow him to exert control over his personal space when he's eating.

Divide his kibble into small amounts so that you have to pick up his bowl to refill it a few times during each meal. After a few days, leave his food bowl down and squat down to add the small portions as he finishes each one. Occasionally, toss a goodie like a cube of cheese or baloney into the bowl while he eats.

When food guarding occurs, you can bet your food budget there are other problems in your dog relationship. Somewhere along the chow line he has acquired the upper paw. He's probably also possessive of his toys or a favorite bone and you just haven't noticed. Go back to the basics (that's obedience training, but you already knew that) to remind him you're the one who buys the dog food and his toys. Make him Sit before he gets his food pan; put him on a Down-Stay for a hour once a day. No on-demand petting or treating. As with meals, he has to Sit or Down submissively before he gets his TLC. Don't worry — he won't mind that. He needs a leader, not a lover.

Play in his toy box and practice there as well. Tell him to "Sit," remove his toy, and give him a tidbit or another toy in return. If he growls or refuses to release, snap on his leash at once and reinforce the Sit or Down, and no more tidbits when he does. Quiet praise, that's all. When you fail to stay in charge, he'll be first in line to take your place!

Recognizing Real Aggression

Not all puppies come with the potential for aggression. But within every dog pack, there's a broad spectrum of personalities, even in a breed like the Golden Retriever, which is famous for its sweetheart temperament.

While play-biting is normal puppy behavior, other symbolic behaviors are definite warning signs that canine aggression lurks inside your puppy's head.

- **Snatching or guarding of toys.** Beware of the puppy who growls or curls a lip when you take his toys away or who snatches them up when you approach.

- **Chronic refusal to let go.** Puppies or dogs who won't release their grip on toys are subtly moving toward an aggressive position.

- **Growling.** While some dogs are naturally vocal, there *is* a detectable difference in their message. Never underestimate growling or allow it for any reason.

- **Refusal to obey known commands, lie down on command, or give up a sleeping area.** He's testing you. Put on his leash and start from scratch.

- **Stops eating when you approach his food dish.** Food guarding is a prelude to a dog bite.

- **Mounts your children or another family member.** Mounting is not a sexual gesture. It's an act of dominance with the dog demonstrating his alpha status. It is *not* cool to dismiss it as a macho, studly act. Tell him "Off!" in a stern voice and offer alternate behavior, a Sit or Down, and then quiet praise. Some experts suggest you distract the dog by spraying it with water or a water-vinegar mix immediately when the dog begins to mount. The key word here is *immediate*.

Getting rough with your dog or puppy will not control or eliminate aggressive behavior. It will, in fact, only heighten his defense response and increase his aggression. *Training* is the key, and the earlier the better. The leash and collar are your best tools, but you also need a good understanding of canine psychology and some assistance from a qualified trainer who will work with you and your dog. It's not hopeless.

People often overlook or dismiss the preceding signals because the behavior may look like playful or innocent exuberance. And most often the aggression doesn't become an in-your-face problem until the onset of puberty. It's also more common in male dogs when the male hormone testosterone starts to flow.

Unfortunately, children are often the first to confront canine play aggression because of their small size and their own high-energy activities.

If you see signs of aggression during play, immediately stop the game. You effectively penalize your dog or puppy by depriving him of his favorite play-mate — you. Repeated displays of aggressive behavior may be evidence of a serious problem that warrants the attention of a qualified animal behaviorist.

Establishing Yourself as Alpha Dog

In order to be an effective golden leader, the alpha person, or top dog, you have to act the part. (Faking it won't do — your dog is smarter than you are.) Leaders do more than just give orders. Your every day interactions can rein-force your alpha position to your dog. If you recall that what is clear to you is not always clear to the dog, you'll know the reverse is also true and that even your very subtle behaviors will be obvious to him. These simple daily maneu-vers will remind your Golden — the insecure dog as well as the one who's got an eyeball on your job — that you're the Big Kahuna.

Your golden goal is a happy and successful life together. To that end, always remember that dogs are groupies by heredity. In order to feel secure, they have to understand the hierarchy of their pack. If a wolf or other pack animal doesn't know who's in charge or he senses a weak leader, he'll try to assume that position for himself because every pack requires a leader (*the alpha dog*) in order to survive. It's that alpha syndrome, the top-dog business I talk about so much, a survival instinct that goes back to the time of Noah. Someone has to set the rules or havoc reigns. Or "Havoc" runs away or even bites.

Dogs are not unhappy or disgruntled with this totem pole arrangement. The truth is, they feel safe and protected knowing that they have a leader who is strong, protects the pack from bad guys, and keeps the other family members in their place. And as social creatures, they are happy knowing they have pleased their leader.

Dogs like and need a strong (but gentle) leader; it defines their world and gives them parameters to follow. Leadership is the best gift you can give your dog. In wild dog packs, everything happens after the leader, the alpha dog, has eaten, been there-done that, or gives permission.

Given that your Golden's pack instincts are so deep and primitive, you should have no trouble achieving leader status if you master good communication skills.

Setting the ground rules

Because play and aggression seem to be opposite behaviors, dog owners are shocked when their otherwise sweet Golden gets a bit testy or threatening during play time. (Hmmm, did he *really* mean to be so nasty? The answer is — yes!) Aggressive "play" like wrestling, tug-of-war, or rough physical play almost always escalates into the real thing (because your Golden is, after all, a dog). As if I haven't already said it a dozen times, obedience is your best insurance against such a happening.

You can (and should) avoid canine "play aggression" by incorporating a few simple ground rules into your most common and everyday interactions with your Golden.

- ✔ **Avoid games that involve direct physical contact such as tug-of-war and wrestling, which are dominance-related activities.** Don't create situations that put you at odds or in conflict with your dog. It will just confuse him and dilute the effectiveness of your training.

- ✔ **Practice the "Come" and "Down" commands every day by incorporating them into all your interactions with your dog, including play.** (This is only after your dog has mastered those commands — see Chapter 9.) One helpful reminder is to do them during television commercials. Promise yourself and your puppy at least one long Down-Stay during every TV evening. These exercises preserve your dog's opinion of you as the head-honcho of his pack. It is *not* mean — your dog will actually love you *more*.

- ✔ **When playing with your dog, periodically assert control by stopping the game and commanding him into a Sit-Stay or Down-Stay.** Don't be grouchy about it — make it fun. Use a pleasant firm voice and always praise him for his compliance.

- ✔ **If your game involves a play object like a ball, tell your dog to "Give" or "Drop it."** If he frequently does not sit or drop his toy, review your training methods and look carefully for other signs that he may be testing you (see the next section) or trying to move into a leadership position. (Understand that these are unconscious canine maneuvers. Your dog will sense your weakness, and his ancient instincts will push *him* to push *you*.)

- ✔ **Just like a child, your Golden doesn't need a buddy (or littermate), he needs a parent (leader).** All humans should be alpha in your dog's perception, but you have to be the boss first before he will identify other people in that role.

- ✔ **Establish your leadership through positively reinforced obedience training.** For the average dog owner, dog-leadership does not come naturally (the cuddle principle). Most people have to work at it, and that means training classes with an experienced instructor.

✔ **Make sure that your children also observe the rules on play aggression.** Unfortunately, children are often the first to confront canine play aggression because of their small size and squeaky voices and their tendency to be more physical in play.

Living successfully with a puppy, even a Golden one, requires a new awareness of your family dynamics. Be alert for signs that your puppy is testing other family members, especially the children. Dogs instantly recognize little people as vulnerable, and they instinctively move to dominate them.

Signs of aggression

Aggression is the No. 1 problem in canine behavior today, and, sad to say, Goldens are no exception. Your Golden must respect every family member and treat outsiders like relatives or he will become an insurance liability and you can end up in court.

This quickie quiz will tell you if your Golden is entering the danger zone.

✔ **Does your dog frequently bite or nip at hands and feet?** Nip that habit in the bud fast. It won't go away by itself.

✔ **Can you approach your dog or touch him when he's eating?** Can you put your hand into his food dish? Does he growl or stop eating when you go near his food bowl? If he stops chewing and just stands there like a stone, he'll soon progress to growling — bet on it.

✔ **Will your dog get off the furniture or bed when you request it?** If he refuses, will he allow you to forcibly remove him? Does he growl or show his teeth if you try?

✔ **Can you take a toy, a bone, food, or any forbidden object out of your dog's mouth without a struggle?** Does he growl, curl his lips (he is *not* smiling), or snatch it up when you approach?

✔ **Will your dog allow you to touch all of his body parts without a struggle?** Can you hold his paws, examine his ears and teeth, or check his belly and his private parts? Does he growl or show his teeth at any time?

✔ **Can each of your family members do all these maneuvers without threat?**

If you or your dog fail even one single question, you have a serious problem that will not go away. Rough treatment is not an acceptable solution. Your dog will simply cave in to his canine instincts and respond more aggressively. You need professional help now. Find a qualified obedience trainer or behavior specialist.

Exercise your leadership

It's imperative when dealing with a dominant or aggressive dog that you become his leader in no uncertain terms. Use these symbolic (to your dog) practices every day to remind your Golden you're the top dog in the house. Remember the big P in Practice and you'll soon do these things automatically.

- **Always enter or leave first when you go inside or outside.** When you leave the house or open the yard gate or your car door, insist that your dog wait while you go in first. (It's part of his obedience training anyway.) That tells him the territory belongs to you, not him. This same principle applies indoors as well. Never step over or around your dog when you walk through a doorway or down a hall. Gently order him to move.

  In my own Golden family, two dogs are rather insecure by nature and will leap up if I as much as step in their direction. My "middle-of-the-roader" will first check out what I want him to do, and my two extremely confident — and dominant — Goldens don't budge an inch unless I tell them to! Fortunately, their early in-depth training established who was top dog in this house.

- **Eat your meals before you feed your dog.** Your dog should not eat before you do. In the wild, the alpha dog chows down first, and lesser pack members snivel in the background waiting for the leftovers. Eat your own meals before your feed your dog. If your dog's meals are scheduled around your own breakfast and supper times, be sure that you feed him after you have eaten. Put him on a Down-Stay or in his crate. Your Golden's canine mentality will get the message. (Of course no begging at the table! That's also bottom-line good manners.)

- **Make him earn his meals.** Require that he sit before you offer him his food dish. Ditto for his cookies. When you give him treats, make him obey some command, Sit or Down or Speak, before he gets a goodie. The plus here is that you're also giving him more opportunities to succeed and demonstrate what he knows, which will build his confidence and your leadership at the same time.

- **Do not pet your dog when he nudges you with his nose or paw (in dog language, ordering you to pet him) or "just because you love him."** As with food treats, petting must be earned by first obeying a command. Give a simple command and then pet upon response. (If he fails to respond to your command, you now have *two* issues to work on!)

- **When you pet your dog, roll him over and rub his tummy.** It's a submissive posture he'll enjoy. This petting principle is not a "forever" rule, just one to be implemented during troublesome behaviors or occasionally as a reminder of who's boss. However, never pet a dog who is growling or continue to pet a dog who growls for more.

Protecting her young

The one exception to most biting rules applies to dams with nursing pups. Even the sweetest bitch will protect her whelp if she perceives a threat. That threat may be unjustified, but you'll never convince her of that; these are her kids, and this is her job! Some bitches won't even allow certain family members near their babies, and maybe only Mom or Dad can enter the whelping room or touch the puppies.

However, most Golden mothers are of the sweet variety and will tolerate visitors if their security person is there to reassure her. But watch her eyes grow wide with apprehension. She's not too happy with strangers near her pups. It's always best to keep things private for the first three or four weeks, until the dam indicates she's ready to have company.

✔ **Implement a 30-minute Down-Stay every day.** All dogs should be proficient on the Down command (see Chapter 9). It's one of your most important (and convenient) training tools.

✔ **Give a command only once.** When you give a command, say it firmly only once and mean it. If he does not respond, help him to perform the behavior, but don't repeat the command. As insurance, never give a command you're not prepared to reinforce, and never give one if you think he won't or is unable to comply. It sets you both up for failure. If you're looking at chronic noncompliance, you already know what you have to work on.

Believe it or not, your Golden will actually feel more secure without those subtle power struggles and will be happier knowing you're the boss.

Aggression and Euthanasia

Sadly, more than 50 percent of all puppies will not be in their original homes at the end of their first year. Behavior problems are cited as the single most common reason for giving up a dog. The majority of those pups will end up in animal shelters and ultimately euthanized.

Adult dogs are equally at risk. Aggression in adult dogs is the most serious behavior problem encountered by veterinarians and dog trainers. According to the Humane Society of the United States, more than 4.5 million dog bites occur annually. Even worse, it's estimated that several times that number go unreported every year.

The real heartbreak with most aggressive Goldens is that they are sweet and loving most of the time. Then, often for no apparent reason, they bite the hand outstretched to pet them. How often doesn't matter. Even one serious bite, even for some imagined provocation, is a serious problem.

That single dog bite, anytime or any place, can have far-reaching consequences. Whether your dog bites you, another family member, or a guest, a host of other problems may arise depending on the state and county of your residence: criminal citations, liability issues with insurance companies, civil suits, small to enormous expenses from emergency room fees to plastic surgery, and the ultimate heartbreak, euthanasia.

Be honest about this. If your dog is a threat to strangers or to your own family, you must take every step necessary to rehabilitate the animal. You'll need help from a professional. You also must be realistic and accept the fact that some Goldens cannot be rehabbed and should be euthanized. If you love your Golden, help him across to the Rainbow Bridge before he hurts someone else and you have to deal with more regrets.

Part IV
The Part of Tens

The 5th Wave   By Rich Tennant

"If you wouldn't throw them out the window, he wouldn't retrieve them."

In this part . . .

This is the fun part. Standard in all *For Dummies* books, the Part of Tens is made up of several short-and-sweet chapters that give you ten or so tips on a variety of topics. Whether it's puppy games or ways to lengthen your Golden's life, you can find a lot of important material in this quick-read part.

Chapter 17

Ten Great Games to Play with Your Puppy

One of the great gifts of golden adolescence is your puppy's joyful exuberance in everything he does. And lucky you — you get to be a part of it! An important part of the total golden experience is having fun together. Puppy games not only enhance the bond between you and your pup, but they also tire him out, a luxury you'll treasure at the end of a busy puppy day. In this chapter, I share my favorite puppy pastimes as well as explain a couple of definite playtime no-nos.

Fun, Fun, Fun . . . and Short!

Make sure that all your play-teaching sessions are fun and successful. Keep them short so that you don't tax his attention span. Take advantage of your puppy's dependence on you and his strong desire to be near you and play with you. His confidence will grow as fast as his little legs and body.

Follow Me!

Your puppy must never discover that it's fun or okay to run away from you, indoors or out, even when you're playing. Teach him to run *after* you instead by inventing games that encourage that behavior. If he's a little slow, pretend that you're racing and simply run in place or take tiny steps so that he can catch you. Whoop and holler, act like an idiot, and tell him "Good boy, Come!" — what a great adventure to outflank your mom!

When your puppy runs away from you, don't run after him because he will consider that a game of chase. To trick him into coming back, kneel down on the ground and pretend you found a treasure. Talk excitedly to this invisible object, even scratch and paw at the ground. Your puppy will come over to investigate, and you can calmly snag his collar.

Puppy Catch

Two people sit on the floor across from each other, 10 or 15 feet apart, with one of them holding and petting the puppy. Have the other person call the puppy with a silly happy voice, "Puppy, Come, puppy, puppy, puppy!" Open your arms wide when you call and praise and hug the puppy when he comes.

You can incorporate a ball or toy into the game and toss the toy back and forth for him to retrieve. Let him fetch the toy, give him a treat to release it, and then toss the toy across to the other person. That person hugs and praises him when he gets the toy, gives a treat, and tosses it back to person No. 1.

Kiss Me, Kate!

Kiss me on command is a snap to teach. (It isn't exercise, but it's something you'll both enjoy forever.)

Puppies, especially Goldens, are automatic licking machines. Just tell him "Kiss, kiss, goood boy, kiss!" every time he licks you. He'll be more than happy to oblige! Puppy breath doesn't last very long, so make the most of this one while you can!

Hide and Seek

Play outdoor fun games like hide and seek. It will help teach the Come command as well as reinforce your protector-leadership position.

Wait until he sniffs the grass or gets distracted. Then slip behind a tree where he can't see you. Peek out to see when he discovers you're gone and comes running back to find you. As soon as he gets near, come out, clap your hands happily, and call him, "Puppy, Come." Squat down with arms outstretched to hug him as he races toward you. Trust me, he will come running!

Fetch!

Sit on the kitchen floor and toss a favorite toy for your puppy to chase and bring back. "Puppy, Fetch." Your word association games start now. As he's bringing back the toy, say "Puppy, Come!" When he returns with the toy, be sure to let him hold on to it for just a moment or two before you take it from him for two reasons.

- ✔ He'll know he's being praised for bringing back the toy.
- ✔ He won't get the idea that you'll take his toy away every time he brings it back.

When he gives up the toy, tell him "Drop" and use that Good Boy praise. If he doesn't release the toy, remove it gently from his mouth while saying "Drop." Throw the toy again with lots of happy talk and praise him as he races across the kitchen floor to take it. He is discovering that fetching is fun and coming back to you means praise and hugs. And he's learning his New Word game. You're already started on "Fetch," "Come," and "Drop."

A second version of the retrieving game uses two toys. Give him the first toy and put the other one in your pocket. Praise him when he takes the first toy and, after a minute, show him the second one and flash it about excitedly. Toss it and when he runs to get it, pick up the first toy and repeat the toss rotation. You can add a third toy if you wish. Pick up the toys as he drops them and continue to exchange toys and let him run around with them in this fashion several times. Remember to back up as you praise him to encourage him to come to you. Get creative and invent your own version of this game. Keep the sessions short and stop the game when his interest level is still high. And *always* stop if he slows down or loses interest.

Okay, I know that's only *five* puppy games. Your job here is to discover or invent five more fun ways to play with your puppy!

No Tug of War

Never play tug-of-war with your puppy or adult Golden with his toys or any other object. Tug-of-war is a dominance game, and your dog should never enter any situation, even in play, where he is at opposition with his boss.

No Teasing, Please

When playing with your puppy, don't do anything to confuse him or make him apprehensive. Kids especially often think it's fun to tease a puppy and show him a toy and then hide it or pretend to throw it. Please don't let that happen. Explain that it will make the puppy distrustful and resentful, and he won't want to play any more.

Chapter 18

Ten Internet Web Sites for the Golden Retriever Believer

*T*he vastness of the Internet never ceases to amaze. Dog lovers in general, and Golden Retriever owners in particular, can surf the 'Net for information about everything doggy, from breed specific information to general care, training, canine legislation, and more and then move on to chat rooms where you can just brag about your special Golden. This chapter suggests several Web sites of particular interest to owners of companion Goldens as well as the die-hard Golden competitor.

Golden Retriever Club of America

`grca.org`

The national breed club for the Golden Retriever offers an excellent Web site that provides a bountiful menu of golden topics and selections. Books, general breed information, regional breed clubs, and local contacts . . . just about everything golden is just a click away.

Encyclopedia of Canine Veterinary Medical Information

`vetinfo.com/dencyclopedia/deindex.html`

This site will give you a brief synopsis and explanation of almost every canine illness and disease, the symptoms, and commonly suggested treatments.

Working Retriever Central

working-retriever.com

WRC includes information on all types of retrievers.

Goldensafield

goldensafield.com

This Web site is not restricted to merely field Goldens as the name may imply. It is dedicated to those enthusiasts who are interested in the improved health, well-being, and functional longevity of the Golden by relaying information on health and research issues.

Golden Retrievers in Cyberspace

golden.retriever.com

This site is dedicated to helping rescue Golden Retrievers and Golden Retriever rescue groups. (Bless them!) It also includes a comprehensive list of links to other Golden-related resources on the Web.

VetGen

vetgen.org

VetGen is a Web site devoted to veterinary genetic disease control research and genetic disease detection services for all purebred animals. Breeders and dog owners combine VetGen resources with other DNA data to target and eliminate genetic disease in their preferred breeds.

American Kennel Club (AKC)

akc.org

AKC is a not-for-profit organization that maintains a purebred dog registry, sanctions dog events, and promotes responsible dog ownership. The AKC Web site offers a wealth of doggy information on health care, training, puppy selection, national breed club contacts, and breeder referral by state and by national breed club, breed registration, and, of course, details on AKC sanctioned events and programs.

Dog Owner's Guide

canismajor.com/dog/guide.html

This collection of previously published articles (from the tabloid of the same name) brings you articles on a variety of dog-related issues of interest to the pet owners as well as owners of the show dog.

Yahoo!Pets

pets.yahoo.com

Even Yahoo! gets into the dog act with its own Web site offering a wide variety of information for the dog lover.

Chapter 19

Ten Things in Your Golden Retriever's Bag of Tricks

In This Chapter

▶ Shining in the ring and field

▶ Mastering basic puppy retrieving

▶ Serving society

*W*hatever your personal golden dream, this breed has proven it can do it all. In this chapter, I applaud the Golden's amazing versatility. You'll be awed and inspired at the vastness of this breed's accomplishments. And maybe, just maybe, you'll be tempted to dip your dog's paws into something more exciting than a daily run around the park and TV talk shows.

Despite the Golden Retriever's ability to excel at almost every activity devised for dogs, about 95 percent of all Goldens serve as all-American bed warmers and family companions. Nevertheless, you should still know what's in your Golden's genetic bag of tricks.

Blue Ribbon Performers: Conformation

If *conformation* sounds a little stuffy, just switch to "showing dogs." Dog shows are basically a Miss and Mr. Golden Retriever beauty contest. The winners earn points that apply toward the future title of show champion, which appears as a Ch. before his name on his pedigree. Show Goldens are judged on the physical properties listed in the breed standard in Chapter 2.

Grooming and Gaiting

If you hope to show your Golden, you have to learn how to *gait* your dog, a term that refers to how your Golden walks and trots. Of course, you also have to spiff him up so that the judge can decide who is the fairest of them all. Proper grooming is an art and one that could affect a judge's opinion of your dog. Gaiting is another major aspect of showing that you both need to master.

You can't teach gaiting by yourself. You need an experienced person to evaluate your dog and help you get started. If you purchased your puppy from a show breeder, work with her to decide if your pup has show potential. Try to find a Golden Retriever club in your area or join a local kennel club where you'll meet other people who show their own breeds in conformation. Attend dog shows and talk to Golden Retriever exhibitors. Your veterinarian can direct you to a breeder or a club so that you can meet other dog show fanciers. If your beloved Golden has no show potential, love him for all his other fine qualities and consider purchasing your next Golden from a reliable breeder with a good track record who will be willing to help you get started.

Obedience Competition: More Than Good Manners

The constant parade of Golden Retrievers on the TV screen, in print ads, and sale catalogs continues to amaze me. One thing is clear: This dog is trainable. Given the breed's tractability and incredible desire to please, most Goldens excel at learning details, which makes them easy dogs to train. In the world of obedience competition, Golden Retrievers always number among the top performers in all categories. In fact, every year more Golden Retrievers become obedience trial champions (OTCh) than any other breed.

Obedience shows are another ring activity, only this time looks don't count. Your Golden will have to master several basic obedience routines (stuff you already learned in basic obedience class) and achieve qualifying scores (a minimum of 170 out of a possible 200 points) in three different obedience shows to earn a title that will appear after his name on his pedigree. It's easy, and it's fun for both of you!

Obedience titles are earned on three levels of competition, with each level presenting a greater degree of difficulty. In the Novice class, you earn a CD (Companion Dog) title, and in the Open class you earn a CDX (Companion Dog Excellent). The Utility class offers a UD (Utility Dog) title.

A dog has to come up through the ranks and earn his obedience titles from the bottom up. Each class also offers placement awards of first through fourth place, so if your Golden performs his exercises to near perfection, he can earn a trophy, too.

If you'd like to dabble in obedience, find a training club or check with a local kennel club for classes in advanced obedience. The American Kennel Club will send you its booklet *Rules and Regulations for Obedience Competition* if you write to the Club. You should also invest in a book or two devoted to obedience training.

Goldens in the Field: Hunting, Hunt Tests, Field Trials, and the WCX

Now you're into feathers and retrieving birds. Does your Golden go bonkers to retrieve, not just birds but even nonbird objects? Is he out of hunting stock? Do you plan to use him as a hunting partner? If you'd like to fulfill the heritage envisioned by Lord Tweedmouth (see Chapter 2), you have lots of choices.

Hunting

If your outdoor passion is waterfowl or upland game and your Golden is from hearty hunting stock, that Golden nose will lead you to unspeakable pleasures in the field. Of course, you'll have to deal with a muddy dog, cockleburs, and other field debris in his Golden coat, but a game bag stuffed with birds is worth it.

Like all performance athletes, a good hunting dog needs fine-tuning before he knocks your socks off in the field. For best results, team up with other hunters or field trainers when your Golden is still young to build good retrieving habits early in the game. A well-trained hunting retriever will be the envy of your hunting buddies, but well trained is the key phrase here. If this is your first hunting experience or your first working retriever, find a professional trainer or people involved in the sport to learn the basic principles of field training that your dog will need to become a good hunting partner. Beg, borrow, or buy a few books on training a retriever for the field.

Hunting tests

Hunting tests are designed for the noncompetitive sportsman who may or may not actually hunt, but wants to work with his retriever in the field. Sponsored by the American Kennel Club (AKC), the United Kennel Club (UKC), and/or the North American Hunting Retriever Association, hunting tests consist of three or more stakes designed to test a retriever's natural abilities with graduated levels of difficulty. The tests are pass-fail, and each dog is judged against a standard of performance and does not have to out-work another dog in order to qualify.

Launched in 1985, the AKC retriever hunting tests have grown into a major event in the world of sporting dogs. Retriever owners and their dogs (real-life hunting dogs as well as retrievers who just love birds, water, and retrieving) work with freshly shot game birds (ducks and pheasants) under simulated hunting conditions to prove their dogs' natural hunting ability. Dogs who complete the requirements as set forth by the AKC rules for hunting tests receive a corresponding title, which will appear after the dog's name on his pedigree.

A *JH (Junior Hunter) title* (the first testing level) requires four qualifying scores or legs. Dogs must complete two simple retrieves on land and two in water at short distances of under 100 yards. The *SH (Senior Hunter) title* requires five legs earned in land and water tests that include multiple retrieves with greater difficulty than the junior test. A *Master Hunter (MH)* needs six legs to earn that title. A Master dog must complete multiple complex retrieving tasks on land and in water and work under more difficult and challenging conditions.

At all three title levels, dogs are judged on their own performance and are not eliminated because another dog did a better job. Because the tests are non-competitive, the atmosphere is more relaxed and friendly, and participants are more supportive of the other dogs entered in each stake. But as with actual hunting, you need to train your dog before you jump in with both barrels. Find a professional trainer or experienced retriever people to work with. You can find working retriever owners in retriever clubs or sportsman's clubs that cater to hunting enthusiasts. Write to AKC for *Regulations and Guidelines for AKC Hunting Tests for Retrievers*.

Wait! There's more. UKC and NAHRA also offer a noncompetitive hunting test program complete with game birds, gun safety provisions and titles for the dog. Rules and regulations are available from both organizations.

Field trials

Field trails are the grand daddy of sporting retriever events and date back to 1931. Licensed by the AKC, field trials are a big step up from hunting tests, and showcase the superstars of the working retriever world. Competition is ferocious, and only the best survive to capture the wins, placements, and points required to earn the title of Field Champion (FC) or Amateur Field Champion (AFC). Field championships are the most prized of working titles, particularly because this is an all-breed sport with Labradors, Goldens, and Chesapeakes competing on the same playing field.

Labradors routinely dominate field trials, with dozens of Labs earning titles annually compared to one or two Golden Retrievers. But it should be noted (in all fairness) that few Goldens run the field trial circuit, so the imbalance may be one of numbers rather than pure talent. However, if you think your Golden has the makings of a trial dog, be prepared for years of grueling training and competition.

Field trials differ from hunting tests because dogs are eliminated on the basis of their performance when compared to that of other competing dogs. Dogs are tested on both land and in water under more rigid circumstances than in hunting tests. The tests are designed on four ascending levels of difficulty to challenge both younger and more experienced dogs. The vast majority of the dogs entered have some degree of professional training, so a novice owner-handler is at a huge disadvantage.

I hate to sound discouraging, but this is an expensive and highly competitive sport that requires enormous dedication to training and a thick hide to endure inevitable failures. With 50 to 100 dogs competing in most stakes, and only four placements awarded, it's no wonder this is often called a loser's game. If you decide to try it, start with the best caliber Golden you can afford, purchased from a reliable breeder with field trial experience (as proven by the accomplishments of the breeder and the parents of the pups).

For the AKC *Field Trial Rules and Standard Procedure* manual, write directly to the AKC. As with hunting tests and hunting, training books and videos abound, and you'll be smarter and more successful if you read a few.

Working certificate tests

Finally, a field event devoted just to Golden Retrievers. *Working certificate tests* are very basic, noncompetitive field tests sponsored by the Golden Retriever Club of America to encourage and evaluate the instincts and natural abilities of Goldens in the field. The dogs are tested on both land and water against a set standard of performance, and they are not expected to perform anywhere near the level of the field trial or hunting test retriever.

Designed with two levels of difficulty, the *WC (Working Certificate)* requires a short (35 to 50 yards) double retrieve on land and two shorter single retrieves in the water. The *WCX (Working Certificate Excellent)* consists of a longer triple retrieve on land, a double retrieve in water, with a few additional requirements to demonstrate trainability in the dog. The tests are sponsored by GRCA member clubs across the country and open to all AKC-registered Goldens. Most clubs hold practice training sessions before the tests to offer assistance to newcomers and club members.

So if your Golden is a retrieve-a-holic or if he loves to hunt a little or a lot, these tests are excellent forums where you and your Golden can show off and have a grand time doing what he loves best. Complete rules and regulations are available from the GRCA secretary or from any area Golden Retriever Club.

If any or all of these events tweak your golden fancy, you can start your puppy field training right in your own backyard. Eventually, you'll have to move to more challenging areas, but basic puppy work is fun, backyard stuff.

Retrieving

Tennis ball, Frisbee, retrieving bumper, fallen branches — if your Golden is like mine, he will retrieve them all, and retrieve, and retrieve until he drops! This dog knows that retriever is the better half of his name!

Whether you plan a serious retrieving future for your Golden or just hope to have a little fun, the right start in retrieving basics will help you both enjoy his natural ability. The most important element in his retrieving life is his inherent enthusiasm for the job he was originally bred to do. Your job is to build on that enthusiasm with encouragement and success. The right start is especially important if you plan to train your Golden for hunting, hunting tests or field trials. He'll need a good foundation in basic retrieving skills. (Yes, he already knows how to retrieve, but he has to learn to do it *your* way.)

Here are some ways to build your puppy's retrieving foundation:

 - **Use a soft retrieving bumper.** Start your 7- or 8-week old puppy on a soft puppy bumper made from an old white sock (because white is highly visible) stuffed with any soft material. A soft paint roller is another good choice. Use your "bumper" for retrieving only, never for play time or any other purpose. If you have a pigeon wing, fasten it to the sock with tape.

 - **Work indoors first.** This is kind of an extension of his puppy-toy-retrieving games. A good place to begin is indoors in a long hallway. Close any doors so that there's no escape route, and he has nowhere to run except back to you. Be sure the bumper is conspicuous on the flooring surface.

✔ **Rev his retrieving engine.** Flash the bumper under his nose to get him excited and then toss it just a few feet in front of him. Throw straight ahead at his eye level, sort of a skimmer throw, because an 8- or 9-week-old puppy has very limited range of vision and can't follow objects that move rapidly up, down, or sideways. Use your "Fetch" command and lots of praise when he retrieves. Encourage his return and praise him once again *while he still has the bumper in his mouth*. (If you take the bumper immediately, he'll associate coming back with you taking the bumper away and will learn not to come back.) Now remove it gently with more praise and toss again.

✔ **Do three retrieves and stop.** Start with three short, easy retrieves a day in the same lesson, *never* more, and less if his enthusiasm fades. Always stop when he's still eager to retrieve again. The biggest mistake most people make is offering too many retrieves until the pup or dog gets bored and tired of the game.

✔ **Move the game outdoors.** Once he gets the idea, move your lessons outdoors on short-cut grass and start with two or three retrieves of 20 or 30 yards, less if he can't follow where you toss it. Increase the distance gradually as he succeeds.

✔ **Use a long line for control.** At some point during this scenario, he's going to take off with that bumper and head for the far corner of the yard. ("This is *my* bumper!") No problem. Attach your 30-foot long line to his collar. The moment he picks up his bumper, call him with a "Come" command and give a gentle tug to remind him to return. (Don't reel him in like a fish. If he still resists, use a series of gentle tugs, only at those moments when he's back pedaling or stops moving toward you.) Run backwards as you're calling him excitedly to entice him back to you. Most retriever puppy owners quickly learn to act wild and crazy to keep their puppies motivated!

✔ **Add a gunner.** Once your puppy is returning without too much resistance, you can add a thrower or gunner to his lessons. As with all dog lessons, when you add any new element to a lesson, back up a step (in this case, shorten the distance of the throw). Still working on mowed grass, the gunner stands 20 or 30 yards away while you hold your pup. The gunner calls "Hup, hup" while you tell your pup to "Mark." Once the pup's attention is focused on the gunner, nod your head to signal for the throw with more "Hups." (No huge throws for little pups.) Release the puppy while the bumper is in mid-air and don't forget to act wild and foolish again on his return. If he has trouble finding the bumper or going the entire distance, shorten the throws until he is successful. Success is the main ingredient in his basic training.

✔ **Train in different places.** Now work with your puppy in different places. Stay on cut grass, but vary the location of your training lessons. With each location change, you will be adding new distractions, so shorten up your throws each time until he's focused on his work. He has to learn to concentrate on his tasks in unfamiliar settings.

✔ **Train with people who know more than you do.** Beyond this point, if you want to pursue field work with your Golden, you'll need a good book or two on training retriever puppies for hunting. If your Golden puppy's a retrieve-a-holic, scour gun dog books and magazines and join a retriever club or hunting club (it doesn't have to be just Goldens) to find an experienced training partner.

Swimming

No doubt about it, Goldens Retrievers are really furry fish, or at least they *should* be. They love the water — lakes, ponds, puddles, and the muddier the better. If you're into swimming and wet dogs, you've chosen the right breed. Swimming comes naturally to Golden puppies, although some may take a little longer to get beyond the puppy-paddle stage.

When introducing your Golden puppy (or Golden of any age) to water for the first time, observe the Golden (water) Rules.

✔ **Never force or throw your puppy or dog into the water.** Your Golden must go in the water on his own. You can lure, entice, cajole, and beg, but never, ever force.

✔ **Don't start with cold water.** Would you bathe a baby in cold water? Positive association applies most naturally to water, too.

✔ **Make his first swim pleasant.** A Golden's introduction to water should always be a positive experience. Start with a beach or pond with a shallow shoreline, warm water, and a warm day. Some Golden puppies take one look at water and dive in head first without a second thought. Most will puppy-paddle at first, but a few will take off swimming like a porpoise.

✔ **Go swimming with your pup.** Put on your aqua shoes and wade in with your puppy. Toss a toy and use lots of encouraging praise. Start in running water up to his elbows or belly, and as he shows confidence, toss the toy a little farther each time. If he gets nervous or refuses, back off and stay in shallow water for a while. Never scold or force. Use your three Ps again — Praise, Patience, and Practice!

Tracking: Using That Golden Nose

Tracking is actually a distant relative of obedience trials, only the dog works independently and follows his nose to prove his scenting ability. The dog must follow a *track,* a path walked by a stranger, across complex terrain that includes twists and turns, fences, hedgerows, and other hazards.

Two AKC titles are offered, and the tests are sponsored by AKC-licensed dog clubs. To earn a *TD (Tracking Dog) title,* the dog must complete a 400 to 500 yard track. The *TDX (Tracking Dog Excellent)* faces a more complex track of 800 to 1,000 yards. Tracking buffs hail this sport as exciting and exhilarating for themselves as well as their dogs! Complete rules are available in the *Tracking Regulations* from the AKC.

Dogs have an estimated 220 million "smell cells" in their noses compared to the 5 million in the human nose. And their sense of smell is said to be up to several million times more sensitive. No wonder your Golden can dig up hidden treasures in your backyard!

Agility

Is your Golden a Frisbee fanatic? Does he climb the kids' slide at the park? Can he leap tall buildings in a single bound, or at least jump on his doghouse? Then he might be a natural for agility.

In agility events, the dogs race through a complex course of obstacles to jump over, crawl under or into, cross over, straddle, or weave through. They are judged on speed and accuracy, earning both qualifying scores and placements for their performance. The sport is open to all breeds of dogs, but athletic Goldens usually excel. Agility enthusiasts have a favorite saying, "Try it, you'll like it!"

Agility clubs are turning up in most major cities, so if you're interested, check with your vet, a local kennel club, or write to the national agility organization listed with AKC. *The Rules and Regulations for Agility Trials* are also available through AKC.

Golden Assistance Partners

Take a healthy dose of all the Golden Retriever activities previously described in this chapter, add the Golden's great willingness to please, and you have the ultimate public servant — and he'll never dip his paws into campaign funds!

✔ **Assistance dogs:** As skilled assistance dogs for the physically disabled, Golden Retrievers pull wheelchairs, pick up books and pencils, turn on lights, open refrigerator doors, and complete dozens of other daily tasks for their disabled person. Goldens easily master complex tasks and minute details and are especially adept at sensing their owner's needs and wishes. Assistance dog owners state emphatically that their dog has made the difference between merely existing and living a quality life.

✔ **Guide dogs for the blind:** Golden Retrievers, Labrador Retrievers, and German Shepherds are the three breeds most widely used as guide dogs for the blind. A guide dog's primary responsibility is what the name implies — to guide his owner in public in heavy crowds, public transportation, traffic, and other busy areas. Guide dogs are raised the same way as assistance dogs — by volunteer puppy-raisers until they are 12 months to 18 months of age, when they enter formal training. Dogs who complete the program are matched to the physical and mental characteristics of the blind recipient.

✔ **Hearing dogs:** Hearing dogs are canine alarm systems for their deaf owners (see Figure 19-1). A Golden Retriever hearing dog will alert his owner to as many as a dozen different sounds: a door bell, an alarm clock, a telephone, a smoke alarm, a baby's cry, a window surreptitiously opened by an intruder. Companion Goldens can easily be trained for this task if their owner suddenly becomes deaf. Some assistance dog providers also train hearing dogs or can refer you to an organization that does.

Figure 19-1:
Hearing dogs also make excellent companions for children.

Nance Photography/AKC Stock Images.

✔ **Drug dogs:** From airports to seaports to land border ports, Golden Retriever drug detection dogs patrol their drug beats in search of illegal narcotics and other contraband substances. Thanks to their superior scenting ability, they can sniff out everything from marijuana and cocaine to cash and alcohol. If there's a downside to a Golden's service in the drug force, it's his huggability and happy personality, which may present a nonthreatening figure to the criminal. Nevertheless, tons of Golden supersleuths work for the U.S. Customs Service and other law enforcement agencies as part of the nation's growing army of drug detection dogs.

✔ **Arson dogs:** Arson detection dogs are trained to sniff out gasoline, kerosene, and other types accelerants that can be used to start a fire. In this area of law enforcement, even modern science has difficulty competing with the Golden nose. Arson officials have recorded cases of canines locating a fire site under inches of ice and water and in places where lab technology failed to find accelerants. In Iowa, a state court set a nationwide legal precedent when it ruled that an arson dog's nose work was admissible evidence in a criminal proceedings. Fortunately, a Golden just thinks he's having fun sniffing around a fire scene.

✔ **Search and Rescue Goldens:** You've seen them on TV, dogs searching through rubble after an earthquake or a bombing, looking for survivors buried under concrete and debris. Known as *Search and Rescue (SAR) dogs,* they work for no reward other than the pleasure of the work itself, finding a human being. SAR Goldens also assist local law enforcement agencies searching for children and people who are lost or victims of suspected crimes.

For more information on canine search and rescue operations, contact the National Association of Search and Rescue (NASAR), P.O. Box 3709, Fairfax, VA 22038.

✔ **Therapists in Golden armor:** Too bad doctors can't invent a Golden Retriever pill. The breed is arguably more therapeutic for the physically and emotionally disturbed than any medication in the marketplace. Take two brown eyes, soft silky fur, a wildly wagging tail, and a dog who senses what you need at any given moment in a crisis, stir well, and pet, and you have a Golden Retriever Doctor Feelgood.

Goldens are active in nursing homes, hospitals, children's wards, prisons, and schools. They work with all ages and all human conditions and make each and every one feel better about themselves or their predicament. To paraphrase Roy Rogers, "Happy tails to youuuuu. . . ."

Chapter 20

Ten Ways to Help Your Golden Live a Longer and More Golden Life

● ●

In This Chapter

▶ Living a healthy lifestyle

▶ Giving sound beginnings for happier dogs

● ●

*T*he average Golden Retriever lives for 10 to 13 years. That's way too short for Golden lovers. Like dog lovers the world over, I wish I had some secret recipe that would magically make dogs live as long as humans do. Although you can't fight some of Mother Nature's rules, you can do certain things to keep your Golden in maximum health, which will translate into a longer life.

In this chapter, I share eight (okay, so I'm a writer, not a mathematician) important suggestions that will help your dog live a healthier, and therefore longer, life. Actually, they are more than suggestions; they are cardinal rules that you should follow if you care about the well being of your precious Golden friend. If I sound like a fanatic on this subject, it's because *I am*.

Keep Your Golden Lean

Obesity is a serious canine health problem that affects your dog's longevity. Indeed, just an extra ten pounds can shorten your Golden's life. The excess weight strains every major body system and predisposes a dog to joint disorders, hypertension and congestive heart failure. My goodness, your dog deserves a better fate than that!

Many veterinarians state that at least 50 percent of all the dogs they see are overweight. Most of their clients don't realize that their dogs are fat or that the excess weight can cause such dramatic problems.

How do you tell whether your dog is "just right?" When the standing dog is viewed from above, he should have a very distinct waist, a narrowing between his rib cage and his rump. You can also do the famous rib cage test: Place your hands on each side of his ribs and press ever-so-gently. You should be able to feel his ribs beneath your palms. If you have to press hard to find those ribs, or if they aren't there at all, then you know what you have to do. His diet starts today!

Check first with your vet to determine your Golden's optimum weight. If he's over by even five pounds, decide what type of food will help you reach his ideal weight goal. Select the correct food for his age, weight and lifestyle. Incorporate more exercise into his daily routine. Whatever he's been doing, he'll need to do it more often, as long as your vet agrees that it's healthy and okay. Skip those table scraps if they are part of the problem. A raw carrot will never hurt your Golden, but a pile of mashed potatoes? That's another story!

Practice Dental Hygiene

The message here is simple. Clean your Golden's teeth, and he will live longer! A survey conducted at one Veterinarian Congress in Vancouver, B.C., determined that dog owners can extend their dog's life by simply providing routine dental care. Other studies show that 80 percent of dogs show signs of oral disease by age 3. Scary, isn't it?

Why is dental care so important? Plaque and tartar buildup on his teeth will cause periodontal disease. Bacteria will then enter the bloodstream through the damaged gums and attack the kidneys, liver, heart, and lungs. Result: early death. As an example, kidney failure, a common cause of death in senior dogs, often starts at a damaged gum line. It would happen to you, too, if you didn't brush your teeth!

The American Veterinary Dental Association reminds you that you are your dog's dentist *and his toothbrush*. Start when he's a baby, get him used to having your fingers in his mouth (great for bite control!), but no matter what your dog's age, it's never too late to start. Although daily brushing is best, twice weekly or even weekly brushing might be a more reachable goal. Find the nitty-griity on how to brush his teeth in Chapter 11. Just make sure that you do it.

Exercise

Your Golden will stay healthy as well as content with a generous dose of daily exercise. Remember, your dog is an athlete who needs to run, play, swim, and do busy, active things. Rigorous exercise will strengthen all his body parts, muscles as well as heart and lungs. I firmly believe that our daily two-mile run has given my Goldens extra vitality as well as extra years. My vet agrees; she is always amazed at their muscle tone and vigor. My 15-year-old Golden did her double-mile trek daily with the rest of our Golden pack until the day before she died; in fact, she couldn't *wait* to hit the trail.

Spay Your Female Golden

Have your Golden girlfriend spayed at the earliest possible age, preferably before her first heat cycle. This one surgical procedure will totally remove any possibility of certain cancers in the female dog.

Statistics show that spay surgery before a female experiences a heat cycle offers 90 percent reduced risk of breast and uterine cancers, pyometra, false pregnancy, uterine torsion, and vaginal and uterine prolapse. Your personal benefits include no messy estrus fluids dripping all over your house and no undesirable suitors hanging around the yard.

Neuter Your Male Golden

The stats are just as good for guy dogs. Neutering will totally eliminate the risk of many cancers that affect male dogs and decrease the risk of several others. Neutered male dogs enjoy zero to reduced risk of testicular cancer, prostate problems, anal tumors, hernias, and testicular infections.

Your personal benefits include absolute birth control for life, relief from hormone driven urges such as aggression toward other males, territorialism on his home turf, neighborhood wanderlust, marking with urine at home and in new places, overt dominant behavior, sexual behaviors such as mounting (your leg!) and arousal, and your own frustration during his hormonal surges when male dogs resist doing what they are told. Altered dogs are also less likely to bite or exhibit temperament problems that could affect your family and neighbors. Your insurance company will love it, too!

There is no downside to spay/neuter surgery. It will not affect your Golden's true personality, and your Golden will still be the silly, affectionate beast you know and love. And he'll live longer, too. Gosh, what more could you ask?

Know How to Take Emergency Action

Become an emergency expert so that you can recognize and handle canine accidents and emergencies. Because my dogs can't talk, I have to be their eyes and ears and always be observant and prepared. In many emergencies, just an extra few minutes could save a life.

Be a Teacher

You already know your Golden does not come preprogrammed or pretrained. It's your job to teach him correct behavior and good manners just as you did with your children, or as your parents did with you. He will be a joy to live with and a welcome addition to the neighborhood as he learns how to be a golden member of human society. Ill-behaved dogs of any breed are at greater risk for accidental death and euthanization.

Socialize

A puppy needs to learn about the world beyond his own backyard if he is to mature into a stable, well-behaved adult. He can't do it alone; you have to be his travel agent. Unsocialized puppies grow up fearful and are candidates for animal shelters, and you know what happens to them.

Index

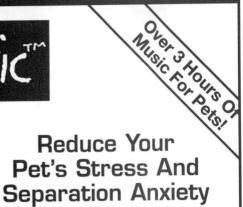

RECIPE "for the" Perfect

GOLDEN RETRIEVER

Kong Dog Toys are used and recommended by veterinarians and dog trainers worldwide. To see how Kong can be utilized to achieve good behavior in your Golden Retriever, send a self-addressed stamped envelope to Kong Company for a free copy of our "Recipe for the Perfect Dog" brochure or simply logon to our website and click **"How to Use Kong"**.

KONG company

16191-D Table Mountain Parkway, Golden, CO 80403-1641 • Phone: (303) 216-2626 • Fax: (303) 216-2627
E-mail: kong@kongcompany.com • Website: www.kongcompany.com   ©**KONG**CO, 2000

Pet owners: check out these other *For Dummies*® titles!

Aquariums For Dummies®	ISBN 0-7645-5156-6	$19.99
Birds For Dummies®	ISBN 0-7645-5139-6	$19.99
Boxers For Dummies®	ISBN 0-7645-5285-6	$15.99
Cats For Dummies®, 2nd Edition	ISBN 0-7645-5275-9	$19.99
Chihuahuas For Dummies®	ISBN 0-7645-5284-8	$15.99
Dog Training For Dummies®	ISBN 0-7645-5286-4	$19.99
Dog Tricks For Dummies®, 2nd Edition	ISBN 0-7645-5287-2	$15.99
Dogs For Dummies®	ISBN 0-7645-5274-0	$19.99
Ferrets For Dummies®	ISBN 0-7645-5259-7	$19.99
German Shepherds For Dummies®	ISBN 0-7645-5280-5	$15.99
Horses For Dummies®	ISBN 0-7645-5138-8	$19.99
Iguanas For Dummies®	ISBN 0-7645-5260-0	$19.99
Jack Russell Terriers For Dummies®	ISBN 0-7645-5268-6	$15.99
Labrador Retrievers For Dummies®	ISBN 0-7645-5281-3	$15.99
Puppies For Dummies®	ISBN 0-7645-5255-4	$19.99
Retired Racing Greyhounds For Dummies®	ISBN 0-7645-5276-7	$15.99
Rottweilers For Dummies®	ISBN 0-7645-5271-6	$15.99
Siberian Huskies For Dummies®	ISBN 0-7645-5279-1	$15.99

Look for these titles in Winter 2001:

Australian Shepherds For Dummies®	ISBN 0-7645-5301-X	$15.99
Dachshunds For Dummies®	ISBN 0-7645-5289-9	$15.99
Pit Bulls For Dummies®	ISBN 0-7645-5291-0	$15.99
Poodles For Dummies®	ISBN 0-7645-5290-2	$15.99
Turtles and Tortoises For Dummies®	ISBN 0-7645-5313-5	$19.99

From the Pet Experts at Howell Book House, Titles of Interest to Golden Admirers:

Books on Goldens

The Golden Retriever: All That Glitters
By Julie Cairns
ISBN 0-87605-041-0
$24.95

The Ultimate Golden Retriever
By Valerie Foss
ISBN 0-87605-196-4
$34.95

Training Guides

Dog Behavior: An Owner's Guide to a Happy, Healthy Pet
By Ian Dunbar
ISBN 0-87605-236-7
$12.95

Dog-Friendly Dog Training
By Andrea Arden
ISBN 1-58245-009-9
$17.95

DogPerfect: The User-Friendly Guide to a Well-Behaved Dog
By Sarah Hodgson
ISBN 0-87605-534-X
$12.95

Dog Training in 10 Minutes
By Carol Lea Benjamin
ISBN 0-87605-471-8
$14.95

Activities/General

All About Agility
By Jacqueline O'Neil
ISBN 0-87605-412-2
$22.95

Canine Good Citizen: Every Dog Can Be One
By Jack and Wendy Volhard
ISBN 0-87605-452-1
$12.95

The Complete Dog Book, 19th Edition, Revised
By The American Kennel Club
ISBN 0-87605-047-X
$32.95

Flyball Racing: The Dog Sport for Everyone
By Lonnie Olson
ISBN 0-87605-630-3
$14.95

Training the Hunting Retriever
By Bill Tarrant
ISBN 0-87605-575-7
$25.95

WWW.DUMMIES.COM

YOUR ONLINE RESOURCE

Discover Dummies Online!

The Dummies Web Site is your fun and friendly online resource for the latest information about *For Dummies* books and your favorite topics. The Web site is the place to communicate with us, exchange ideas with other *For Dummies* readers, chat with authors, and have fun!

Ten Fun and Useful Things You Can Do at www.dummies.com

1. Win free *For Dummies* books and more!
2. Register your book and be entered in a prize drawing.
3. Meet your favorite authors through the IDG Books Worldwide Author Chat Series.
4. Exchange helpful information with other *For Dummies* readers.
5. Discover other great *For Dummies* books you must have!
6. Purchase Dummieswear® exclusively from our Web site.
7. Buy *For Dummies* books online.
8. Talk to us. Make comments, ask questions, get answers!
9. Download free software.
10. Find additional useful resources from authors.

Link directly to these ten fun and useful things at **http://www.dummies.com/10useful**

For other technology titles from IDG Books Worldwide, go to **www.idgbooks.com**

Not on the Web yet? It's easy to get started with *Dummies 101*®: *The Internet For Windows*® *98* or *The Internet For Dummies*® at local retailers everywhere.

 IDG BOOKS WORLDWIDE

Find other *For Dummies* books on these topics:
Business • Career • Databases • Food & Beverage • Games • Gardening • Graphics • Hardware
Health & Fitness • Internet and the World Wide Web • Networking • Office Suites
Operating Systems • Personal Finance • Pets • Programming • Recreation • Sports
Spreadsheets • Teacher Resources • Test Prep • Word Processing

IDG BOOKS WORLDWIDE
BOOK REGISTRATION

Register This Book and Win!

We want to hear from you!

Visit **http://my2cents.dummies.com** to register this book and tell us how you liked it!

- ✔ Get entered in our monthly prize giveaway.

- ✔ Give us feedback about this book — tell us what you like best, what you like least, or maybe what you'd like to ask the author and us to change!

- ✔ Let us know any other *For Dummies®* topics that interest you.

Your feedback helps us determine what books to publish, tells us what coverage to add as we revise our books, and lets us know whether we're meeting your needs as a *For Dummies* reader. You're our most valuable resource, and what you have to say is important to us!

Not on the Web yet? It's easy to get started with *Dummies 101®: The Internet For Windows® 98* or *The Internet For Dummies®* at local retailers everywhere.

Or let us know what you think by sending us a letter at the following address:

For Dummies Book Registration
Dummies Press
10475 Crosspoint Blvd.
Indianapolis, IN 46256

™
...FOR DUMMIES

BESTSELLING BOOK SERIES